What others have said about
LIMITLESS LIVING
A Guide to Unconventional Spiritual Exploration & Growth

∞

"Dr. Kinser's LIMITLESS LIVING invites us to discover the mystery of faith in our lives. In a beautifully written work, Dr. Kinser takes us on a spiritual tour, welcoming readers of all ages and beliefs. He provides numerous examples and illustrations, including nontraditional approaches to spiritual insight. Dr Kinser affirms life and spreads joy. Readers can benefit from his unique perspective of spirituality in a 21st century world.
A must-read!"
Christopher S. Walsh, M.D., Board Certified Radiation Oncologist;
Fellow - American College of Radiation Oncology
Mid-Rivers Cancer Center

∞

D1715980

"Here is a breakthrough book by a courageous writer whose life exemplifies limitless living. He is a great teacher through his writing and through his presence."
Margaretha K. Finefrock, CLO/Wrangler of The Learning Project, and author of: *Pilgrimage of the Heart*; *Mountains Diminish Under Foot*; and, *The Art and Ministry of Teaching*

∞

"It is a privilege and an honor to have Prentice Kinser quote from my death experience when I met the Risen Christ and was conducted through the four realms by Him. Prentice is a 21st century priest and the type of minister we need to lead our young people to greater understanding of how great our God is and how far out God stands ahead of us all."
George G. Ritchie, M.D., psychiatrist and author of: *My Life after Dying—Becoming Alive to Universal Love*; *Return from Tomorrow*; *The Place We Call Home—Exploring the Soul's Existence After Death*; *Ordered to Return, My Life After Dying*; and *The Challenge*

∞

"Rev. Kinser has created a remarkable and important book which I would highly recommend to everyone. Science has now documented the mind/body connection and its importance to our health. In addition, research has begun to show that connecting with the religious and spiritual dimension of our lives provides powerful tools for prevention and reversal of disease, as well as achievement of optimal wellness."
Sandra A. McLanahan, M.D., Integrative Medicine Physician; Executive Medical Director of Integral Health Center; Former Director of Stress Management Training for the Preventive Medicine Research Institute, founded by Dean Ornish, M.D.; and, co-author of *Surgery and its Alternatives, How to Make the Right Choices for Your Health*

∞

"This is an extraordinary book on spirituality and the myriad ways to access guidance along this path of healing into Limitless Living. A must-read for everyone who is on this journey or interested in embarking on it. I loved it!"
Pat Reppert, RN, "Goddess of Garlic," Founder of Hudson Valley Garlic Festival, and author of: *Mad for Garlic Cookbook, A Cookbook for Garlic Lovers*

∞

"By turns humorous and meditative, the author explores and shares his spiritual journey and encourages his readers to do the same. He provides a wonderful resource on topics from theology to T'ai Chi, Native American traditions to meditation, and other avenues for limitless living!"
Anonymous, RN and Nurse Practitioner, Nursing School faculty and yoga instructor

LIMITLESS LIVING

A Guide to Unconventional
Spiritual Exploration and Growth

May all your living be limitless!

Prentice +

The Rev. Dr. Prentice Kinser III

All Biblical quotes, unless otherwise noted, are from the *New Revised Standard Version Bible*, Copyright © 1989 by the Division of Christian Education
of the National Council of Churches of Christ in the United States of America,
published by Thomas Nelson, Inc., Nashville, Tenn.

T'ai Chi illustrations by Philip McKenney.
Cover ocean photo Copyright © 2007 Prentice Kinser III.
Cover sunset photo Copyright © 1996 Corel Word Perfect, adapted and
used with permission.

This book is not a substitute for the medical advice and supervision of your
personal physician and/or nurse practitioner. No exercise program should be
undertaken except under the direction of your health care provider. If you are
now or have been in the care of a psychiatrist, psychotherapist or other mental
health care provider, seek their advice prior to beginning any exercise or
meditation in this book that may impact your emotional state.

Publisher's Cataloging-in-Publication Data
Kinser III, Prentice (The Rev. Dr. Prentice Kinser III), 1939-
Limitless living, a guide to unconventional spiritual exploration and growth
1st ed.
   Includes bibliographical references, index, diagrams, and T'ai Chi images
   Library of Congress Control Number: 2007907180
   ISBN-13: 978-0-9798584-0-6
   ISBN-10: 0-9798584-0-2

   1. Spirituality—Theology—Faith.
2. Guardian Angels—Meditation—Mindfulness.
3. Reincarnation—Near Death Experiences—Mind-Body Healing.
I. Kinser III, Prentice, 1939-   II. Title

Published by:
ANCIENT OTTER PUBLISHING™
PO Box 53, Montross, VA 22520
www.ancientotterpublishing.com

Printed in the United States of America
Published October 2007

CONTENTS

EXERCISES

All exercises in this book are included as educational experiences, and are not to be mistaken for therapy or care. Some readers may find some exercises to be too psychologically and/or physically challenging. In case of any question or concern, please consult a health care provider or counselor. If you have had an emotional disorder, talk with your mental health professional before using any exercise or meditation in this book.

Acknowledgements

I am grateful to George Ritchie, M.D., Brian Weis, M.D., and the late Ian Stevenson, M.D., for their courage to go where few physicians have gone before as they explored their near-death experiences, cases suggestive of reincarnation, and encounters with past life recall both in their own lives and with patients. Their groundbreaking publications have given encouragement to me and to other health care providers, therapists, and clergy who have moved into these unconventional areas of research, study and spiritual growth.

Many other authors are mentioned throughout this text and in the Bibliography, which recognizes that we all stand upon the shoulders of past explorers who continue to open for us new paths of spiritual discovery and growth, thus helping us move toward *limitless living*.

I am indebted to my wife, Mary Ann, who read and re-read this book to help me clarify that which is often shrouded in a cloud of unknowing. Thanks go to: my sons, Mark and 'PK'; to my daughter Patricia; to my daughter-in-law, Aleta Meyer; to my grandchildren, Alex, Sacha, Quinn, and Morgaine; to my sister, Pat; to Marsha and Jim Peterson, Anne and Ed Brooke, and Maggie Finefrock. Their presence and love in this lifetime helps keep me centered. I also thank my son-in-law, Chris Woods, for the T'ai Chi photos that formed the basis for the sketches produced by the artist Phil McKenney in Chapter Seven. I am especially grateful to my "eagle-eyed" editors: Mary Schweitzer and Doug Britton.

Thanks go to *all* family, friends and parishioners who encouraged me to complete this work before I move on into the next great adventure. They helped provide the motivation to keep me going.

Credit must go to the Board of Directors of Blue Ridge Pastoral Counseling Centers who first encouraged me in the early 1990s to record the stories that were emerging in my clinical practice which make up part of this text. Please note that even where clients and/or parishioners have given permission to use their stories, or where people involved are now deceased, I have chosen to disguise identities to honor the privacy of individuals and families. The contributions of those clients and parishioners, though anonymous, are immense.

My deep appreciation also goes to Faye and Bill Richardson. They contributed office space for a counseling center in Warrenton, Virginia, and remain dear friends. Little did I know then what was opening up to me in 1982 when a mutual friend said, "You must meet my weird friends Faye and Bill." They also introduced me to the A.R.E.®1 which has been a part of my own *limitless living*.

Also, special thanks go to Katey Denner, LCSW, who donated office space in Sterling, Virginia, and was a good friend and colleague as I weathered the challenges of earning a doctorate.

And finally, thanks to the many fellow clergy who have advised and supported my spiritual pilgrimage: Jim Cunningham, Tom Clifford, Howard LaRue, Mark Engle, Jenks Hobson III, Hal White, Milt LeRoy, Vic Malloy, Mary Fran Hughes-McIntyre, John Westerhoff, Craig Anderson, Harry Pritchett, the late Bob Hall…forever my Bishop, and the late Urban T. Holmes…forever my Dean. Some of you might consider parts of this work heretical. So I don't credit you for the heresy, but I thank you for your love. Our lives are dedicated to the same Master and Lord!

Prentice Kinser III, D.Min.

---

[1] The Association for Research & Enlightenment, Inc. (A.R.E. ®), is a not-for-profit organization, founded in 1931 by Edgar Cayce (1877- 1945), to research and explore transpersonal subjects such as holistic health, ancient mysteries, personal spirituality, dreams and dream interpretation, intuition, and reincarnation.

DEDICATION

∞

*This book is dedicated to the
clients, parishioners and friends
who boldly shared their stories so others
may find courage to explore theirs.*

∞

*And I especially dedicate this book to my wife,
children and grandchildren who have made
every moment of my life an adventure in
limitless living.*

∞

The Rev. Dr. Prentice Kinser III

Most people think we are physical beings

who occasionally have spiritual experiences.

The truth is we are spiritual beings who are now

having this physical experience of life on planet earth.

∞

Introduction

A warning is in order. This book is clearly labeled as a guide to "unconventional" spiritual practices, i.e., it contains material that is unorthodox. To be orthodox means to "conform to accepted standards and established practice." If you want only traditional spiritual direction please look elsewhere; this text is not for you. I do have a list of some good conventional publications in the Bibliography. There is a vast wealth of such traditional guidance, most of which can be of great benefit in a spiritual journey. I have not tried to duplicate here that kind of assistance.

However, if you wish to explore areas that some may consider outside of the accepted and standard then you have chosen an appropriate resource. Perhaps it is not by chance that you now hold this particular book at this specific time. More than one master has told me that the right teacher is sent when a person is ready. Some of my best teachers have appeared in the form of books to which my hand was drawn, as though by some unseen force. On more than one occasion I felt books "jump" off the shelf into my hands or "pull at me" from the Amazon.com web site.

You may be only curious and just beginning to search. That impulse of curiosity is not something that "killed the cat" but rather it is

Holy and is driven by the Spirit of God, or Allah, or YHWH[2] to move us toward knowledge and faith.

My purpose in writing this book is twofold.

FIRST, I share these pieces of my spiritual journey, these spiritual explorations, insights, and exercises, with the hope that other spiritual pilgrims may be encouraged to search their own inner depths and there encounter the Infinite Mystery of God. In the process, I pray the reader becomes more open to *limitless living*.

Often pain or difficulty draws us to look for meaning and truth. The 23rd Psalm of the Jewish Bible (the Christian Old Testament, King James Version) states: "The Lord is my Shepherd, I shall not want. He *maketh* me lie down in green pastures; He leadeth beside the still waters. He restoreth my soul...." The pain and problems of life allow God to *make us* lie down for a while so we can have our souls restored. Four years ago I experienced the illness commonly known as "shingles." My physician instructed me that I must rest and remove all stress for a minimum of six weeks. That was easier said than done for a busy parish priest. Fifteen years earlier, ten days after bypass surgery, I had insisted on officiating at the burial service of a dear friend in my parish. As with many clergy, I often was torn between the needs of the people in my parish, my family needs and the needs of my own physical, spiritual and emotional health. When I learned of my shingles, I had many parishioners who were much sicker than I and feeling much greater pain; so how could I take six weeks to recover? However, my doctor added, "If you do not follow these instructions then the pain you now feel will probably last not just for six weeks but for six months to a year, and perhaps even longer. However, if you totally rest and relax the pain

---

[2] YHWH is the Hebrew name for God. Hebrew has no vowels; therefore one cannot pronounce this Holy Name. I do not wish to exclude any expression of faith in a divine power in our search for limitless living. Scott Peck, in his book *The Road Less Traveled*, talks of the stage of mysticism in psychological growth in which a person comes to have a more universalistic view of the transcendent and infinite mystery we call God or Allah or Jehovah, etc. This book comes from that more mystical perspective. I will usually use the tradition of my faith when I talk of "God," but I use this name as an inclusive term not an exclusive one.

should subside in two or three months." With such a stern warning, I followed his instructions, and spent some serious time being quiet and listening to the holy silence…even in the midst of hurricane Isabel which almost killed my wife, Mary Ann, and me. (more later).

It has been my experience that in listening to the silence we may hear that still small voice which leads us to the still waters deep in our souls. Usually it is in such silence where healing must originate, and from which new endeavors can commence. It is in those deep inner places where we encounter that infinite Mystery we dare to call "God," experiencing a Truth that passes all understanding, and thus are free to live a life that is limitless.

Saint Paul, in his second letter to the Corinthians, said: "Now the Lord is the Spirit, and where the Spirit of the Lord is, there is freedom." (2nd Corinthians 3:17) The late Karl Rahner, SJ (1904-1984), a profound Roman Catholic theologian, suggested that when we are burdened with problems or upset and not feeling free, those are the times we need to move deep into our hearts where God's Holy Spirit dwells with infinite freedom.[3]

For me, it was during those weeks of rest and listening that this book finally found the guidance to move toward completion.

But I am not saying that being in such silence is ever easy or comfortable. Sometimes we must see ourselves in ways not seen so before. Almost always we will find silence to be a new place, even if we have been there many times before. It is in such silence or new places that mystical experiences are rooted. We may need considerable encouragement to adventure into new places, especially if we have heard those places may be dangerous or even "bad." Spiritual activity that appears to have mystical roots can be threatening to a logical, rational, analytical mind. Traditional Christianity and Judaism have even discouraged the more mystical elements of their faiths.

---

[3] A theme of his book, *Prayers & Meditations*, Karl Rahner, Seabury, 1980. Rahner, a German theologian, had a major impact on my own theology.

For example, in the past, Orthodox Jews, except Rabbis, have been forbidden to study the Jewish Kabbalah[4] because it has been seen as too "dangerous" for one not thoroughly grounded in the Torah. Likewise, Christian mysticism has been seen as acceptable for the monk and rare Saint, but to encounter it in an ordinary member of a conservative Christian denomination could almost be cause for "shunning," "excommunication," or removal from the worshiping community. Some have condemned mystical spirituality as being "occult," not realizing that simply means "beyond the range of ordinary knowledge or mysterious." According to that definition, all faith based spiritual activity might be considered "occult."

It is my hope that by sharing some of my more non-ordinary spiritual explorations, which have been part of my life both as a lay person, as an Episcopal priest, pastoral counselor and psychotherapist, and by sharing similar experiences of friends, parishioners, and clients who have given me permission to do so, the reader may be less intimidated by their own logical hesitations or by the conservative elements of their faith traditions. A friend recently said to me, "You know, one of the special things you have done is expose me to all sorts of new possibilities which I could then choose to pursue and explore or not."

However, our work in these areas may make those around us somewhat uncomfortable, if not hostile. Many years ago I happened to tune into a morning TV show during which the American novelist, Irving Wallace (1916-1990), was discussing one of his novels and its unattractive Christ figure. He noted that he had wondered for years, "What would make a believer out of me?" He then said, "It would take such a miracle that the miracle would not only make me a believer but also a quack, who may not be very attractive to some people." Touching the Mystery of God can turn our lives upside down. And then if we are so bold as to talk about these things, the fearful in our midst may condemn us, and the rationalistic may scoff and ridicule.

---

[4] A body of esoteric wisdom in the Jewish tradition. *Kabbalah for the Layman*, by Dr. Philip S. Berg is a good introduction. The literal meaning of the word Kabbalah is "Receiving."

Nevertheless, problems, pain and difficulties in life have a way of emboldening us. I survived a heart attack in 1989 and subsequent bypass surgery in 1990. I endured a painful resignation from my parish in 1992 where I had served as Rector for eleven years. I watched the divorce of both of my sons and the anguish caused to them and their children, and I felt like a failure because I could do nothing to save their marriages. Also, over the years, numerous clients and parishioners have shared stories of terrible anguish and suffering, and I have been with many during some of the worst events of their lives. And through it all I have seen how, almost without exception, these events may lead us to those still waters where our souls can be restored. Therefore, I now feel more willing to share as much of my story as may be useful for others to hear, although parts of it may be quite unorthodox. A friend, who has also endured much pain and been near death more than once, said to me, "When you have been close enough to THAT door to hear the angel wings flapping, you look at life in a totally different light, and you have a new boldness to say what you really feel like saying." I feel a new desire to share more of my story than I normally would in a parish setting, and a willingness to test whether or not there are others who wish to hear. Actually I would be quite happy if only my children and grandchildren were to read this book, but I do hope others will find it valuable, too.

My SECOND reason for writing this book is, having lived sixty-eight years of this current lifetime and almost thirty years as a priest, I am learning that in order to proceed with my own spiritual journey I must share with others that which I myself have received as gifts. Native Americans had a wonderful tradition called the "giveaway" (a tradition that has not been totally lost). When a member of a tribe became "rich" that person would gather friends, family and other tribesmen. He would then give to each person part of his riches after having spent a great deal of time trying to choose the gift that would be most useful to the recipient. By doing this they believed they would then be open to continue to receive further riches.

I have been told that a remote genetic part of me is connected to the Powhatan tribe, to Pocahontas, and to her many descendants -- of which I am one. So I feel a connection to this tradition.

Like those early American brothers and sisters, I think I have experienced so much, I have benefited from the teachings and guidance of so many, I have received such spiritual riches, that I MUST give away some of those riches or be blocked from further growth. So I am writing this book to help me, as well as you, thus opening up my heart and soul for new adventures that have already begun.

My background is quite varied. While in college I worked as a surgical scrub nurse. I've been a chemistry and physics teacher, a businessman and real estate broker, a parish priest, pastoral counselor, psychotherapist, and clinical hypnotherapist. I have a bachelor's degree in philosophy with a minor in the sciences, a master's degree in business administration, a master's degree in divinity, a doctor of ministry degree in pastoral counseling and psychotherapy. I am also a board certified clinical hypnotherapist, and am certified as a Pastoral Counselor and a Fellow in the American Association of Pastoral Counselors. Several years before I decided that the ordained ministry was my call, I even attended medical school for three semesters.

I have conducted seminars and workshops in many parts of the United States and teach occasional courses as adjunct faculty at a college in Virginia. And I have served as a Rector, Assistant Rector, and Interim Rector in numerous Episcopal churches in Virginia. I currently serve as priest and Rector of two Episcopal parishes in the Northern Neck of Virginia. This diversity of life experience and education has carried over into a diverse spiritual pilgrimage, usually quite orthodox, but occasionally somewhat unorthodox.

At the same time, I recognize the great potential for fraud and deception in the area of spirituality. The need to believe can be so great that individuals may accept as helpful and holy that which is dishonest and a hoax. Or perhaps just as bad, we may simply accept someone else's honest misunderstandings of that which is perceived, or of what one thinks they perceive.

Belief that something is possible may stimulate the hypnotic effect of seeing or hearing things that are not there. I have come to recognize that the old guideline is false which says: "I'll believe it when I see it." The truth is: "I'll see it when I believe it." If we believe something strongly enough we will generally find evidence for that belief, even if we have to unconsciously manufacture or fabricate the evidence. The converse is also true, i.e., if we believe something is impossible then it will be almost impossible for us to see the evidence of such phenomenon. Even some of the most reputable scientific investigators have reported this unconscious inclination and have gone to great lengths to protect their research from such bias.

That is why I strongly recommend testing any spiritual guidance, direction or communication you receive while doing the exercises contained in this book or while participating in any other spiritual exploration. Appendix A provides a process for doing what Holy Scripture calls "testing the spirits." I have found this useful and effective. I also suggest that you find a spiritual guide, i.e., someone further along the spiritual path you have chosen to explore, who can walk with you for a while. Talk with your minister, priest or rabbi. A call to the American Association of Pastoral Counselors can put you in touch with therapists, many of who have been trained both in pastoral counseling as well as in theology and the exploration of spiritual matters. You may have to do a little checking to determine whether or not the minister or therapist is open to unorthodox explorations, or doesn't automatically fall into the reductionistic trap of labeling the "non-ordinary" as abnormal or even "sinful" and "the work of the Devil."

My past exposure to philosophical questioning and business analysis, and my training in the scientific method, does cause uneasiness in presenting untested spiritual phenomenon. The very nature of spiritual exploration provides anecdotal data that is difficult to replicate. Good research is being done in many places today in order to document certain types of spiritual activity that can fit into scientific, double-blind studies. However, much that I share here comes from one-time, personal experiences. What makes this kind of data more believable is the fact that these experiences are not as rare or as unusual as may be thought. Popular literature is filled with similar stories. As I have taught classes, led workshops, preached sermons, and discussed these topics in diverse settings, I have often been surprised (though less so today) by how frequently people come to me to share their unusual spiritual experiences.

Since some of my spiritual experiences have come from outside orthodox Christianity, I want to make it clear that I do not speak for the Church. I have neither sought nor received approval of this book from my Bishop or any other ecclesiastical authority. However, as an Episcopal priest, I am bound by canon or church law not to preach heresy. I hope it is clear that what is contained in this book *is not* what I preach. What I preach is, as Saint Paul said so well, Jesus Christ crucified and resurrected to new life. That new life is so radical[5] that I believe it sets us free from fear so that we may choose to live with love and hope, and we can freely participate in this adventure of life with joy. And yet even within that context of the life and freedom, which we find in Christ, some of the material in this short treatise may be considered by some to be heresy. The late Dean of my seminary[6], The Very Reverend Urban T. Holmes, who I will mention later because he played such a large part in my formal theological training, once said to me, "Prentice, if you are going to be faithful to your call to be a shaman and priest in your community, then sometimes you must be willing to go beyond that which is accepted by Church 'authorities' and to move into areas that some will say is heretical." Thank you, 'Terry' … I have followed your advice.

Throughout most of my adult life I have felt an acute dilemma. I love to write. I have been writing on scraps of paper, in spiral ring notebooks, in speckled hard backed journals, and on computer floppy disks and hard drives. I have tried my hand at novels, prose, and theological reflections. I have written over 1300 sermons, uncounted numbers of required papers for classes, graduate theses, and finally a doctoral thesis. Through it all I have felt the thrill of seeing

[5] The word "radical" literally means, of or from the root; the center, foundation, or source of something; or extreme change.

[6] The School of Theology, University of the South, Sewanee, Tennessee.

my thoughts on paper. But therein lies the dilemma. Once upon the paper or on the computer screen, I'd begin to compare my paltry compositions with the great writing of those authors whose books I greedily consumed whenever I could. At one point while working on my doctorate I almost quit the process as I imagined my thesis being reviewed and critiqued by scholars. My childhood memories of cringing before the stare of a teacher instructing me to stand and give my answer to some easy question when that answer was totally lost in the horrible state of complete embarrassment, had me wondering if I might sit before the faculty review board and be unable to open my mouth. Having preached all those sermons and led countless workshops and classes over the past forty years was no comfort whatsoever. Deep down inside, I am still the shy little boy who quit taking piano lessons at age six because the instructor required all her students to be in a recital. So I can honestly say, it was only by the power of the Holy Spirit that the doctorate was completed, the review was successfully traversed, and this book was ever considered.

So how can one who feels so limited by introverted inhibitions ever conceive of the idea that there might be such a thing as *limitless living*? In lives filled with external and internal limitations, with handicaps and illnesses, with pains and sufferings, with doubts and questions, with real and imagined foes along the path of life, where do we find such limitlessness?

Just the fact that you hold this book in your hands is testimony to the concept of *limitless living*. As with all of life, nothing we do is done alone. I realize that psychologists have bemoaned the fact that "we are born alone and die alone." More than one author has said something to the effect of, "I was, being human, born alone and will die alone." But I think that is not true. Just as a mother and father start a life in the passionate union of sperm and egg, as a mother painfully and yet joyfully gives birth, as we are held to be fed and learn to walk and talk and read and drive and fly, we are always surrounded by others. Even when we look around and see not another soul, I believe we are surrounded by a great cloud of witnesses who encourage us to run this race of life to the finish. And the testimony of many near-death survivors is that at death others are there to greet us and help us through the door to the other side.

So we are not alone, and we are not limited by the visible restrictions and strictures of life. My experience is that there is more going on in this life than we can ever imagine. Great forces are at work as we open our hearts and souls to the grace of God and to the presence of other souls. And this book is written with the hope that it may contain hints, or Gretel-like[7] pebbles along the trail, so others who follow may experience the limitless nature of life that I have found everywhere.

I hope the raw data of these personal explorations provides stimulus for further study, not blind acceptance. Please be a "doubting Thomas" when looking at all things new and unusual. Doubt is good. It is an essential part of a mature faith process. And if you don't like what I have to say here you can pass it off as the wild ramblings of an old priest who has sipped too much communion wine.

I do not think I say anything profoundly new. Rather, I am sharing some of my stories and those of others. In so doing, perhaps the reader may be able to connect her or his story to THE Story of our loving Creator.

I have arranged the anecdotes in logical groups, not chronological order. In that way you, a book club, or a study group, can look at one chapter at a time to examine a particular type of spiritual exploration; and you are invited to delve further into those areas of special interest or attraction by using the exercises included within some of the chapters, or by doing further study using the footnotes and books recommended in the bibliography. Explore where you feel called and do not be limited by my structure or organization.

Most of the exercises presented here begin with a relaxation and centering process. In Appendix B there are three different tech-

---

[7] On the first attempt of the mean stepmother to have her woodcutter husband take his children, Hansel and Gretel, into the forest and leave them, Gretel left a trail of pebbles along the path so they could find their way home. For our purposes here I am looking at the importance of following the more feminine, intuitive, right-brained path.

niques for accomplishing this. These are designed to help you move deeply into the exercises and receive the greatest benefit possible. And great benefit is possible!

Jesus said: "I have come so that you may have life and have it to the full." (John 10:10) Elsewhere he said: "I have told you this so that my joy may be in you and your joy be complete." (John 15:11)

The Buddha said, "Follow the way joyfully through this world and beyond.... Live in joy, like the shining ones.... Look within. Be still. Be free from fear and attachment. Know the sweet joy of the way!" (The Sayings of the Buddha)

The Holy Koran says: "God is the Light of the heavens and the earth. High above our petty evanescent lives, He illumines our souls with means that reach our inmost being. Universal is His light, ...pure, ...intense.... All nature sings to the glory of God." (S.xxiv.35)

In the Talmud we read: "Father Elijah, of happy and blessed memory, used to say: Heaven and earth testify that to a scholar who studies the Bible and traditions for the sake of God, and who supports himself, the following verse applied: 'When thou eatest of the labor of thy hands, happy shalt thou be, and it shall be well with thee.'" (Seder Eliyahu Zuta, ch. 15, p. 197)

Too often we consider our lives "limited" or our spiritual experiences incomplete. Yet, as can be glimpsed in these and many other holy writings and in the stories that follow, we live in a universe of unlimited supply, of abundant light, love and joy. I hope this unconventional primer will help you experience more of that abundance through *limitless living*.

A wise Bishop once said to me: "Prentice, your spiritual explorations may take you into dangerous and unchartered territory. However, if you keep a strong foundational faith, such investigations need not be dangerous, and you will find that many others have also trod these same paths."

I begin this book with a look at such faith and how it enhances our efforts to experience *limitless living*. You will note that the first chapter has more of the theological and psychological underpinnings for such unorthodox spiritual activities and explorations. This is important material.

Yet, a caution is in order. Some readers may initially find Chapter One too "heavy" or burdened with excessive verbiage. To avoid getting bogged down in the theological and psychological discussions, feel free to skip those sections that are not now of interest, or simply move on to Chapter Two. Later you may wish to return for a deeper look. However, please remember, YOUR SPIRITUAL PROGRESS IS NOT LIMITED BY YOUR UNDERSTANDING.

Often spiritual breakthroughs occur prior to a logical comprehension of the processes involved. As Frederick Buechner suggested in his book *Wishful Thinking, A Theological ABC*: even when we are not sure where we are going, faith means we go anyway.

Chapter 1

FOUNDATIONAL FAITH

S everal years ago an attractive woman appeared at my office without an appointment. Fortunately, my last client had just departed ten minutes earlier, and I was free for about two hours. I invited her to be seated. She gave me her name, Pamela, but asked that I call her Pam. She started to tell her story. She had moved her residence several times, had been divorced twice, and was feeling lost. By attending different churches, she found some churches were having internal struggles that quickly became projected onto each newcomer. Pam wanted peace, and found only discord. She had wandered into various occult groups, but again each group was insisting they had the only "right way" or the one "real truth." To become a part of their group, one was expected to accept their philosophy, their faith, and their interpretation of reality. Again, no peace.

Finally, in desperation, Pam had just started walking in our small town. Why here? It was where her car had needed gas, and she needed food. As she walked around she passed my office building and saw my name next to the door, so she came in. She did appreciate the fact that the town police department was right next-door, as that made her feel safe. And there was "The Rev. Dr." in front of my name. Although several times she had not found help from "religious" folks, which "The Rev." implied, she thought the "Dr." meant that I might be open to more possibilities than what she called "the accepted dogma of a particular institution or organized religion."

So this woman overcame her reluctance to seek "religious" help because my office was next to the police department, and there was a "Dr." which implied advanced training. Also, under my name were the words: "Pastoral Counselor and Clinical Hypnotherapist." Pam said that spoke volumes to her, i.e., the combination of counseling and openness to hypnosis seemed to put me in a different kind of category.

So there she sat across from me. As Pam talked her feet gradually curled up under her legs, while her arms alternated between being held tightly to her chest and dangling so her hands could cling to each other, as though they had nothing else on which to hold. When I asked her to take a deep breath, tears started to well up, and, when she realized I was comfortable with tears, she started to weep. Behind her sobs were the words spoken over and over, "Oh God....Oh God....Oh God," also with an occasional, "Oh Shit....Oh Shit....Oh Shit!" (A fit juxtaposition of phrases, I thought, since God is sometimes easier to find in the excrement of life than in places we ordinarily look for Him/Her. Please note that since "God" is referred to in many holy scriptures as having both masculine and feminine characteristics, e.g., God the Father and Creator, as well as the mother hen who shelters her brood under her wing, I will usually refer to God as "Him/Her," despite the awkwardness of such a formulation. Actually, I believe any reference to God, the ultimate and infinite mystery, must be inadequate and incomplete. The Hebrew use of "G_d" also seems appropriate. Both will be found here.)

It is when I am in the presence of such deep need as being expressed by Pam that I am driven to the core of my own faith which gives me the courage to try to touch the face of God in each person I meet. When I talk with a new client or counselee, I find it essential to gently hold in the back of my mind the important pieces of my faith.

I believe we are not accidental sparks of life set afloat in a dangerous and mindless cosmos only to quickly fade and die, never to see life again. Also, I believe the basic and fundamental nature of creation is LOVE. This infinite LOVE, numberless eons ago, spoke into the void and began a process of spiritual and physical life so complex and so infinite that we can see only a minuscule part of the whole.

This creative force of LOVE is also incarnational; it comes and dwells among us. It is so personal to each part of Its creation that It is closer to us than our own breath.

I gratefully admit a bias of one who has experienced this force in the life and death of Jesus of Nazareth, and in the risen truth of the Christ. My life is centered in what the Christian New Testament calls the Light of Christ, or the Word or Logos. That Light, that Word gives me purpose and strength to continue to do that which the Mystery of God calls me to do.

I also believe that traditional Christianity is not the only place where this Mystery is experienced. If Christ was, is and shall be universally present, which is a fundamental part of my faith, then that Presence has been, is now, and will be expressed and experienced in many different religions and through varied spiritual practices.

The former Presiding Bishop of the Episcopal Church in the U.S., The Most Rev. Edmond L. Browning, while speaking at Christ Church Cathedral in 1991, said that one of the steps in sharing our faith is to "hold up our conviction that Jesus Christ is already at work in every human being. This is our Anglican heritage of incarnational thinking. We do not take Jesus Christ to others. Rather we listen to others to hear where Jesus Christ is already at work in them."

C. S. Lewis, in his book *Mere Christianity*, asked what difference Jesus has made to humanity. He then suggested that by becoming "a son of God" he changed us from created things into begotten things, thus moving us from a biological form that is temporary into something that is timeless and spiritual. In this way Jesus has already done the hard work as He saved us, although we must make that salvation our own. What makes this so special is that the Christ has come down into humanity. Therefore we do not have to scramble up some spiritual mountain through only our own efforts. Lewis says that all we need to do is open ourselves to the man who was both a real man and God, and then He will change us into timeless beings[8] (or as I discuss in this text, "limitless" beings).

I am amazed at how often that same Light of Christ brings a person such as this new client, Pam, to my door at the only time of day when I could have seen her. As I listened to her, I could hear how the Lord truly had been her Shepherd, and was now leading her to the comfort of still waters where she might find peace and healing.

It has also been my experience that this Presence of Christ or the Mystery of God is rich with surprises. Many people are not prepared for surprises and live a fearful faith.

The Rev. Dr. John Westerhoff, a former professor at Duke University and an Episcopal priest, has studied and written about stages or styles of faith. (I strongly recommend any of Westerhoff's books. See the Bibliography for details.) John conducted a Christian education workshop in Roanoke, Virginia, in 1979 while I was serving there, and the following discussion comes from notes I made at that workshop. I think they are helpful in understanding why we react differently to different spiritual experiences.

Westerhoff suggested that a person functioning out of a "dependent style of faith" tends to copy the faith and practices of others and recognize faith not so much as a theological affirmation but as an affective or emotional experience. A person in a "belonging style of faith" primarily wants to belong to or be part of a group or faith community and to hear absolute or final answers, not the paradox and ambiguity that is rooted deeply in all faith. On the other hand, someone in a "searching style of faith" wants to question and doubt everything being presented. And finally, an individual in an "owned style of faith" (what Dr. Scott Peck, author of *The Road Less Traveled* and other popular works, calls the "stage of mysticism") has a maturing faith and is eager to explore that which is new, uncertain, and unfamiliar. An owned faith is usually more mystical. All mysticism seems to be based on personal experience, which is later processed and understood within a faith context.

---

[8] C. S. Lewis, Mere Christianity (NY: Macmillan, 1952), pp.156-157.

Although there resides in us some part of all the styles or stages of faith, I find the most joy in being a mystic. I leave to others more equipped for such things to be the "defenders of the faith" or apologists for orthodoxy. I prefer to be on the spiritual frontiers "pushing the envelope" of faith.

Pushing the envelope is an aviation term that means pushing an aircraft to its limits, especially in the context of flight-testing. In the world of aeronautical engineering the envelope is the collection of curves that describe the maximum performance of an aircraft. To push the envelope is to take the aircraft to the edge of what it was designed to do and try to take it beyond.

In the world of spiritual exploration pushing the envelope would imply moving beyond accepted boundaries of orthodox religious beliefs and practices. I may make mistakes as I push the envelope and move out beyond that which seems indisputable, but it is in such uncertainty that I also experience excitement and passion, puzzlement and surprises, hope and fulfillment, and, as the title of this book suggests, *limitless living*.

The late Very Rev. Urban T. Holmes, Dean of my seminary (The School of Theology, University of the South), shared with my fellow classmates and me the following model for thinking about spiritual matters. As with all models it is limited and only a pale reflection of truth. Nevertheless, it has helped me better understand and teach about this dimension of our lives.

Using Dean Holmes' model, we first try to visualize the separation between *that which is infinite* (e.g., God, YHWH, Creator, Ultimate Truth and Energy, The Christ, Buddha, Infinite Mystery, etc.) and *that which is finite* (the world of our day-to-day experiences which is both physical and spiritual). The names we use for that which is infinite often depends on where we were born, the religious background of our family and significant teachers, and on the spiritual experiences we have had along the way.

This boundary between the finite and the infinite is fuzzy and the Energy of the Infinite moves freely across it. The Energy is unlimited and infinite in space and time (see Figure 1.1).

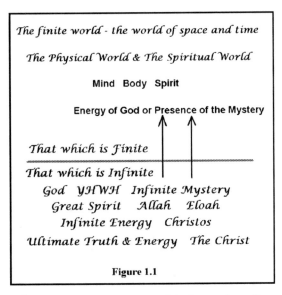

The finite world - the world of space and time

The Physical World & The Spiritual World

Mind Body Spirit

Energy of God or Presence of the Mystery

That which is Finite

That which is Infinite

God YHWH Infinite Mystery
Great Spirit Allah Eloah
Infinite Energy Christos
Ultimate Truth & Energy The Christ

Figure 1.1

When we are born, we move across this boundary from the infinite into the finite physical dimensions of space and time (Figure 1.2).

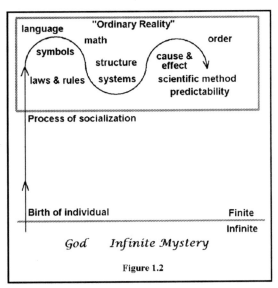

language   "Ordinary Reality"

math   order

symbols

structure   cause & effect

laws & rules   systems   scientific method
predictability

Process of socialization

Birth of individual   Finite

Infinite

God   Infinite Mystery

Figure 1.2

Gradually we are socialized and learn to live in this finite world.

We learn to exist within family and social structures. We use sensory data and language to maneuver and function in what we come to see as "reality" and which some now call "ordinary reality." This is the realm of structure, law and order, scientific method, systems, cause and effect. Here we trust the predictability of life and the systems we use to order our lives. And, because we have come to believe that we are finite and limited beings, we are unable to perceive the truly unlimited.

Many of us pass through life thinking this ordinary reality is the only reality. And then at death we move back across the boundary into the Infinite Mystery of God (Figure 1.3).

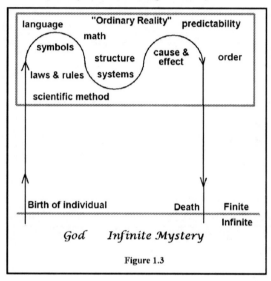

Figure 1.3

Sometimes our ordinary reality is pierced by *Something Else*, something that gives a glimpse of the realms outside our ordinary empirical data and safe structures. I believe Christ was one such piercing of the veil. And there are other, more frequent occurrences experienced by monks and saints as well as by more typical people like you and me. These experiences may be mediated or activated through music, poetry, art, good liturgy, meditation, prayer, etc. Such encounters with the Mystery are the essence of this book. Regardless of the mechanics that enable our experience of God, suddenly one moves from the realm of ordinary reality into nonordinary reality (Figure 1.4).

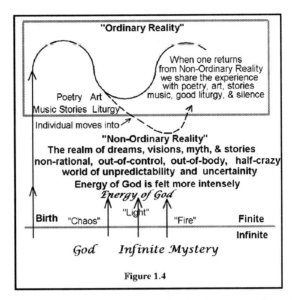

Figure 1.4

The dimension of non-ordinary reality is the area of myth and music, of unpredictability, of being out of control. It is the world of dreams and uncertainty, of visions and experiences of the psyche or soul, and is "half-crazy." When one moves in the dimension of non-ordinary reality and then returns, one realizes it is impossible to describe exactly what has happened. In order to share experiences with others one must resort to music, poetry, stories, prayer, art, liturgy, i.e., the very things that help us move into that non-ordinary reality.

Mystics who have frequently been in non-ordinary reality, close to the boundary between the finite and the infinite, speak of a roaring "chaos," of a flaming abyss, or of an overwhelming white light. Here in non-ordinary reality, one sees burning bushes that are not consumed by the flames. Here one learns to "fear the Lord," because it is here where true awe is experienced which, when intense enough, becomes awe-full.

Experience of this realm has convinced me that what we perceive as a boundary between the finite and the infinite, and between ordinary and non-ordinary reality is actually illusion. Infinity is here in this present moment, in this here and now, in this "I and thou" (Buber[9]), and all of this is One.

Therefore, God is encountered as omnipotent (all powerful), omnipresent (present everywhere, in everything), immanent (present here), intimate (personally present, i.e., may be personally experienced), and transcendent (beyond human understanding or surpassing all limits we may try to impose on God).

Our finite minds cannot grasp this unity within and throughout the diversity. Theoretical mathematics and simple stories come closest to capturing and conveying this truth. I am not a mathematician, so I tell stories.

However, since having a strong faith is a prerequisite for bold spiritual exploration and *limitless living*, we are faced with a quandary. Bold faith develops from taking leaps of faith into the unknown and finding that there is a loving God to catch us. If we are too fearful to take leaps of faith, how can we develop bold faith?

Fortunately we are not trapped in that quandary. I have found that Life, or God, will send the teachers and life events needed to teach us what we are here to learn. I have also discovered that God's Spirit is gentle and will not force us to move faster or further than we can handle.

My new client, Pam, sitting across from me in my office, was gently led to our small town and to my small office.

And I will go so far as to say that I believe she was led by the Infinite Mystery of God. But in saying that, I am also saying that this Mystery used very ordinary restlessness, psychological discomfort, chance events, a car needing gas, a person needing food, and on and on, to bring about such a leading.

So God presented Pam with choices. But she had the choice. The final decision of whether or not to enter and risk talking with me, was her choice – coming out of her courage. I think that is often the

---

[9] Martin Buber, *I Thou* (Scribner's; 2nd edition, 1958). Buber (1878 – 1965) was a Jewish philosopher and educator whose work centered on religious consciousness and interpersonal relations.

place of Grace, i.e., there is a spark within each person, which sooner or later is allowed to expand and fill the heart with new boldness.

But what had happened to this soul? Why had life for Pam become such an impossible problem rather than a great joy? How does one develop, as a soul and a person?

It appears that somewhere during the process of growth and development a moment occurs when part of an infant's experience in the present moment is an awareness that the self is an individual (or a "me") that has had an experience and will have more experiences.

This encounter with the self is an essential step in the formulation of the individual. Harry Guntrip, one of the seminal authors in the field of object-relations theory[10], has indicated that as we move toward self-development we are doing so because of the basic need for object-relations.

The "objects" can be parents, family members, and even "transitional objects" such as stuffed animals or a piece of a blanket. These objects are essential building blocks for our sense of self and for how we ultimately relate to the world around us. The awareness of self enables the "me" to step out of the experience, to stand outside of the "me" or self and perceive and share the perceptions.

But it must be remembered, *the sharing of the perception of experience is always one step or level away from the actual experience* (Level One — Figure 1.5).

As mentioned earlier, the sharing must be expressed in symbols, language, music, art, stories, poetry, rituals, etc., to help another person have some awareness of our experience (Level Two — Figure 1.5).

Later, as the human spirit grows and learns, the individual may begin to think about how other humans have reflected on their experiences, and their reflections are then related to other past

---

[10] "Object relations theory" is an adaptation of psychoanalytic theory that says, as we develop, we form attachments to "objects."

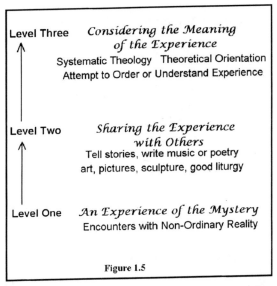

Level Three   *Considering the Meaning
of the Experience*
Systematic Theology   Theoretical Orientation
Attempt to Order or Understand Experience

Level Two   *Sharing the Experience
with Others*
Tell stories, write music or poetry
art, pictures, sculpture, good liturgy

Level One   *An Experience of the Mystery*
Encounters with Non-Ordinary Reality

Figure 1.5

reflections. One then tries to develop a system of understanding, a way of ordering the experiences of the individual and of others, and thus attach meaning to the reflections, to the symbols, and to the experiences (Level Three — Figure 1.5).

In religion that final step might be called systematic theology; in pastoral counseling and psychotherapy it might be called a theoretical orientation; for most people it is simply a way of thinking about something they have experienced.

Occasionally, people accept such reflections about the Mystery as a substitute for an experience of the Mystery. But such reflections or systematic ordering of reflections is two steps or levels away from the actual experience, because we are now using signs and symbols to represent the reflections about the representations of the experience. I contend that when people say they reject God or don't believe in God they are actually rejecting or questioning the way others have represented God or systematically ordered their thinking about God. God is beyond our rejection.

These representations or reflections may have power to draw others into our experience. Still, the experience is always equivocal, i.e., there is always a "surd", or something left over or left out -- something beyond language, understanding, comprehension and reflection.

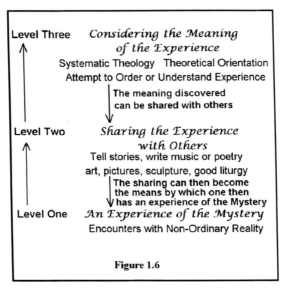

Figure 1.6

And sometimes this process can cycle back upon itself (Figure 1.6) as the meaning and understanding gathered at Level Three is shared with others at Level Two. Then that sharing itself can become a resource through which the individual may be led to have a personal experience of the Mystery at Level One.

As you read this book, I hope it is clear that part of my purpose here is to invite the reader into his or her own experience of the Mystery. This is done through the sharing of my own experiences or stories and the experiences of others. I also share some of my theological reflections upon those stories. And finally, I offer some simple exercises that enable the reader to experiment with the processes involved. A good attitude to have as one tries the exercises is to think of them as experiments. In an experiment, one cannot fail. Rather you simply get more data or information, and perhaps you will encounter non-ordinary reality or have your own experience of the Infinite Mystery of God.

[Please Note: I realize this may sound like a lot of psychological or theological mumbo-jumbo, but stick with me a little longer ... there

is light at the end of the tunnel – and maybe an experience or two of the Mystery!]

So let us return to our discussion of what happens to an individual as one grows. As the self continues to develop, many different systems of ordering experience may be attempted as an individual tries to makes sense of, or find meaning in, their experiences and in the reflections on their experiences. As the individual collects experiences, and grows in a family system and social/cultural context, certain developmental processes are needed so that the fullest potential of the individual can be expressed. Abraham Maslow talks of the need hierarchy; Erik Erickson talks of stages in a life cycle; John Westerhof talks of styles of faith (mentioned above); Scott Peck talks of stages of psychological growth (also mentioned earlier); Harry Stack Sullivan brings to our attention the importance of "tenderness" and empathic linkage" with mother; Heinz Kohut defined caretakers as self-objects and brought a new emphasis to the vital interrelatedness of the parent-child unit; and there are many other valuable ways of ordering the process of human growth and development. Clearly this process may be short-circuited, stunted or blocked in many different ways.

Sometimes the individual, because of blockages and disruptions, begins to reflect negatively on their personhood or self and on life, and begins to anticipate that the future will be a negative or closed system that will always be the same. It is as though a trance is being utilized which has become defective and dysfunctional. They mentally order past experiences so that they come to believe that their story is a closed story, locked within a kind of circle in which they feel: "I am unacceptable; the past is haunting; the future is fixed; all is bad; and, there is nothing outside this wall or circle."

This is where my new client, Pam, had found herself. She had come to my office because what she had tried was not working, or what worked in the past was no longer working now. Her story had become closed down. She saw no way out, and hoped that someone like a counselor may help her find a different path. That small spark of hope, I believe, is the presence of God or the presence of Grace.

Because it seems no human goes through a perfect developmental process (i.e., accidents happen and life is full of events that hurt and bring loss and distress) there will be some elements of such a closed story in all people.

But life provides opportunities for something else to happen, for the "surd" to break through (often experienced as "absurd"). Also, the human organism can't permanently stay within a closed system - unless there is extreme dysfunction. Therefore, a break of some kind usually occurs. This break could be an infinite number of different events and/or experiences (internal or external). We can verbally symbolize the happening as a *radical experience* or a *life shock* that breaks through the old wall or circle.

In this way we have the chance to begin to realize that our story is not closed but open. The old order has the potential of being transmuted or transformed into a new order: "I am accepted and acceptable; the past is approved; the future is open; and, all is sacred and exciting."

I knew Pam was deep in pain, and not able to guess what her future might hold. Often when in such pain, despair, and depression, we feel we can never change and life will never change. However, when working with such a client, if I hold a more positive frame of reference or perspective, that can allow the individual to have a "safe space" in which to begin to see that the radical experience or life shock or pain in which they find themselves is actually a positive thing which may enable them to break free from a previous frame of reference or understanding and move on in their lives in changed and exciting ways.

However, this more open and altered frame of reference is sometimes a scary way to order life because it is open and different. Like the Israelites, who wandered in the open wilderness (wild place) while many wished to return to slavery in Egypt, an individual may think he or she wants to return to the safety of the closed walls of the old way of ordering life, and to cling to old transitional objects. To put it another way, an individual often wants to return to the old "trance." To help an individual discover the courage to continue to explore and begin to experience their story as an open story it is often necessary that the person be with others where there is a ministry of presence. Such a ministry lives out the truth of an old adage that states: "I don't care how much you know until I know how much you care."

I believe pastoral counselors and other therapists, as well as priests, rabbis, and other clergy, are often called on to be present with people in crisis or distress as they explore their story and bring light into their inner shadows. Sometimes a friend holding the hand of another, simply being in the silence together and listening to each other's stories can provide that ministry of presence. And usually all of us, at one time or another, need to be with someone who will listen to us without trying to fix us. The hope is that by being with each other in this way we may see that the haunting demons of the past are not things that possess us and destroy community, but are in reality mistaken representations of reflections. This healing process seems to happen best in an atmosphere of hospitality in which we say, "Tell me about . . . ."

As Pam began, over the next several weeks, to share her story in a safe place that held her as acceptable and her story as sacred, there came a re-membering process. This helps the person put himself or herself back together (i.e., to re-member), and to re-order life as holy, whole, and healthy. This particular client remembered a seemingly insignificant mystical experience that had occurred while she was in college. That memory became a focal point for Pam to begin to rediscover her center and to recover her vocation.

As we work to help others heal, or as we struggle to find healing within ourselves, we will often find that this process of remembering and reordering may begin in very small ways. Perhaps just a momentary glimpse of a long forgotten path where one has found meaning and truth, or a new path or a new order begins to emerge, which helps us feel hope and continue the movement toward health and wholeness. Sometimes we must hold the hand of another for a longer period of time, until the fear of the new order is less than the fear of returning to the old order.

As I try to create a holding environment of accepting presence, in addition to the faith discussed earlier, I also gently hold in the background of my mind the different theories or ways the story being shared might be ordered or understood, e.g., as part of a developmental disruption in which object relations are not adequately formulated, as the result of a dysfunctional family system, as a failure to adequately represent a behavioral experience, as a spiritual need, as an activation of a state dependent memory, etc.

Usually this therapeutic process requires some element of faith on my part that there is *something more*, and, for me, the nature of this *something more* is loving and creative. Even if an individual client cannot be there with faith, my presence is a presence of faith, i.e., just the fact that I have been ordained or set-apart as a priest implies a faith perspective to all that happens in my office. Likewise, as any of us sit with a friend who is in deep anguish, blocked or overwhelmed by life events and/or circumstances, we can best be there if we have allowed our faith to deepen as we have gone through the tests life throws at each of us. Some of the greatest healers among us are those who Henri Nouwen called "wounded healers," i.e., those individuals who have been deeply wounded in their lives, but have moved through their woundedness to healing and hope.

An aspect of the experience of a person in this healing process may be an experience of grace that is part of the mystery of life. Then an individual may begin to see his/her story is part of *The Story*, and more fully become the human being they are called to be. And I believe, deep within each individual, there is a spark of the Grace that is always trying to move one toward health, wholeness and full humanity. At the core of that movement I have found a growing openness to learning and faith.

There are many truths that can open us to the possibility of learning and to speeding up the process of our faith development. Here are four of those truths that can help us move toward a limitless faith and *limitless living*. More will be shared throughout this book.

Truth One, *the more we give away the more we will receive.* This is a sound stewardship principle that applies not only to money but also to all of living. I mentioned in the introduction that Native Americans believe they would get nothing more until they had given away what they had already received. This also applies to spiritual gifts. It is hard to be open to the movement of the Spirit if we are closely grasping things, people, past learning, theories and theology. So an important lesson is to hold onto things, ideas, and opinions in a gentle way, always ready to let go.

Truth Two, *forgiveness is essential*. This means we must be ready to forgive ourselves for our failures and mistakes, AND do the same for others. As we let go of the past we can fully live in the present, and we discover that there never was anything to forgive. In his book *The Healing of Persons*, Dr. Paul Tournier, a great Christian physician, discusses many cases he handled in his medical practice. In some of these cases he saw a direct relationship between the physical illness of his patients and their being in the midst of broken relationships, or still clutching anger or resentment or guilt that blocked the possibility of forgiveness. He noted his amazement at the frequent speed of physical recovery when reconciliation was accomplished and/or forgiveness was experienced. Even when some relationships cannot be healed or where no physical illness is involved, there may be healing within ourselves that comes from choosing to allow forgiveness to work in our lives. As we forgive others our lives are changed so that we no longer have to feel like we are strangers in a foreign land, no longer disconnected from ourselves. We are discovering a stronger kind of wholeness or "at-one-ment" that opens us to the possibility of a changed life and fresh hope.

One of the powerful messages of the story of the prodigal son in the Gospel according to Luke (15:11-32) is that we do not have to remain as we are or where we are. As we open ourselves to the life-changing forces around and within us we find we have the power to choose, the power to intentionally allow the love of God to work in our lives. This brings forgiveness and wholeness and reconciliation and new life.

Truth Three, *we learn to live by living*, we learn to pray by praying, we learn to fly by flying, etc. A variety of exercises are presented in this book. Other writers have shared experiences and tools for learning. Look for those resources that will help you on your own path. Pick and choose. Ask for help from the Holy Spirit, and prepare to be surprised.

<u>Truth Four</u>, *relax and enjoy the journey.* The longer I live and experience more as a priest, pastoral counselor, psychotherapist, husband, father and grandfather, the more I am convinced that the opposite of faith is neither doubt nor unbelief but fear. Therefore, try, as best you can, to step out in faith. Do not cringe in fear.

Fear is seldom related to something happening right now, in this moment. Debilitating fear is a dread of something that <u>may</u> happen in the future. Most fear I encounter in clients and parishioners is about that which has not yet, and may never happen. So a truism I frequently try to share is: "Never suffer future pain." Live in the present. As much as I love imagination, it is this talent that can create the greatest fear.

Ernest Hemingway talked about the natural fear soldiers feel before a battle. He believed that cowardice usually came from being unable to stop the imagination, and that the greatest gift a soldier could acquire is to live totally in the moment, with no before or after. Recently I was talking with a high-ranking Army officer just back from Iraq. He said that, as soldiers prepare for going into battle, one of the things often suggested to help them remain calm is to imagine that he or she is already dead. At first I thought, "What an extremely insensitive thing to suggest to a soldier, who soon may very well be dead." And then I came to see that what is being suggested is actually an attitude of non-attachment that helps one become free of anxiety about results. This freedom from anxiety would naturally help a soldier be more clearly alert to the moment thus helping him avoid a sniper's bullet or an improvised explosive device (IED). Such an attitude of non-attachment is one of the gifts of Buddhism. It is a gift from which we could all benefit.

Psychiatrists and psychologists tell us that much in our lives is driven by our fear of death. We all know we will die. But the more we deny that reality, the more we repress that fear, then the more it unconsciously controls our lives and blocks our full and abundant living. That is why it is so important to remember these ancient words: "Yea, though I walk through the valley of the shadow of death, *I will fear no evil*; for thou art with me; thy rod and thy staff, they comfort me." All of our lives, from birth to death, are lived in that shadow of death. As we remember that we are not alone, "for thou art with me," we find comfort in the reality of the present moment.

I vividly remember a fellow priest telling me about the death of his mother. He was feeling anxious and upset. Things were feeling unreal. He felt he wanted to get "things under control." So he was trying to get a handle on his feelings as he drove home alone from the hospital immediately after her death. As he drove he asked himself, "What is going on? What is happening to me right now?" After thinking for a while he said aloud, "I am an Episcopal priest whose mother has just died." That was a true statement; it was reality but not all of reality. It sounded like it was something that had happened to someone else. So as he continued to drive he continued to think. In a while he said, "I am a man who has just lost his mother." That was getting closer ... but still not the full truth, so he continued to wonder. Next he spoke into the noise of the moving car, "I am a human being who has just had a very important person torn away from him." Now he was starting to feel the pain and some of the grief, but he knew he still had a way to go. Finally he had to pull over to the side of the road and speak these weeping words into the silence, "I am a little boy who has just lost his mommy!!!" In these words he had gotten to the deep core of his experience. In that moment of being with his own terrible pain, not running from it or hiding from it, he was beginning his grieving process and moving back into *limitless living*.

True *limitless living* must be done right now, in this present moment. There is no other time to live than in the NOW! And the more we grow in faith, confident that there is more to this life than ordinary reality, and that the basic nature of all reality is Love, then the more we can move beyond fear and pain and reach for hope and peace. The word "confident" literally means "with faith." And confident living truly is *limitless living*.

If we find ourselves becoming fearful it helps to look around at our current location. CENTER ourselves in the present. NOTICE the sounds of the birds, the color of the trees and plants. If possible, hold the hand of a friend or spiritual partner. Then ASK, "What in this present moment do I fear?" "What is the worst that can happen?" Recognizing the worst can free us to experience the best. Having done so, then proceed to live, love, and learn!

I believe one of the great fears we face in life is that of being totally alone. That had been a significant part of the pain for Pam, sitting in my office. And, before finding the courage to walk into my office, she felt like she had always been alone in the past, would always be alone in the future, and that no one else in the world really cared. As she continued her healing process over several months, Pam came to accept such feelings as a gift, not a curse.

Henri Nouwen talks of the importance of being alone. As we embrace that aloneness, rather than running from it, the fearful silence and empty space can be converted into creative solitude. Since fear produces hostility, this movement from aloneness to solitude is paralleled by a movement from hostility to hospitality.

Hospitality is our ability to be at home with ourselves and allow others, and God, to be at home with us. Hospitality also provides space for growth. That was what I was trying to provide for the new client in my office – a place of hospitality.

It is my experience that the loving and life giving power of God always surrounds us, even if we are too busy or fearful to realize it. In solitude we become more aware of this truth and allow that power to flow through us, to make its home in us --- energizing us for our journey of faith. We can allow that power to envelope us in Love. *Limitless living* acknowledges that Love, accepts that Love, grows in that Love, expresses gratitude for that Love, and gives that Love to others. That last phrase is of special importance.

We are on this journey not only to complete ourselves or to find fulfillment, love and wholeness for ourselves, but also to be enabled to give that love and healing to others. Pam, after a few months of sitting with me, of healing some old, painful memories, of remembering previous mystical experiences, of following her own spiritual explorations, and of reflecting daily in her spiritual journal, was able to return to her vocation of teaching and to her deep love of being a writer. Both of these are ways Pam now gives to others some of what she has been given.

I am reminded of a story about a small child who was being put to bed by her mother. She had said her prayers, and her mother had turned out the light and gone from the bedroom. The little girl started to cry, and her mother immediately returned and asked what was wrong. The little girl replied, "I'm in here all by myself, and I'm lonely." The mother responded, "But remember, God's spirit is here with you." The little girl, with pouting lips nodded and said, "I know. But I want someone in here who has skin on 'em."

That, I think, is our job: to enflesh the love of God, to be that mysterious presence with our families and friends, and with everyone we meet. That truly is *limitless living*.

Chapter 2

EARLY REFLECTIONS

I include content from my early childhood and youth to suggest that we all, as Wordsworth said, come into this world "trailing clouds of glory." Children seem to grasp spiritual realities more easily than do adults. Perhaps that is why Jesus said that we must receive the Kingdom of God like a child or we shall not enter therein.

Reflecting on our early lives is a worthwhile project. As we allow our minds to drift back into our early years we can ask the question: "Where do I see the hand of God moving in my life?" We may be surprised by what we see, and seeing allows us to be like a child -- more accepting of God's Kingdom. I once did an exercise with a parish vestry (the governing board of an Episcopal church) to help them remember times God had touched their lives, followed by a time for sharing. The depth of experiences remembered surprised me. That also became a time for quite a few tears, not a regular part of vestry meetings.

Below is an exercise to help us see how God has been working in our lives.

EXERCISE 2.1 – Exploring Early Memories

1) Allow yourself to go through the relaxation and preparation described in Appendix B.

2) In your mind tell yourself that you want to go back in time and examine a significant moment in your childhood where God was especially active.

3) "Listen" for a feeling, a word or a phrase and follow that to the early memories; make any brief notes that will help you recall what you see, feel, or hear.

4) When you have finished ask yourself, "Why was I shown this particular event, or moment or time?" or "What can I learn from that memory that will help me now?"

5) Record what you have learned in your journal (Chapter 5 has more information about journals).

I must point out that some of our childhood experiences and memories may not be happy or will not appear beneficial. But we can learn a great deal from them, they still have much to teach us.

Once, during a weekend workshop, I was going through a deep meditation and felt great pain in my chest. Using the pain as a guide I followed it back to an amazing early memory, which I think was from when I was in the process of being born. The birth canal was squeezing my chest. My heart was being crushed. I felt I was dying, but I wanted to live -- so I struggled on for life. But I also said to myself, "I will never allow this to happen to me again."

As the years went by I often blocked myself from pushing beyond those unconscious limits. For example, in high school track my race was the 220-yard dash. I was good but not great. The coach wanted me to try the mile. When I started running endurance type of distances, I began to feel a squeezing pain in my chest and would stop. It was the same early pain and the same promise I had made years ago, "I will never allow this to happen to me again." Because of that promise, I backed off and refused to move through the pain.

I now understand how we unconsciously allow early guiding beliefs (picked up from our experiences and parents) to limit our lives.

Here is an exercise that can be used to help remove these blocks.

EXERCISE 2.2 – Removing Blocks

1) After becoming relaxed and centered, ask to be shown a guiding belief that you have which is blocking or hurting you right now. (For example, I picked up a early guiding belief that "I am stupid," because I could not play some of the games my first grade classmates could play.)

2) Once you have identified this negative guiding belief, begin to rephrase that belief in its positive form, e.g., "I am smart" or "I am creative and can do many things."

3) Since a great deal of emotion went into forming that original belief in your mind, you will need to put a lot of feeling into driving that belief from your mind and spirit. Sometimes it helps to yell your positive statement as you pound a pillow with your fists. Do this for 10 to 20 minutes and record the results in your journal.

I spent most of my first six years on my grandfather's farm while my father was in North Africa and Italy during World War II. Those years were rich with learning about the earth and people. I clearly remember being about three or four years of age. I put my hands down into freshly plowed ground and smelled its richness. Even then I knew intuitively that the soil was alive.

Recently theologians and scientists have begun to think of the earth as a living organism, not just a big ball of rock floating in space. This theory has been called the "Gaia Theory," which is actually not a new one. American Indians, the true Native Americans, have for centuries talked to and tried to work in harmony with their "Earth Mother" who, they believe, is alive and responds to them.

During my early years, I would lie on my back against this Earth Mother, looking up into the stars at night. Somehow I felt a part of all of this, even as a child. As strange as it may sound, I knew I was at home amongst those stars and at the same time I was a part of the earth.

An uncle gave me a new concept of the magnitude of our planet by telling me that my father, all the way across the ocean in North Africa, could see the same stars I was seeing. My four-year-old self was beginning to grasp that there was something beyond the mountain behind our house. I sensed the expanse of space and the idea that people on the other side of the earth were in this same space, and it sent my mind reeling. It was like a shaman's bang to the side of my head[11], and I glimpsed the light and infinite mystery of God.

My grandfather, a Methodist lay pastor who was later ordained, was one of my great teachers. He would arrive early on Sunday mornings to prepare our little country church for services. On one especially cold Sunday morning I was with him. I was five years old. He had gone down into the church's dark basement to try to bring heat into this holy space. Peering down the steep steps into the shadows I could see him shoveling coal into the furnace. The light of the flickering flames began to dance in the darkness mixing with the moving shadow of my grandfather.

Even today I can remember wondering if the shadows were real or if my grandfather was real? Were the flames the real source of light and heat or did wood and coal get the light and heat from another place? And in the middle of the flickering questions and light, I felt "something else"---something as vast as the heavens on a starlit night, and as close to me as my rapidly beating heart.

Here was an encounter with the deep world of unconscious (or subconscious) experience. Perhaps I was encountering images from my own inner, genetic memories or from what Carl Jung called the "collective unconscious." I felt fear and awe (note the relationship between "awe" and "awful"). I was intrigued by the mystery. I believe I touched "God" there in the basement of that country church, and that "hound of heaven" and mover in the dark basements of our unconscious world has never let me go.

My grandfather was the agent for another of my early experiences of the Mystery. Often he took me on his rounds as he delivered

---

[11] A shaman is a religious leader or medicine man, especially in primitive cultures. One of the techniques of a shaman is to strike a student in a certain place or with a certain word to bring a heightened state of awareness.

Betsy Ross bread to remote areas of rural Virginia, near Charlottes-ville. On one particular morning when I was about five years old, we started out in his rickety old bread truck long before dawn. I dozed off and on, listening to his humming or singing some favorite hymn. Suddenly I was wide awake. Just outside of my window was a drop of hundreds of feet down a sheer cliff!

I looked out over what I expected to be a view of the rolling land below, which I had seen before in these Blue Ridge Mountains. But on this occasion there were clouds stretching as far as I could see. Never before had I been above clouds. What a thrilling sight! The sun was coming up on the distant horizon and was turning the tops of some of the higher clouds into beautiful shades of purple.

While I was looking out at a scene that was totally new to me, on a different level I felt I had been here before. Although I didn't then, and am only now beginning to, understand, I *had* seen these clouds prior to that morning. I had flown above the earth and seen its in-credible splendor. I had been, and was then in that moment, with "God." I was a part of the Mystery! We all are part of that Mystery.

You might try the following exercise 2.3 to have your own special encounter with the Other.

Please do not use this exercise if you have been diagnosed as having a Dissocia-tive Disorder, Borderline Personality Disorder, Schizophrenia, or have psychotic episodes, or hallucinations.

EXERCISE 2.3 – Moving Out of Body

1) After you are relaxed, centered, and have surrounded yourself with the protective Light of Christ, allow your mind and spirit to open to your present location. Look around the room, then close your eyes and listen to the sounds and en-counter the smells. "Feel" your space.

2) Then, in a childlike way, imagine that you can move up and out of that room. Feel or see yourself going up through the ceiling, through the roof, up above the trees, up above the clouds. Look down and see your town or city far below. It may take a while to be able to move up out of your body. For some it is instantaneous. Most people may need to ex-

periment with different techniques. For example, some have found it helpful to imagine that you sort of roll out of your body, like rolling out of bed. In this way you are initially looking down at your body, and then you can turn your attention upward toward the ceiling; move closer and then through the ceiling into the space above and then on out through the roof.

(Note: Please don't be discouraged if at first you don't succeed. This is not a contest, but rather like a science experiment. It can't be done wrong. Enjoy the process. Regardless of how far you get, there is always benefit if you can free yourself from expectations. Occasionally, if I am blocked, I will simply "play like" my consciousness is moving up out of my body and up into space. The more you play like it is happening the closer you come to an experience of it happening.)

3) Continue moving up above the earth. See the earth as an astronaut would see it, round, blue and beautiful, with patches of swirling clouds. Keep going up, out by the moon; see its craters as you float by.

4) Keep going into space, past the most distant planets and then on through the stars. Go only as far as you are comfortable. Look and listen. Feel the infinite dimensions of this universe. See as perhaps God sees.

5) Return to earth more rapidly, back into your space and record what you have seen and felt. How does this new perspective influence the way you look at things?

I must have heard much about God in those early years because we had to go to church every Sunday, rain or shine. My mother told me, however, that I usually went to sleep during the sermons and would often loudly complain that the preacher, my grandfather, was making too much noise. But when asked many years later, during a seminary class, who had first ordained me to be a priest, I knew immediately it was my grandfather, The Reverend Linwood R. Whitten, or 'Daddy Whit' as all the children and grandchildren called him.

I think almost everyone has a 'Daddy Whit.' Think back to your childhood and try to remember significant adults in your life. Was there an aunt or an uncle, a grandmother or grandfather, a family friend or neighbor, who had a positive influence on your early growth and development? Try to recall ways they helped you, showed you how to cook or work on a car, or tie your shoes, skate, sew, read, spell, etc.

Since my mother had eight brothers and sisters, and we lived with my grandparents, there were many strong and helpful adults in my life. One of the powerful images I have of those early days was lots of family gatherings where there was always large amounts of laughter. Please remember that those were the 1940s (more stories about this time will come in later chapters) and we had no TV to occupy our time. We enjoyed many games such as "Capture the Flag," "Rover, Red Rover," "Hide and Go Seek," "Dodge Ball," "Blind Man's Bluff," "Hot Potato," "Musical Chairs," "Simon Says," and a wonderful, all weather game called "Jenkins Up." (I recently found a website that describes many of these old games, found at: www.kellscraft.com/gamessec1.html.) Sometimes just remembering old family games, or games played with friends, can take you back to earlier years.

Although some memories may be painful or difficult, it is good to not hide from those. If there were memories of abuse, you may want to talk with a professional to help you resolve any persisting impact.

However, for the purpose of simply gathering images that reflect some of your spiritual origins, you may have to go no further than remembering times at church or Sunday school, or recalling religious rituals in your family such as Shabbat or Passover, Iqamat, Namaz, or Janasa.

All such events, and many others, can be a focal point for our soul memories that can also bring back to our consciousness memories of receiving special guidance, spiritual hunches, and that is the topic of our next chapter.

The Lord is my shepherd, I shall not want.
He makes me lie down in green pastures;
He leads me beside still waters; he restores my soul.
He leads me in right paths for his name's sake.
Psalm 23:1-3

Chapter 3

SPIRITUAL GUIDANCE

One evening, about thirty five years ago (when I was still a real estate broker in Charlottesville, Virginia), my wife, Mary Ann, and I were watching TV. I started to feel restless and had the strong impression that I was to go somewhere. I did not know where. I told Mary Ann what I was feeling and decided to drive around town to see if I could get any clearer direction. Fortunately she was accustomed to my sometimes-strange behavior and was not overly concerned.

I started driving to our Episcopal church north of Charlottesville. I was then serving there on the Vestry, was Junior Warden, and a Lay Reader. I reasoned, "Perhaps something is wrong at the church, and since I have a key then maybe I can help resolve the problem." When I pulled into the parking lot there was a large group of people coming out of the parish hall. "Ah Ha!" I thought. "This MUST be where I am supposed to be. I didn't know of any meeting here tonight!"

But back in the recesses of my unconscious mind, where imaginative faculties meet the rational mind and where spiritual guidance seems to be mediated, I could almost hear the words: "No, this is not where you are to go...keep driving." As I looked more closely at the people in the parking lot, everyone seemed to be laughing and talking … no obvious problem. So I turned down the street next to our church and kept driving.

A short way into this residential area my headlights caught the image of a man struggling to climb up the embankment next to the road. He started to stagger out into the street, and then I saw a car that had gone off the road and down the hill.

"This must be where I am supposed to be," I thought. "I am here to help this man." I lowered my window as the man leaned against my door. "Can I help?" I asked, eager to play the Good Samaritan.

"Noooo, I donn't thunk so," was the slurred reply. The man's breath reeked of bourbon. "I thunk I missed my driveway," he continued. "I live just over there," pointing to a nearby house.

I drove on, a little discouraged but still feeling the restlessness, knowing I was supposed to go somewhere. Next I came to an office building owned by a friend. "Perhaps I am supposed to be here!"

"No, keep driving," came the internal guidance.

Driving over a railroad bridge next to a small shopping center near the University of Virginia I saw two police cars parked in front of a small bookstore. I served on the Advisory Board of that store.

"So this must be where I am supposed to be?"

"No, keep driving."

Finally, I pulled up in front of a Roman Catholic Church near the University. I was part of a charismatic prayer group that met there once a week -- but not on this night. I knew the doors were always open, so I went in.

In the corner where the reserved sacrament[12] was kept, I knelt, surrounded by silence and flickering candlelight. "What do you want?" I whispered into the silence.

I then could hear these words very clear in my imagination, "I have been teaching you guidance and obedience. Now go and be with your family."

---

[12]Bread and wine that has been consecrated in an earlier service of Holy Eucharist.

There is one thing I have come to especially appreciate about that mystery we call God: She/He has a sense of humor.

I chuckled to myself and went home, thinking this episode was over and the time really wasn't wasted. The restlessness was gone, and I was learning to listen and hear on an inner level.

The next day I was getting ready to eat lunch at a sandwich shop run by a friend. My Reuben sandwich had just arrived. Suddenly I felt that restless feeling again, but this time it was stronger.

"Get up and go," I heard in my mind.

"Hey, come on! My sandwich just got here, and the Reuben is my favorite!"

"Get up and GO!" This was more than a gentle nudging.

I got up and went, after taking a quick bite from my sandwich and telling my friend to save the rest and I'd be back later to pay. I felt a "pull" to start driving west on Route 250 out of Charlottesville. Approaching a subdivision where I had a home listed, I slowed and got ready to turn, thinking in my logical mind that this must be where I was to go.

"No. Keep going straight," the inner guidance directed.

I kept going out into the country...five...ten...fifteen minutes. Each time I slowed down, thinking maybe it was time to turn, or go back, I got the clear direction to continue.

A year earlier I had sold an old farmhouse to two potters, Alice and Jack. They planned to make the house into a pottery and retail shop. This house was about twenty minutes from town. Alice and Jack were business partners. I had not thought about them for several months.

As I drew closer to their property I *knew*, "This is where I am supposed to go!" Just as I pulled up behind their house, Alice came running out of the back door.

"Help, help," she screamed. "Someone is beating up Jack."

Without asking questions, I ran with her into the house. In the front hall was a very large man lifting Jack up against the wall and banging him against the plaster.

I walked over to the stranger and put my hand on his shoulder. He turned and looked at me with a surprised look on his face, then collapsed on the floor, dropping Jack to the side.

"Get up," I said to him, "and follow me outside," which the stranger did, as Alice rushed to help Jack.

I sat on the front porch as the man paced back and forth in front of me. This continued for about ten minutes. Two or three times he stopped, looked into my eyes, and asked, "Is today Sunday?" When I replied that it was not, he continued to pace.

Finally, a Virginia State Police car pulled up in front of the house. The officer handcuffed the man as he scolded him for "getting away again." After they had gone, I turned to the couple that had been huddled behind the front door while we waited. "What in the world is going on?" I asked.

They related that fifteen minutes earlier this stranger had started knocking loudly on their front door and saying he needed help. When they let him in he asked Alice to call his mother who worked at a bank in Charlottesville. Alice told the mother that her son was in their house and where they were located.

The mother was quite distraught, saying that her son was a mental patient at a state hospital about thirty miles away and he must have escaped, which he was fond of doing. She said he would usually find drugs, and that would send him over the edge. The mother asked Alice to put her son on the phone.

The stranger, after listening to his mother for a few seconds, became very angry. He ripped the phone from the wall, turned, grabbed Jack and started banging him against the wall. We guessed the mother had called the police.

I drove up at exactly that moment, and the rest you know.

I do not pretend to understand all that happened, but note: I received my first impression that I was to leave the sandwich shop at least ten minutes before the stranger had even arrived at the couple's house!

Some have said this is a case of "precognition."

However, my faith is simpler. I believe I was directed by a Higher Power, by God, by Guardian Angels, or by the Holy Spirit to go to that house because I could help. This kind of thing has happened to me numerous times, and to many people I know. This case is the most dramatic, but not necessarily the most significant.

I had another such experience of unconventional guidance while serving as Rector of a parish in northern Virginia. That small town church had a very old Bible that was kept in an unlocked glass case in the receptionist's office. Many times the room was unoccupied and I worried about the safety of that special treasure. The vestry had refused to install an alarm or a more secure case. I purchased a small padlock that could at least fit the little hasp on the front of the case. However, six months later I discovered the lock had been cut and the Bible was missing.

Calling the police we were quickly overwhelmed with detectives dusting for prints and asking about the presence of strangers. Because we frequently had transient visitors stopping at the church to ask for help and we were not sure on which day the Bible was stolen, we realized it would probably be impossible to identify who had taken it. The vestry did offer a $5,000 reward for anyone who could provide information that would lead to the return of the Bible. (Only later did we learn from the Smithsonian that our Bible was worth more than $80,000.)

Not long after we had publicized the reward I got a call from a woman who said she was a psychic and asked if she would receive the reward if she told us where the Bible was located. I said, "Absolutely!" We arranged a time for her to come to the church. When she arrived she suggested we sit in the room where the Bible had been located, so we went into the receptionist's office. I pulled down the shade on the door and locked it, not wanting a stray parishioner to suddenly come into this rather unusual meeting. After we were seated in front of the empty case the woman pulled out an Ouija board (used to spell words received in supposed spiritualistic communications). I declined the invitation to participate in her Ouija session, saying I would sit quietly in prayer.

As the "psychic" began to do whatever it was she was going to do, I closed my eyes and moved into a meditative space opening myself to and asking for guidance from the Holy Spirit. As my meditation deepened I saw in my mind's eye an image of a very thin, somewhat emaciated man in the living room of his home. That was over 20 years ago, but when I think about that even today I can see that image in my mind. It was that clear. On a shelf in that room was a green, plastic garbage bag that was wrapped around a large object that I knew was our Bible. There was a kind of glow emanating from the Bible, and every time the man walked near it, this light expanded to enfold the man with what I understood to be the healing light of Christ. As I saw this image I received in my mind this message: "The Bible is not to be found now. It has work to do." At the same moment I got this message the psychic sitting across from me suddenly exclaimed, "Wow, I'm not supposed to be doing this right now. Something is not right." She immediately put away her Ouija board and, after some brief pleasantries, she departed. I never heard from her again.

I heard nothing from anyone else about our missing Bible. Then one day, about ten months after the Bible had disappeared, I received an unsigned, handwritten letter with no return address. The writing was quite shaky. When I opened the letter a small key dropped from the envelope. The letter was from a man who wrote that he was dying of AIDs. He said he had taken our Bible, explaining that his life companion, many years earlier, had purchased the Bible in an antique book store in England because he recognized some of the names in the family tree that were handwritten on the inside cover of the Bible. He knew they had lived at one time in our parish. It was the understanding of the writer of this note that the Bible was going to go to him when his companion died, also of AIDs. But, when the will was read, he learned that the Bible was being given to our church. The man felt it was his Bible and an important reminder of his companion, which was why he had taken the Bible. But now that he was soon to die, he wanted to return the Bible to us. He said the key was to a locker that contained our Bible and was located at the Richmond Amtrak station. He also asked that the reward go to AIDs research.

I called the detective who was handling the case. He said he would pick me up in ten minutes, if I wanted to go with him to Richmond. I did, and we were off on a very fast trip. I remember roaring down Interstate 95 going about 100 miles per hour with the lights flashing and the siren howling. He said he had called ahead to ask for a bomb squad to be there, because this note could be a hoax. However, when we arrived we were told there were no bomb squad members available at that time. I told the detective that I would go ahead and open the locker. I had a strong, inner assurance that the letter was authentic and that all was safe.

We went into the station which had been cleared of passengers. I went to the locker and inserted the key. I must admit that there were a few drops of perspiration on my brow as I turned that key ... remembering that we are a people of faith, not of absolute or rigid certainty. When I opened the locker the first thing I saw was a green garbage bag wrapping the Bible in exactly the same manner I had seen in the image that had come to me ten months earlier. Another affirmation of the faith I so strongly hold and which holds me!

As an unrelated aside, a reporter later questioned if we would give the reward to AIDs research as had been requested. The vestry of the parish had voted to honor the dying man's petition, which I told the reporter. Somehow the story got twisted and it went out on the AP wire that our church was refusing to give the reward to AIDs research.

Over the next several days I received numerous calls from national TV networks, from the *Washington Post* and from several other major newspapers, all wanting to interview me about our refusing to give the reward to AIDs research. When I informed them that the AP report was incorrect and that our vestry had voted to give the reward to St. Jude's Children Hospital earmarked for AIDs research, each reporter quickly hung up, no longer interested in the story. Since then I have refused to be interviewed by reporters, always telling them they can hear me on almost any Sunday morning often at three different services.

A member of another parish where I once served shared another very special example of spiritual guidance. He was a Colonel in the Army and his wife was a government consultant. They usually drove to work, in Washington, D.C., at different times. But one morning his wife said she wanted them to drive together. After work, when he picked her up, she suggested they visit their daughter who was a boarding student at a private school about an hour's drive away. He asked if she wanted to eat dinner first, and she was insistent that they go right away to the school.

Several times along the way he asked if she were sure she didn't want to have some supper, but each time she became even more certain they were to go to see their daughter as soon as possible. When they arrived at the school they quickly went to her room in the dorm. As they walked into the room their daughter started to turn but fell to the floor in a convulsion. She had never had such an episode before, and no one else was in the room with her at that time. They immediately called for help and did all they could to clear an airway and make her comfortable. A doctor later said that had they not been there when this happened there was a strong possibility she might not have survived.

Another interesting part of this story is that when the call went in to the local Rescue Squad, at the moment it was announced on Squad radio, an off duty Squad member was driving by the gate of that same private school. He immediately drove to the dorm and provided more experienced help until the Squad truck arrived.

Both husband and wife would start to cry when telling this story. In their minds there was no question that they had been led by God to be there at that moment when they were needed to save the life of their daughter.

Another story comes out of my own personal experience. Actually this contains two separate but connected stories. The first story began on the weekend of September 8th, 2003, when Fran (not her real name), a dear friend and parishioner at St. Peter's Church, Oak Grove, had a heart attack. She was admitted to the hospital in Tappahannock, but I did not hear of this until Sunday morning just before our worship service at St. Peter's. Fran had also sent word to me that she was doing fine, and (being aware that I had been recently diagnosed with a severe case of shingles) she said for me not to worry about visiting her right away. However, while I was taking a shower on Monday morning, I had the strong feeling, "Fran is not going to make it." Mary Ann and I quickly dressed and drove to the hospital in Tappahannock. The intuition of impending death had been so strong that when we entered the Coronary ICU, I was expecting to see Fran comatose or on the verge of death. However, as we approached her bed she smiled warmly and said with energy, "I thought I told you to stay home and rest. I'm doing fine!"

We had a nice visit with Fran. Then the three of us joined hands and had a prayer for her healing. I anointed her (placed a cross on her forehead) with oil blessed by my Bishop and pronounced a final blessing, after which she said to me with a great smile, "And right back at you!" We departed feeling wonderful that Fran was doing so well, and I remember saying to Mary Ann as we got to our car, "Well, so much for my intuition that Fran isn't going to make it. She is doing great!" It wasn't until later in the day that we learned that Fran died fifteen minutes after we left her room. Thank God I had listened to that spiritual guidance, and I pray that the simplified "last rites" Mary Ann and I were able to have with her was a comfort at her crossing.

The next story began several weeks before this last event off of the coast of Africa as a tropical depression that was to become hurricane Isabel. The day after Fran's death it became clear that hurricane Isabel was now coming up the Atlantic coast and was starting to take aim at North Carolina, but was still not threatening much of Virginia. However, by 1:00 PM, Thursday, September 18th, when the hurricane struck Cape Hatteras, North Carolina, it was clear that Virginia was in danger. We stocked up on food and batteries at the local Food Lion and settled in to watch the hurricane on TV. It was expected to move more inland, between Richmond and Charlottesville, and not be a problem for the Chesapeake Bay or our area of the Northern Neck of Virginia. But by 7:00 PM it was clear that we were on the dangerous, eastern edge of the storm where the expected winds were to be no greater than 75 to 80 mph. (However, because those winds were moving unobstructed up the Bay, we learned later that we on the Northern Neck got full hurricane force winds of 100 to 120 mph.) By 8:00 PM, the winds were howling and the power went out. I tuned my portable radio to the FM station that gave us the audio of TV Channel 6 (CBS) out of Richmond. We were getting tired and because of my shingles and the importance of my getting plenty of rest, we decided to go to bed. I set up battery-powered lights in the bedroom so Mary Ann could read as I listened to the latest hurricane reports. The severity of the wind became greater.

In spite of my great fatigue, something was tugging at my intuitive faculties and I suggested we move into a front bedroom, away from the tree behind our house. But as soon as we got settled in there, I had another strong spiritual urging, "Get out of bed and go downstairs...NOW!" Especially after what had happened on Monday concerning the warning about Fran's death, we both felt we should listen to that guidance. We moved back down into the den. We had been there for no more than three minutes when we felt the entire house shake and heard a terrible, roaring boom, the sound of breaking glass and of wind gusting through the house. We rushed upstairs and discovered that the window in our bedroom had been torn out and the sheets ripped from our bed. It was evident that the tree beside our house had blown over and in the process one of the limbs had come into our window and across our bed where we would have been if we had not listened to the warnings to move. That particular limb had broken in a previous storm and had a sharp pointed end. I have no doubt that one or both of us would have been seriously injured or killed by that limb had we been in the bed!

Mary Ann did remind me later that when we had first been sitting in the den, she had suggested that we just stay there rather than go up to bed. As I have frequently observed, women often hear intuitive or spiritual guidance quicker than men, but they seem to be less inclined to trust that guidance...as had been the case with Mary Ann. Still, it is clear, I had been "told" to get out of our bedroom just in time to save our lives, although the storm wasn't supposed to be that severe.

In a similar way I have been "told" to visit the hospital when I knew none of our parishioners were there. But when I arrived I have found a member just admitted, or in the emergency room needing pastoral support. These have not been rare or isolated events. And I do not think I am a special case. I have talked with many other clergy and lay people who have been trying to "listen" to guidance from what they call God, the Holy Spirit, their Higher Self, etc. They also report that when they respond to what I call "holy hunches," they usually find someone in need, something needing to be done, or an important opportunity.

Just a few months ago a member of my current parish said she had been driving back from a shopping trip. On the previous Sunday I had discussed in my sermon the importance of frequent moments of thanking God, of how gratitude and grace are related, and how the more grateful we are then the more open we become to God's grace. As she was crossing the bridge across the Rappahannock River, she was thinking of these things and was actively thanking God for everything in her life. Suddenly she had a strong feeling, almost like a voice in her mind, telling her to drive home by a different route. She didn't like that route because it had so many curves. So she ignored the thought, and resumed thanking God. Again she got the same feeling, and again resisted the suggestion and continued on. Finally, as she passed the turn to that road she got the clear impression of words in her mind, "OK, if you aren't going to turn -- then at least SLOW DOWN NOW!" The feeling was so strong that she immediately put her foot on the break and slowed to 45 mph on what was still a 60 mph highway. As she came to the top of a hill, there was a major accident involving multiple cars. The accident had happened just moments earlier. If she had continued at her earlier speed, she would have been in the middle of that pile of mangled autos!

Recently I was at the office when a parishioner came in for a visit. She said she was just at the local drug store and someone had said that another member of our parish, I will call her Joan, was critically ill and perhaps close to death. I had been visiting Joan and taking her home communion for seven years, and she had become another good friend. At my last visit, prior to Easter, she had been weak but not critical. However, as soon as I heard Joan's name I "knew" there was no "perhaps" about her situation, and that I should go out to her home immediately --- which I did. I stayed for over an hour, visiting with her family and being with her, although she was in a coma. The doctors had told the family that Joan might live another 48 hours. I anointed her with oil and had had a final prayer with her, knowing in my heart that this was the last prayer I would have with her. I returned to our church, and, twenty minutes later, I received a call from Joan's son saying she had just died. Both the parishioner who heard the news at the drug store and I had felt a strong hunch that death was near.

My guess is that many, if not all, of us have had similar kinds of "hunches," such as "Slow Down" or "death is near." Most people simply call these "coincidences." I like to call them "God incidences," or as mentioned above, "holy hunches."

Now I must readily admit, not all of these hunches lead me to some need. Three months ago on a day off from parish duties, Mary Ann and I had started driving to Richmond, Virginia, to do some shopping. We had traveled about five miles when I got a strong feeling in my gut that we were not to go, so I told Mary Ann. Immediately she said, "I can't believe it … I was just getting ready to say that I don't think we are supposed to go to Richmond today." We heard of no wrecks on the highway we were to travel, of no danger, no flood, no obvious problem, and we still do not know why we both got that same feeling. Many times I do not understand why I have "heard" this call to "Go," or "Don't go." Nevertheless, I trust that there is a higher Power with infinite knowledge and love, and I am willing to try to serve that Power. I strongly believe that, even when there are no obvious and dramatic results of our obedience, God is at work in beautiful and loving ways.

I admit I have not always obeyed these hunches. Once, on a Sunday afternoon in 1980, I was totally exhausted after preaching at three services and teaching a Sunday school class. I got the "nudge" to go visit an elderly friend at a nursing home. Two days earlier I had taken communion to her, anointed her with oil, and had a long visit with this dear lady. We both knew she was dying, but the doctors said she would live at least another two months. On that Sunday afternoon, I was too tired to go out again, and felt I had nothing else to give. So I didn't go to visit my friend.

That afternoon she died! Fortunately, a retired priest in our parish had received a similar nudge. He responded, and had been with her when she died. For a long while I felt very guilty about that. Finally I realized there were other things to learn in that failure. I saw that God is not dependent on me alone, or on any one individual.

That, I think, is a piece of the wisdom of the Christian understanding of the "Body of Christ." Each individual is part of the larger whole; we all contribute to or detract from the common good. Each of us has different gifts and abilities to offer. And we each are called to do the best we can, no more and no less. And even our failures can work for good. I think we will find that failures are among our best teachers. I believe it was that failure in 1980 which helped me listen in 2003 to the guidance to immediately visit my friend Fran prior to her death, and the same for my friend Joan.

And that continued to inspire me a short while ago when another friend and parishioner was in the hospital approaching death due to a massive stroke. It was late Tuesday afternoon, and I "knew" I was to visit her in spite of terrible storms in the area. I drove the 30 minutes to the hospital in Tappahannock and had a final visit with my unconscious friend (she died later that night).

As I left the hospital I noticed a line of black clouds to the East and tuned my car radio to a local station. There was a tornado warning for the area. I hoped to get out ahead of the storm and make it home before it hit, however the rain kept increasing. Massive black clouds were swirling overhead as I crossed the bridge over the Rappahannock River, and torrential rain was pouring down as I reached the end of the bridge. The car in front of me suddenly came to a complete stop. I was barely able to slide to a stop just two feet behind him, and then realized there was a terrible wreck ahead on the opposite side of the two-lane highway. I wanted to keep rushing ahead of the storm. However, I "knew" on an inner level that I was to go to the car that just crashed into the guardrail and was then hit from behind by another vehicle. I noticed that a few people had gotten out of the cars that were behind the wreck, but no one would approach the front car. I walked over to that mangled wreck and could see a large man slumped against the left side door, from which the window was broken. As I got closer I could see a woman wedged in behind him. I tried to get a neck pulse for the woman but there was none, and I saw there was no breathing. The man was unconscious and quite bloody but still breathing. However, I could see his breathing was shallow and ragged ... death was approaching, and I understood why others were staying away from this car. Most people feel helpless when they are around death.

I felt a deep inner peace as I prayed for both the man and the woman and then talked with the man who was dying. Although he was unconscious, and the woman was already dead, near-death reports lead me to believe a person's soul can often hear what people around them are saying as they leave this life. Since I am quite comfortable being with people who are near death, I believe God put me there at that precise moment, to be with those individuals who were going through the gate to their next adventure of life. With the help of another person we did attempt to open the car doors, just in case we could try CPR, but the car was too crushed. So I stayed with the couple for about five more minutes until he died, too. Another man and I then directed traffic in the pouring rain until State Troopers and the Rescue Squad arrived. On one level, I felt there was so little I could do for that couple since I was not EMT trained and did not have the equipment necessary to cut open the crushed vehicle. However, on another level I knew I was there to offer whatever I could at that moment – and in some way that which I was able to offer was connected to the Infinite Mystery of our loving God.

As we struggle to offer our gifts, and to openly receive the unlimited gifts that are available to us, it is very important that we listen, on that inner level, for guidance. Sometimes the "guidance" may come in the form of very rational planning and decision-making or from a friend or neighbor who, knowingly or unknowingly, points us in the right direction.

I hope these stories have helped you see that we can also hear guidance on an inner, spiritual level. We usually hear this deep in our minds where the creative and imaginative faculties are most active. At other times we are simply placed in situations that call forth the gifts we have received and are somehow connected to God. But sometimes it is hard to determine when we are receiving *genuine* guidance from God and when we are experiencing an overly active imagination.

As mentioned earlier, once a classmate at seminary asked Dean Holmes, "couldn't such feelings be JUST my imagination?" Dean Holmes slammed his hand down on the podium and said, "Don't ever say, 'Just my imagination!' If God is to speak to us He must use our image-producing faculties -- our imaginations; that, ladies and gentlemen, is one of our most precious, God given talents!"

Exercise 3.1 is designed to give you a chance to try your skills at listening on this inner level. If you receive clear guidance to do something and it seems appropriate, then I hope you will act on that guidance.

However, if the guidance seems strange or unusual, requiring you to totally change your life, such as Saint Paul's conversion, please talk with a spiritual guide and "test the spirits" as discussed in APPENDIX A. Although Paul did not seek a guide, one was sent to him. Elsewhere, Paul suggests that we search out a spiritual friend to help evaluate guidance.

EXERCISE 3.1 – Spiritual Listening

1) Go through the relaxation and centering described in Appendix B, and surround yourself with protection.

2) Have a pad of paper or your journal open on your lap. If you are comfortable working at a computer, boot up your word processor, place your fingers lightly on the keyboard, and then get relaxed and centered.

3) Close your eyes and open yourself to the presence of God, the Holy Spirit, your Higher Self, or your Guardian Angel. Ask this presence to help you remember times when you

have felt most distant from God. Open your eyes enough to list these or type them as they come to mind. Don't try to analyze or understand, just list. Put down anything that comes to mind.

4) Now ask this presence to help you remember times when you have felt closest to God, when you have been able to "feel" his/her presence, when you have heard guidance, or received "holy hunches." Again, simply list. At first, most people say they have never had such hunches or intuitions. But when given time to reflect more deeply, almost always there will be recall of significant guidance being received. This exercise helps us awaken these intuitive faculties.

5) Next, ask if there is someone you are to visit or something that you should be doing at this time. Listen carefully for the name of any individual or perhaps you will get a picture of some situation. Open yourself to God's guidance. (Please do this ONLY if you are willing to respond to that guidance as best you can within the time that you have.)

6) Record in your journal anything you receive for later reflection and possible action.

Agnes Sanford, a wonderful spiritual guide, author, and friend, once told me that she would get up every morning and spend time doing this kind of listening. She planned her day around the directions received, and would do only those things that God had directed her to do. She said that a few times each year she received no direction, so she sat in her meditation chair for most of the day! I must admit that I have never taken my "listening" to that level of obedience. However, I do not make any major decision without first spending considerable time simply listening.

After what you sense is an adequate length of time, bring this exercise to a close with a brief prayer thanking God for what you did or did not hear! Both are OK.

I strongly recommend that you record any "hunches" and "leadings" in your journal and how you responded. Gradually over time you will build up more confidence concerning your ability to discern what is fairly reliable guidance and what is not.

I realize one of the dangers that may come from reading about the mystical experiences of others is that one might begin to think that all such experiences are accompanied by flashes of lightning or clashing cymbals.

I have found that a mystical experience may be as simple as a hunch or impression that helps us in our lives or work. We may be led to avoid doing something that could have created major problems for us or for others. The inner direction we get that helps us make a decision in such a way that it brings benefit to us and to our loved ones can also be thought of as a mystical experience.

So as you read about mystical moments in my life and in the lives of others, I hope you will keep a sense of humor and perspective about all of this. Please remember that most writers will not record the day-to-day experiences of life but rather the occasional and exceptional events. But it is also worthy to note that it is in the everyday moments where *limitless living* usually takes place. It is in the simple acts of breathing in and breathing out, of eating a juicy slice of a peach, of seeing a child born, of looking at the stars at night, that we realize we are totally surrounded by and filled with the Infinite Mystery of *limitless living*.

Chapter 4

GUARDIAN ANGELS
& DEPARTED SOULS

I think we have loving, caring, nurturing, teaching, spirits with us each moment of our lives, whether or not we believe in them. I call these helpers "Guardian Angels," others call them "Spirit Guides," "Teachers," our "Higher Self," etc. Sometimes they walk on this earth with us, as did my 'Daddy Whit.' However, most of the time, these Guardian Angels are with us even when we aren't aware. Holy Scripture has many references to these "spirits" or "angels" who are here to help us and guide us[13].

Although I believe I have been in regular contact with my Guardian Angels throughout my life, I made my first recorded contact on August 16, 1987 (the day before what some have called the "Harmonic Convergence"[14]). I was in the middle of a two-week Clergy Development Conference in Bethlehem, Pennsylvania, sponsored by the Alban Institute, and was planning to take the weekend off with family at my sister's home in New York State. Near there was the site of one large gathering of "Convergence" participants, in

---

[13] There are 109 references to angels in Jewish scripture, or the Old Testament, and 171 references in the New Testament. Some have called the Book of Revelations the "Book of Angels" because it alone mentions angels 68 times. A fascinating and revealing study is to look up some of the references and see how these helpful spirits have moved in the lives of people in the past.

[14] The Harmonic Convergence was a loosely-organized New Age event, when groups of people gathered in various sacred sites and "mystical" places all over the world to usher in a new era. It occurred on August 16, 1987, a date based primarily on the Mayan calendar, but also on interpretations of European and Asian astrology. (http://en.wikipedia.org)

Woodstock, New York I did not feel led to go to that gathering but planned my own observance on my sister's farm.

The night before this "New Age" event, I was asleep in the college dorm where the Clergy Conference was taking place. College party noises, then breaking glass across the field in front of my dorm awakened me. I wrote the following in my journal:

8/15/87, Saturday, 1:25 AM. (I described the sounds outside.) Wide • *awake now. Have turned on a white sound generator to cover outside party sounds.*

Today is the day before the Harmonic Convergence and the beginning of a new age. This evening I did Tai-Chi as the sun was setting and felt I was saying "good-by" to the present age, actually feeling some sadness at the passing. Strange?

Time is actually an illusion. All things and all time is now, there is only the One which encompasses the All. But these things such as time and space help our limited, finite minds function within the One -- to differentiate ourselves for a while so we can work on what we are here to do, prior to moving back into the One.

I have the feeling that I am to let my pen start writing without mental review:

(The following words were then written in handwriting very different from my own.)

Oooom is the sound we use to tie down the infinite sound which started this all at the beginning and which is the source of this all, but we can never tie that infinite, unknowable force in any way. It simply IS as we ARE.

Who are you?

I am your Guardian Angel, your friend in light. My task is to watch over your mission and help you stay on track. [Upon reading this, a good friend who knows me well remarked that this was an impossible task!]

Why do you speak directly with me now?

I have been speaking with you throughout your life as conscience, hunches, special urges, insights and so on . . .

I start wondering about what was happening to me, and there is a pause. Then the writing continues.

Try not to review what is coming through, just write -- OK?

OK. Is there something you want to let me know now?

Yes. Do not be overly concerned about the Harmonic Convergence. This will be going on for many years, and there will be plenty of time for you to accomplish what you are here to accomplish. However, there is a specific task for you as this time period begins and your participation is vital. You are one of the beings who have a special mission to love this part of the universe. The way you loved that apple was an exercise to prepare you for loving this galaxy.

The day before, as part of our morning spiritual exercises, I had done what is called a "Zen walk" through an apple, taking about an hour to savor and finally consume it. I treasured each bite and loved the apple for sacrificing its life for me. I shed tears over that apple and felt tremendous closeness to it as another living entity. The strange handwriting continued in my journal.

Do not limit your love and concern for just the Earth. Hold this galaxy you call "Milky Way" in your hands and love it the way you loved that apple. Love all the atoms and combinations of atoms, the suns and planets, the clouds of matter, the swirling gasses, the energy and light, the darkness and black holes, the life forms as varied as the species on this world.

Love them all! This will be your gift to the galaxy -- not to take credit for -- but because it is important. The galaxy needs your love as we make this harmonic shift, to keep it from splitting apart. Hold the galaxy in your hands and, along with several thousand other beings, your love will keep this galaxy functioning -- in love, for the purpose of love.

Is this just my imagination? (In spite of what I said in the previous chapter about Dean Holmes' admonition to never say this, I still

seriously question all paranormal events, and always tend to wonder, "Is this pure fiction?"[15])

*What if it is? You know you must do this -- because you are here to
love, to learn love, to be love, no matter what!*

Yes. I understand.

*This is one of the reasons you have learned Tai-Chi, so you can
learn a Galaxy Form that will become part of your daily spiritual
discipline.*

I realize this conversation may sound rather strange, unreal, and
perhaps even delusional, but for me it was very meaningful. That
was the first of thousands of what I believe were direct conversations with the Guardian Angel I named "GA" (for "**G**uardian **A**n-
gel"...not very creative but at least I can remember the name).
There seem to be several other Guardian Angels also helping me at
this time, with which I have also had conversations. Evidently I
need much help.

I think I am not unusual or exceptional in this contact with my
Guardian Angels. I believe, and the experiences of many others
agree, that we all have Guardian Angels. These angels never block
our direct contact with God. However, they are close friends who
walk with us and support us. They are loving agents of that Mystery
we call Almighty God.

But here I must add a warning. From what I understand, there may
be other "spirits" in this world that are not concerned about our
welfare and are not agents of light and life. I have not experienced
them, but some say these "spirits" are departed souls who chose not
to leave this plane of existence or who are so trapped by their

---

[15] The late 1980s did see a tremendous geopolitical shift, especially the
fall of communism. Many esoteric prophecies had predicted, the Harmonic
Convergence would usher in a five-year period of Earth's "cleansing," where
many of the planet's false structures of separation would collapse. Shortly after
this event, the American stock market collapsed, followed by a significant stand-
off in China's Tieneman Square, the ending of apartheid in South Africa, and
finally the collapse of the Berlin Wall. Many believers in new age philosophy
point to these events as being indicative of a major cosmological shift.
(http://en.wikipedia.org)

earthly concerns that they cannot escape. These spirits may appear to be giving us wisdom. But when we examine their communications we realize it is often garbage – the workings of small, dark minds.

Therefore, (as I have suggested in Appendix B, Step 4) when we are talking or working with our Guardian Angels or doing any spiritual exercise, it is wise to first surround ourselves verbally and spiritually with the protective Light of Christ, or whatever spiritual source you find to be safe and protecting. This is important. Those who do not protect themselves in this way occasionally report experiencing dark or negative forces or spirits. That has not been my experience, which I attribute to having a strong foundational faith, a support system within a community of faith, and to using such protection.

If you have not yet formally met your own Guardian Angel, and would like to do so, try this next exercise after you have followed the protective procedure in Appendix B. I have successfully introduced many people to their Guardian Angels through this simple process. These steps may seem too easy. Try to remember, we do not have to make anything hard or difficult. Often we feel we must earn or deserve contact with the Holy Spirit or with our Guardian Angels. The Grace of God is a free gift. Our entire lives are surrounded by and filled with gifts!

EXERCISE 4.1 – Meeting Your Guardian Angel

1) After you are relaxed and centered, from your spiritual center mentally ask, "Are you there?" or "Will you talk with me?" Direct your question to your primary Guardian Angel. (I usually find that most of us have more than one, located at different places around our bodies.)

2) If you are doing this exercise to secure genuine help and not just out of curiosity, you will usually get a rather quick and sometimes surprising response. More often than not within a few moments you will intuitively hear or feel a clear "Yes." Consider that "yes" to be an invitation to continue your conversation. Feel free to ask questions of your Guardian Angel. You may want to see if a name, image or

symbol is associated with your Guardian Angel. If you do not get an immediate response, that does not mean you have no Guardian Angel. Relax, smile, and try again later.

3) Record any direction or conversation with your Guardian Angel in your journal. (I have sometimes found it helpful to sit at my word processor or typewriter so I can rapidly record what I receive.)

Another important activity is to test what we are being given, especially if it is guidance to be acted upon. This is a procedure I frequently recommend throughout this book. Please see "Apendix A – Testing Spiritual Guidance."

My reception and recording of spiritual communication can sometimes be confusing and perhaps incorrect. Therefore, I rarely report to others what I think I receive from my Guardian Angels (or from the Holy Spirit). Looking back in my journal I see entries in which I thought I was receiving guidance. However, a later writing has shown that some of this "guidance" was perhaps incorrect or I had interpreted it incorrectly. Such experiences keep me humble. I am *very* cautious about ever saying, "God told me this," or "God told me to tell you....," etc. When I do feel directed to share something that may be from my contact with God or my Guardian Angels, I always try to couch it in these kinds of terms: "I have been getting the feeling that I am supposed to share something with you. However, I am not certain whether this is from God or from me. Please, test this yourself for its truth and reliability."

For example, my Guardian Angel informs me now as I am writing these words that many who read this book will do so primarily from a desire to only hear about the unusual, the super-natural, or extraordinary. That is natural curiosity. But, at its worst it might become voyeuristic spirituality, which will only leave us feeling empty and depressed. We may think, "Why can't I do that?" or "There must be something wrong with me because I haven't experienced anything like that."

True curiosity, at its best, is a desire to learn and to know, a drive to explore. Each of us has already been on a rich spiritual pilgrimage whether or not we realize it. My prayer is that this book will take you deeper into your own inner resources. Investigate the spiritual parts of yourself and of the Mystery. Use the reflections contained in this book to spark your own reflections. Use the exercises in this book to further your own spiritual adventure. Anything I have done, you can do. You are special. Your experiences are unique. Your Guardian Angels are yours, are with you and are ready to actively guide and support you.

I close this discussion of Guardian Angels with one piece of faith. Often people have come to me feeling like they have failed at some spiritual exercise or in working with their Guardian Angels. I believe that when we are open to the energy and power of God and are following our spiritual paths with high ideals, aimed at furthering Love in our lives and in this world, then we really can't "fail." As we strive, seek, and struggle with love in our hearts everything we do is already successful.

I accept what St. Paul said in his letter to the Christians in Rome: "We know that **all things work together for good** for those who love God...." (Romans 8:28) So even our mistakes and failures can work for good!

Departed Souls

We now move to the topic of "departed souls," which may not be that different from "Guardian Angels." Some have suggested that Guardian Angels are actually departed souls who have taken on the task of helping those of us still in our earthly pilgrimage. When I asked GA about this I received a very simple answer, "Some are and some aren't."

Knowing that most of my readers will not have conversed with departed souls or Guardian Angels, I realize this topic may make some scratch heads in wonder and disbelief. That is a natural and healthy response to something that is outside of our day-to-day experience.

On the other hand, others may say, "Yes, something like that has happened to me!" The number of times someone has said this to me is so large that, over my almost 30 years of priesthood, I have lost count of how often. But it is clear the frequency is major. That being the case, I am convinced that something is happening that is beyond ordinary reality. What I am speaking of is the experience of regular people seeing deceased loved ones.

I usually hear such reports only after I have preached a sermon or told a story in which I mention such events, and make it clear that I accept this as a possibility. My most recent experience of this was just ten months ago. I happened to be talking on the phone with a parishioner, a member of our Vestry (a church governing board) about a totally different matter. I mentioned how much I liked the TV show "Ghost Whisperers," but that I was disappointed with the recent tone of some story lines where the spirits were being portrayed as more and more violent and threatening—probably just to boost ratings. I said that my experience with departed spirits was that they were loving and concerned.

My friend and parishioner immediately said, "You mean you believe that stuff?" I replied that I had talked with many people over the years that had experienced, both in dream states and in normal waking consciousness, meeting departed loved ones. Sometimes this was a family member from another part of the country who would wake them in the middle of the night at exactly the time they died far away. Others have seen a brief presence of that loved one not long after a person's death.

My friend immediately said, "I can't believe you are saying that! I thought I was crazy and wouldn't tell anyone about this. But, right after my father died, I woke up in the middle of the night because of a banging on the sliding glass door to our bedroom. I looked and there was my father knocking on the glass, and with him was grandma – who had died many years before. I think she was helping him move on into the next life. I knew he was close to death, but I didn't know until the next morning that he had died at approximately the time I saw him outside of our bedroom. I believe he really was there!"

I said, "That is exactly what I think also." My friend asked, "So you don't think I'm crazy?" To that I replied, "If you are, then thousands upon thousands of other people are also crazy."

I guess I should have said, "Well maybe we are all a little half-crazy," in the sense of that model I mentioned in Chapter One. In that model, when we move into the area of "non-ordinary reality" we are moving in a "half-crazy" world in which burning bushes may not be consumed by the flames, and where loved ones may appear to us after their death.

But, as I have said before and will say again, with most such events in non-ordinary reality, the reports of these experiences are personal, individual and anecdotal. This means it is difficult, if not impossible, for science to verify through replicable experiments that such occurrences really do happen. It is only in telling stories of these experiences that we learn of them, not through the collection and mathematical manipulation of data to prove a hypothesis.

We are a people of stories. Stories help to give meaning to our lives. Stories help us remember, especially in the sense of re-membering or putting ourselves back together. The experience of death is a tearing and dismembering thing. We feel torn apart by the loss of a loved one. As we share stories, we are remembering, which allows us to be put back together so we can move on with our lives.

That is why I think such encounters with departed spirits are so valuable. The discussion of them should be encouraged, not questioned or derided as being wishful dreams of the bereaved or empty delusions of the deranged. I believe such encounters are real. They happen often enough to normal, ordinary people, that either all of us are deluded or the boundary between life and death is not as clear as we suppose.

A rabbi once told me of an ancient Jewish custom which suggests that when a person dies the body is not to be moved for two or three hours in order to help the person make their transition to the other side. Doesn't it seem logical that such a long held tradition would have developed only if people of the past had experienced the spirits of loved ones who were making the transition from this life to the next life?

Now I must agree with other mental health professionals that some such experiences may very well be the result of emotional trauma, which stimulates flashes of memory of a loved one. The experience of hearing a door slam and knowing that a departed spouse is walking into the house is stereotypical of this type of event. But at the same time, I believe we need to accept the possibility that we may be actually encountering a loved one when we feel a slight touch on our cheek when no one is in the room with us or when there is a momentary flash from the corner of our eye that looks like our departed spouse is sitting in her favorite chair.

Believing it is possible allows us to be open to, and accepting of the experience. But I realize that such experiences may also evoke fear. We fear the unknown, and so much TV and movie drama likes to portray encounters with "ghosts" as being terrifying or even dangerous. That is sad, because if we expect such an experience to be fearful, then we will feel fear when a departed loved one reaches out to touch us in some way as they make their transition to the next life. I invite us to realize that this can be a warm, loving event that can help both of us make the transition and can especially help us start the healing process of grieving their loss. When we can accept the possibility that our loved one has moved on into their next adventure of existence, then we are more able to continue this life here, while still holding a holy hope of eternal life with those we love.

I also realize that sometimes telling such stories may make us sad. I have to say that it is OK to be sad; it is important to be able to let ourselves cry. Tears are an indication of not just our hurt but also of our love. When someone we love dies, we care, we hurt. Something terrible has happened, and we can't pretend it has not. Our loved one is no longer physically with us here and that hurts! It hurts really badly.

Sometimes the loss of a pet can hurt as much or even more than the loss of another human being. That may sound strange, and yet that pet was so dependent upon us and was often more present to us on a day-to-day basis than a husband or wife. A husband or wife has their own life to live and an independence that is critical to their own emotional survival and health. But a pet is there with us totally and completely. And when that pet dies, the loss is total and complete.

Five years ago our Golden Retriever "Dodger" died. He had been my good friend for fourteen years. Our daughter had helped raise Dodger from a small pup. We had shared so many good times together. When Dodger died I had such deep, soul wrenching grief, with sobs and moans of inner pain so profound that I wondered about my own health. When he was alive Dodger and I would take long walks together, and I would talk with him about my deepest problems and greatest concerns ... and he would listen with loving eyes and a knowing smile as though he really understood. Anyone who has owned a Golden Retriever knows what I'm talking about. And I expect anyone who has loved any attentive dog or cat knows about this type of behavior.

So after Dodger's death, I still took my walks and felt that Dodger was walking with me, that he was still listening to my problems and concerns. One day my then eleven-year-old granddaughter, Sacha, went walking with me. I told her that I would still talk with Dodger when I went on such walks. When she got home she immediately went to her father, my son, and told him, "I don't think Grandpa is doing too well. He thinks he can still talk to Dodger."

Even children are becoming so overwhelmed with "ordinary reality" and the science surrounding its comprehension that imagination and mystery are being squeezed from their lives. I pray that we will help our children keep alive the mystery. Tell stories. Especially tell unusual stories that expose them to the possibility that non-ordinary reality does exist, that life after death does exist, and that more is going on in this world, in this universe, than we can begin to imagine.

Not long ago I was talking with a parishioner and she said, "You know, you are kind of weird." My honest reply was, "Thank you." I then explained that our word "weird" actually comes from an Old English word "wyrrd" which means "of or related to the supernatural." It is my hope that I, as an Episcopal priest and as a human being, will always be somewhat weird, i.e., that I will always be related to the supernatural. So if someone calls you weird for learning about non-ordinary spiritual activity, then I hope you will express your genuine gratitude for the profound compliment.

Chapter 5

JOURNAL KEEPING
& RECORDING DREAMS

I once read about a psychiatrist who required all of his patients to keep journals. Often he gave them assignments to carry out in their journals. He realized, after many years, that the greatest healing results were not obtained by his active counseling but by the patients' individual work in their journals. Likewise, great spiritual growth can come from following one's own inner guidance and keeping journal records. It connects our inner and outer worlds.

While I was a young child I didn't keep a diary, thinking that was only for girls. So I have missed the fun of being able to go back and read some of my earliest thoughts and reflections. I first started keeping a kind of journal when I was about twelve. Our family had a recreational farm fifteen miles from our home in Danville, Virginia. That farm became a spiritual and emotional haven during my teenage years. I would wander our sixty-five acres of woods and fields feeling like they were thousands. Sometimes I would spend hours lying on the moss next to a stream, peering into the waters and watching the movement of life. On other occasions I would watch a bird building a nest, follow the track of a deer, or sit on our highest hill watching an approaching thunderstorm. Once I wrote a poem about a dead tree, and another about the sounds of darkness. I drew sketches and captured moments.

I remember much of this because I recorded my thoughts on loose-leaf notebook paper as a kind of primitive journal. I had not yet discovered the wonderful invention of Mead composition notebooks

(I like the ones with the black binding and black speckled hard covers) to record thoughts, ideas, prayers, poems, etc. I believe readers seriously interested in spiritual exploration would be wise to keep a journal. A journal is not a record of daily events. Rather it is a place for you to report on special insights, spiritual experiences, new questions or perspectives, learnings, hopes, fears, beliefs, dreams, etc.

For years my journal writing was free of structure except for recording the date and time. Some of my earliest reflections did not even have a date, so I must guess when they were written. I now recommend a minimum framework, which will give your writings greater utility if you later study or review your spiritual pilgrimage. You may want to include a date and time, and perhaps the weather. (There is some speculation that certain types of barometric conditions actually enhance spiritual activity. Perhaps later researchers may be able to use our reports.) Some journal keepers record phases of the moon or other astrological data.

Simply writing reflections and thoughts pull them out of the momentary sparks of mental processes and give them substance and greater potential for learning. Most of the stories in this book would have been lost if it were not for my journals. Sometimes my journal notes are from my own internal perspective. On other occasions I am an observer of a journey, a recorder of events, seeing symbols and meanings I would have missed were it not for the journal reflections.

I received the following suggestions about keeping a journal while in seminary. Although I have no record of the source, I still find them useful.

"A journal says something about who one was today in the context of life and who he/she is at the moment of writing. A journal is a continuing confrontation with oneself in the midst of life. By writing a journal one makes concrete one's own relationship with oneself.

"No matter how well one thinks he remembers and retains his thoughts and fantasies, changes and revisions are unconsciously made each time we think about them, unless we have subjected ourselves to the discipline of writing it down in black and white.

"It is all too easy to convince ourselves that we were not hostile or infantile yesterday unless we read the clear evidence of it written down yesterday.

"In the journal all the relationships that are important to one's own life can be set down, explored and encountered anew. The mere act of careful and honest description made tangible by being written down is an important step in clarification. The gathering of insight can occur naturally and spontaneously and is cumulative as the work progresses." (source unknown)

I like to use my journal as a place to record conversations with my Guardian Angels and with God, as has already been seen in the previous chapter. More will be said about this in later chapters on meditation, channeling and conversations with the Masters.

Remember that your journal is a private record. It can take any format that you wish to use. My wife, who knows true shorthand, often uses such notations in her journal. Others develop their own form of abbreviations that will have meaning only for them. I never write in my journal with the idea that it will be read by someone else. These are for me, for my own personal use, to further my own journey into *limitless living*.

In addition to recording portions of your spiritual journey, your work with a journal can utilize formal exercises to deepen your awareness or increase your understanding of what has gone before and where you are going next. For example, I have led spiritual growth groups in which we utilized the following exercise to raise awareness of our religious journeys.

Exercise 5.1 – Exploring Your Religious or Spiritual Journey

1) With your journal at hand, take time to relax (as suggested in Appendix B), and then drift back in you memories to your first memory of being in a church or other religious center. What was it like? How did it make you feel? What religious behavior did you observe in the adults? How did

that first experience influence your later spiritual journey? Record your observations in your journal.

2) Try to remember what you were taught by parents or guardians about religious or spiritual experiences, and record these in your journal. Was religion or faith important to your parents or guardians, and how did their attitudes influence your attitudes? Did your family have prayers at special times, at meals, at bedtime, and other special events? Record.

3) Was there a major spiritual event for you such as First Communion, Confirmation, or Bar/Bath Mitzvah? Record what that was like for you and how it still impacts your life.

4) When did you first start to question the dogma of formal religion and how did that make you feel? Was there support for your spiritual questions or was doubt condemned as evil, and how do those attitudes still impact your journey? Record your reflections.

5) Record some of your most meaningful religious or spiritual experiences outside of formal religious settings, for example, walking at night under the vast dome of stars and feeling great awe and wonder at the infinite mystery of it all. How have such experiences expanded your sense of that which is "holy" or "divine?"

6) Sometimes it is helpful to create a spiritual or religious "time line" in your journal, with your birth on the left and a straight line that goes through the years of the past and moving out into the future on the right. Then record on that time line the positive and negative events, rituals, conversions, revelations, etc., with the positive events above the line and the negative below the line. This will give you a visual representation of your religious past and perhaps some indication of future hopes and new directions for your journey.

As mentioned above, keeping a journal may also be a valuable aid to your emotional or psychological growth. I suggest to almost all of my pastoral counseling clients that they keep a journal to support the work we do together. However, I will say here and repeat again below, if you are currently or have in the past been in psychotherapy, it is essential that you first discuss this with your mental health professional since some parts of the following exercise (4.2) may be contraindicated for your particular problem. These suggestions can also be helpful if you are working with a spiritual director. By discussing your journal observations with your therapist or spiritual director you can integrate those into your spiritual journey.

I have found that using a journal increases our ability to express ourselves just by learning to write our thoughts and feelings on the pages of our journal. That will naturally enhance our self-expression during counseling sessions, or just in our day-to-day conversations with colleagues and friends.

Although the following suggestions may be helpful for those who are in psychotherapy, working with a spiritual director, or simply wishing to deepen their spiritual journey, one must use caution and common sense when engaging in any exercise that changes one's emotional state. If there is any history of dissociative disorders, delusional thinking, or psychotic episodes, then it makes sense to avoid practices that will move one into a dissociative state, i.e., when one feels separated from one's self or from logical, rational processes or split off from our core of consciousness.

Since much spiritual thinking involves a kind of movement into non-ordinary experiences outside of our day-to-day logical thinking, we need to be aware of when we are in such a non-ordinary state and when we move back into ordinary reality. Most people can learn to move easily and safely between these states of consciousness and need not worry about any danger of "being caught or trapped" in a weird spiritual experience. When a healthy person moves into a deep trance state or self-hypnosis, there is no danger of being unable to return to a waking state. If alone, such a person in a deep trance state can simply drift into normal sleep and then awaken when ready to do so.

However, individuals with any history of dissociative, psychotic, or delusional episodes should avoid deep spiritual exploration, unless done under the supervision of a mental health professional or trained spiritual director.

Exercise 5.2 – Journal Keeping While in Psychotherapy or When Working With a Spiritual Director

*(If you are in therapy, **do not** utilize this exercise until you discuss this with your mental health professional, and then use your journal work as a adjunct to your therapy.)*

1) Record your reasons for being in therapy or for working with a spiritual director. What is the nature of your problem, pain, depression, despair, hopes, fears, etc.? Record in your journal your response to the following questions.

2) What are you now doing that is not working? What is working? Often we go into therapy because what we have tried to do in the past has not helped, and we see no other alternatives. How long has this been going on? Observe how other significant people have made this worse and/or have helped. Try not to put all the blame on the other person. Record how have you have contributed to this problem or situation.

3) Try to express your anger and/or frustration in your journal rather than hold those feelings inside. Initially this may be helpful. Later, if we express our anger or replay a painful event, over and over, then we may simply reinforce the trance state we have been in, which can make it even harder to see a solution or a way out.

4) What old expectations do you hold that may be having a negative impact on this problem? How might changing your expectations have a positive impact or expand your spiritual journey?

5) Have you seen any new possibilities, or received any intuitive hints as to how this problem might be resolved immediately, or over time?

6) After discussing the above thoughts and reflections with your therapist and getting an O.K. to continue, you might try one or both of the following:

7) Move into a relaxed state and ask yourself, "What am I feeling at this very moment?" Then imagine where in your body this problem is having its greatest impact, e.g., in

stomach, chest, arms, etc. Focus on that location in your body, and then gradually listen to what that area may be telling you about new directions and new possibilities. Record these observations and discuss them with your therapist. It has been suggested that just learning to focus attention on where in our body we are feeling the impact of our problem drastically increases our ability to heal or recover from that problem.[16]

8) Move into a relaxed state; then try to imagine a symbol or some physical representation for your problem. Imagine that symbol or image in the room with you. Then move around that image, see it from behind, from above, from below, then drift away from it. How does your perception of the problem change when you change your physical perspective? Record your observations and then discuss these with your therapist.

9) Finally, ask yourself: "What blessing or gift am I being given in this problem?" If you can see no gift present, try taking a deep breath and as you breathe out allow a slight smile to be on your face, even if you do not feel like smiling. Then, keeping that smile, look again at your problem and try to see the gift or blessing that is present. Record your observations and discuss them with your therapist.

Somewhere along the way I found the following journal-writing suggestions with which you may wish to experiment: A) write an unsent letter, making believe you are telling someone what you like and/or dislike about them, which can provide a catharsis. Although this is an undelivered letter it may clarify your feelings and offer an opportunity to resolve unfinished business. B) Explore some of the roads you did not take in your life. Imagine that you had taken that job which you didn't take, or married that other person, and how your life would be different today. C) Imagine where you will be one month from now? One year? Ten years? This helps us get in touch with the direction we want to follow in our lives, what we want to do and be, and in the process awaken our intuitive and

---

[16] Eugene T. Gendlin, Ph.D., *Focusing, 2nd Edition* (New York, Bantam Books, 1982), and other books by Dr. Gendlin.

creative wisdom. D) Freeze-frame happy moments. Remember the good feelings. Attach a word or phrase to those feelings. I call this "Creating a Positive Resource State."

As we record in our journal a detailed description of a very positive moment, and recall the associated emotional and physical elements of that state, we can later utilize those feelings as a positive resource to promote our relaxation, stress reduction and emotional healing. Neuro-Linguistic Programming[17] suggests creating an "anchor" for such feelings by, for example, touching the back of our hand at a specific place as we experience such a resource state. By doing so, many people have found it easier to return to a fuller experience of those emotions. I have found the following to be just as resourceful: simply record in your journal the happy or relaxing moment; find a word or phrase that represents that moment; then by simply saying that word or phrase in your mind, you can bring into the present some of those positive feelings your have recorded and thus expand your own *limitless living*.

Dream Work

I have observed that recording dreams in our journal is another powerful way to help us move toward *limitless living*.

If I report a dream in my journal I start that record with the large word "DREAM" in the margin so I can quickly go back and find these. Dream analysis often follows not just one dream but the flow of many dreams over many months. In searching for old dreams you can quickly get bogged down in reading all your journal musings. Labels in the margin can help you rediscover special dreams and themes.

While in seminary we were required to record our dreams for several months in a separate dream journal. We were then told to look for the primary symbols that occurred repeatedly and write a creative fairy tale using those symbols. This was a technique designed to increase our intuitive functioning, and it worked quite well for most of us.

---

[17] Joseph O'Connor and John Seymour, *Introducing Neuro-Linguistic Programming* (London: Harper Collins Publishers, 1990), p. 69-75.

One very powerful dream occurred during this period. After recording it I went back to sleep. The next morning, I did not remember having recorded the dream or having dreamed at all. Later in the day I looked in my journal and found this report:

DREAM February 1976: I am in a grocery store. There is a great commotion over in another part of the store. I move in that direction. I hear a roaring, swirling sound mixed with deep groaning noises, as though the building were moving.

A crowd has gathered around a section of shelves. I push through to look. I see that a portion of the shelves has disappeared and in its place is a gaping hole filled with a swirling chaos from which these noises are coming.

We start discussing what this might be, e.g., a time warp or a overlap with another dimension of space. We notice that the area is slowly moving down the aisle. Where it has been is now just empty space in the store. Someone suggests that this is some kind of being that will gradually consume our planet.

I remember the idea that in the chaos we might encounter God. I ask for a rope, which I tie around my waist. The others are instructed to pull me back in 30 seconds.

I go through the space and am totally in another world or dimension. Colors swirl about me. Time feels different. Just as I am getting some kind of bearing I am pulled back into the bright light of the grocery store and people are asking me questions. I tell them I must go back, that something is calling me to return. I untie the rope and push back through the opening into the swirling, groaning chaos.

I glide gently amidst changing colors. The colors move through me, become part of me and almost sing within my body. Each color seems to have a tone associated with it, so I am surrounded by and filled with floating, swirling melodies. This is a beautiful sensation and I notice I feel no fear of the unknown.

I am not falling but floating, as though in water, but I notice I can breathe that in which I am floating. I decide that the molecular density of this space must be the same as my body but is still gaseous with an atmospheric pressure that allows breathing.

I realize that by changing the position of my body and moving my arms like I am swimming a frog stroke, I move freely through this space with the sensation that I am flying. I spend a good while just doing loops and dives and power stalls – going straight up then flipping over backward into slow spins.

The air is fresh, cool and full of energy so I do not get tired.

Soon I start feeling that there is somewhere I must go. I take off my shirt to use as a sail, for I have noticed there is a slight breeze within this swirling, colored, music-filled material.

I hold up my shirt, lie back and begin drifting along, awestruck by the beauty in which I am floating.

After a while I begin to hear a new sound, like waves breaking on a shore. There are creatures now swimming near me. They look a little like otters, but are different somehow. We swim together toward the shore.

I realize I can now walk but am still surrounded by the same material. So I can glide or swim along or settle back down and walk.

I am taken to meet someone. I move into the presence of a pure white Light and I feel totally loved. Just as the colors and music surrounded me, and swirled through me, now I feel love doing the same thing....

Later, as I reflected on this dream, I felt again this love flowing through me. The experience was so real that I truly felt I had been in the presence of God! This was a very special dream, and yet it was more than a dream… perhaps like a vision. I share this to show how such dreams are pathways to God, as dreams have been throughout human history. Another reason I include it here is to point out that I would not have remembered this dream if I had not been actively recording my dreams in a notebook next to my bed. I had made a commitment to myself to try to remember and record dreams, so when I awoke during the night it was a natural thing to do. It required little conscious effort.

Many people tell me they do not dream or they can never remember them. The following suggestions may help.

EXERCISE 5.3 - Dream Recall & Guidelines

1) Have your journal next to your bed, open, with a pen ready to record anything you remember. Before going to sleep say a short prayer or simply suggest to yourself that you will remember what you need to remember.

2) If you awaken during the night and remember any part of a dream, record all you can at that time. Do not wait until morning.

3) When you first awaken, lie quietly and still. Let your mind focus on the first thing that comes to the surface. Even if you don't recall a dream, your first waking thoughts may remind you of the content of your last dream and allow you, with practice, to remember more details of the dream.

4) Always record your dreams in the first person, present tense as if they are happening in the present moment, as I did in the above example. As you write in this way further recall, and sometimes more detail, is generated.

5) Record anything you can remember about a dream, even if it is only one image or one feeling. After several weeks of making such records you may see a pattern to these images. When you first start recording dreams you may only get a glimpse of a face or a building. Don't be discouraged.

6) Always be careful in interpreting your dreams. Some people may give you a quick analysis of the meaning of your dream. However, that is what the dream means to them. Only you can discover the true meaning of your dream for you. I like to assume that my dreams represent a message to me from a deeper part of myself. Only rarely do I encounter a dream that seems to contain a message from God, but always be alert to that possibility. Jung suggests that each part of your dream is actually a part of yourself. Even though you may be dreaming about a person you know in ordinary reality, think about what that person may represent within you.

7) Also be alert to the possibility that your dream is telling you something literal. If you dream that there is $1,000 under the rug in the hall, first look under that rug. Then start looking for other meanings.

8) Find a spiritual guide who can help if you want to become involved in serious dream analysis. Ask your priest, pastor or psychotherapist to recommend someone knowledgeable in this area or someone who has special training in spiritual guidance.

Some people find Jungian dream analysis to be quite helpful. The late Carl G. Jung (1875-1961) believed that many dreams are messages from our unconscious minds, often in the form of archetypes or symbols. In my own dream studies, I have talked with such dream symbols to receive guidance and insight. However, such dream work can occasionally be traumatic, or bring about sudden insights that may be shocking, and should be undertaken only with professional guidance.

Finally, through a study of rapid eye movements (REM) and other physiological signals, while individuals are asleep, and of associated blood chemistry changes, dream research has shown that the process of dreaming is necessary to our psychological health. Every person dreams every night, unless there is some pathology or medicine blocking that process or when sleep is often interrupted so normal dreams cannot happen.

When one goes without dreaming for more than three nights hallucinations will occur – which is one cause of many truck accidents when drivers on long hauls have been kept awake with drugs or too much coffee. That is also why in hospital intensive care units, where sleep is frequently disrupted by medical procedures, noise of other patients, and pain medications, patients will often see strange things or have other hallucinations (now given the clinical designation "ICU[18] syndrome/delirium" manifested by a variety of psychological reactions, including fear, anxiety, depression, hallucinations, and delirium).

---

[18] Intensive Care Unit

So whether or not we remember our dreams, they are still working for us as we sleep. For this we can be truly thankful!

Journal writing and recording dreams are just two resources for spiritual guidance or spiritual awakening. In the next chapter we will explore some of the most valuable pathways into *limitless living*...meditation, mantras and chakras.

Chapter 6

MEDITATION, MANTRAS & CHAKRAS

I f you read only one chapter in this book, I hope it will be this. Here we come to the heart of any serious spiritual journey, the essential element in spiritual growth, and the most accessible doorway into the Mystery of God: meditation.

Meditation is a central part of Biblical prayer. The great "prayer book" of the Bible, the Psalms, has many references to meditative activity, e.g.: "Let the words of my mouth and the meditation of my heart be acceptable in thy sight, O Lord, my rock and my redeemer." (Psalm 19:14) "I commune with my heart in the night; I meditate and search my spirit." (Psalm 77:6)

Meditation is traditionally thought of as silent, wordless emptying of the mind so that we may come to know God who is already deep within our innermost being. However, meditation can take many different forms and involve a vast array of practices.

Meditation in each religion tends to take on the flavor of that particular faith. For example, The Very Reverend James C. Fenhagen[19], former Dean and President of General Theological Seminary in New York, has suggested that the real purpose of meditation in Christianity is to live more deeply in Christ so that Christ might live through us.

My experience and faith is that this will happen, regardless of which faith tradition we are a part, because I believe Christ Consciousness

---

[19] More than Wanderers, James C. Fenhagen, p. xii.

is universally present. Karl Rahner, the Roman Catholic theologian, once proposed that as people say "Yes" to life they are actually saying "Yes" to the Christ and are therefore anonymous Christians.

Non-Christians may not like this universal association of Christ with all affirmations of life and within all spiritual centering. I think it matters little what we name that presence of Love and Light, which I have called "Christ." Perhaps using no name at all is most effective, because any name tends to carry with it theological associations and previous images that may distort our actual experience of Infinite Mystery.

By using meditation we can become so intentionally centered and receptive that we begin to sense the Nameless Silence before which we must stand in awe. The late Thomas Merton seemed to speak from experience when he reported that at the center of each person is a point of nothingness which is the presence of God within us[20], and that this place is one of pure truth and poverty, like God's name written in each of us. I believe that this point of light is that toward which we move when we are in meditation.

Years ago, while deep in meditation, I began to experience a series of images. I had cleared my mind of thoughts and settled into a deep silence. Suddenly I felt myself moving through a long tunnel. It was as though I were on a bobsled, moving with lightning speed down a sloping shaft. I kept going down, flashing past lights and levels, too fast to see any features along the way. My observing mind told me I was going deep within myself, but another part of me felt out of control and not a little frightened.

After what seemed to be a long period of rapid movement downward, my passage slowed and the space became illuminated. As I slowed to a stop I could reach out and touch what felt like cold, wet walls of a cave.

I was in a hall with two openings. The one to my right was an ornate doorway with an ornate brass knocker. The one to my left was a low entrance into what appeared to be a natural cave. From my

---

[20] Conjectures of a Guilty Bystander, Thomas Merton, p. 158. Through his many books, Merton has been one of my greatest teachers.

studies I knew the left direction was often more intuitive, left handed and feminine -- often the place where God may be more fully experienced. So I started crawling through this low opening. After going about fifty yards on my hands and knees, which became scratched and bloody, I came into a large room. The sound of flowing water filled the space.

In the center of the room was a large pond with a brightly glowing fountain of "living water" spurting up five feet over the surface. Supported on this column of water was a glistening crystal sphere.

I was drawn closer to this sphere and looked within; suddenly realizing it was filled with a dark substance that I knew was manure. I felt I was being shown the innermost part of myself. At first I felt revulsion. But then the thoughts became clear in my mind that "humus," from which the word "human" is derived, is that rich, physical substance in which life can grow and flourish.

I next was drawn into an opening at the bottom of the pond, from which the living water was pouring. Again, down and down I went, more rapidly this time, and now totally at the mercy of that which drew me to Itself. After another long passage I was suddenly, without transition, face to face with such sparkling splendor that I had to fall to my face and cover my eyes.

Even with my eyes shut the radiance of this Presence showered through me and filled me with awe and Love. Words cannot adequately describe what I experienced. This was beyond human language. Theologians call this a "numinous experience," because they like to put names on such things. But a name cannot describe what, for me, was an encounter with God. Meditation was the doorway for this experience. I did not seek this experience. It sought me. It was an overwhelming gift.

One of the best descriptions of using meditation to move into a mystical experience of God comes from the writings of one of my favorite authors, Susan Howatch. Although fictional, I could not help but think that her report was based on someone's genuine experience. Her hero had moved slowly into meditative space, and then gradually moved beyond an awareness of his own presence in the experience. Finally he was able to say, "For one radiant second my fingertips touched eternity."[21] That is one goal of meditation.

While talking with Bill Moyers about myth, the late Joseph Campbell said that one could handle only a few of these kinds of experiences in one lifetime. Fortunately (or unfortunately?), not all meditation ends with such encounters with God. Most meditation accomplishes several other functions.

First, meditation is a way of clearing out garbage in our lives, of cleansing, and preparing ourselves for further work.

Second, meditation develops an inner knowledge of the self. St. Augustine said, "Let me know myself, Lord, and I shall know Thee."

Third, meditation provides a discipline, a framework for all other spiritual activities, thus enriching them and rendering them more "in tune" with the Infinite.

Fourth, meditation can help us achieve harmony and balance between our physical and spiritual lives, and between our left-brain and right-brain activities.

Fifth, meditation can help us reach our day-to-day goals in life.

If meditation is this valuable why doesn't everyone do it? Part of the answer is found in our previous education and training. We live in a post-Aristotelian world where empirical, scientific thought and methods dominate. We learned to be active and accomplish goals. We learned to study for tests, to follow directions, to make concrete plans and then measure the results of our efforts.

Meditation does not fit that masculine, left-brained, cause and effect type of thinking. When we first try meditation we may feel a little guilty because we are "wasting time," we are not actively "doing something" or accomplishing anything.

Anyone who has done Transactional Analysis[22] can identify the "critical parent" within saying something like, "You really *should*

---

[21]Susan Howatch, *Glamorous Powers* (New York: Alfred A. Knopf, 1988), pp. 379-380.

quit this foolishness and get back to work." It takes a firm, adult commitment to the importance and value of meditation to continue your practice in spite of such self-parenting judgment.

A good friend in a former parish, who has taught an A.R.E.[®23] study course which stresses the importance of meditation, regularly asks me, "Have you been meditating lately?" Even after all these years of using meditation with amazing results, I sometimes find myself drifting away from the daily discipline of taking time to meditate. Her question helps bring me back to this rich treasure.

So how do we mine this fertile source of spiritual, physical and mental blessings? It is helpful to be clear about what is NOT meditation.

Prayer is not meditation. Prayer is active talking with God, which is extremely important. If God is to be our friend, then, as in all friendships, it is important to talk regularly with that friend. But such conversation is not meditation.

Contemplation is not meditation. Contemplation is the active process of focusing the mind upon some worthwhile passage of scripture, poetry, art, etc., often with specific steps to follow. You will find in Appendix C a contemplative exercise I call "Praying the Scriptures."

Most structured spiritual exercises, such as those of St. Ignatius, are not meditation. These can be very valuable as avenues toward spiritual growth, but are quite different from pure meditation.

To help the reader better understand what meditation might be, I will share a personal account from my journal of one period of meditation. Please note that most of what goes on during this account is not meditation but rather my attempting to enter into a meditative state.

---

[22] "Transactional Analysis" popularized in the book, *I'm OK, You're OK* (Thomas A Harris, MD, Harper & Row, 1967), which helps us see how we may act out of different modes such as Parent, Child or Adult. There was an update to that work with the book, *Staying OK*, by Amy Bjork Harris and Thomas A. Harris, MD (Harper & Row, 1985).

[23] See footnote #1 on page two.

I spend about ten minutes getting relaxed and centered as described in Appendix B. I then focus my attention on my breathing. I watch the air going IN....OUT....IN....OUT, etc. I allow any thoughts that pop into my mind to flow out with the old air, and I bring fresh, clear, imageless energy in with each IN breath.

This regular breathing brings an inner calm. Physical stress drains from my body. I could easily go to sleep if I were not sitting up. My legs start to hurt because I am sitting on a prayer cushion in a half-lotus position (legs partially crossed). I allow my legs to hurt, not focusing on the pain ... just letting it be there.

The pain seems to be helping me move to a deeper state. I am no longer conscious of the pain. Breathing has shifted to the background. I am surrounded by the silence, filled with the silence, absorbed into the silence, and become one with SILENCE.

Although I do not actively think about it, I know I am empty and yet filled with JOY and LIGHT. I am a space traveler in the cosmos, timeless, infinite, boundless, eternal, and only a speck in the Mind of God. I touch the infinitely large and the infinitely small, and know that I am nothing and everything. I am one with the ONE.

I continue in this silent state for a while, feeling Pure Energy flow through my physical body, Pure Spirit flow through my soul, and Pure Thought flow through my mental body.

Slowly a gentle tugging pulls me back into awareness of the room I am in. I hear the sound of the noisemaker I use to create "white sound" as a background to cover outside noise. My legs need to move.

I stretch my legs and allow the feelings of peace and joy to move into my conscious awareness. I remain seated for several minutes as I move back into full wakefulness. When I finally stand and look out my window, the colors of the sky seem richer, the air seems fresher, I feel more fully alive.

Not all meditation has this same content. Sometimes I just feel tired and never seem to get anywhere. At other times meditation becomes a stepping-stone into some other spiritual adventure or process. But always, meditation for the spirit is like air for the body. It is essential.

If you look at an actual meditation exercise you see it is quite simple. As I said above, meditation is like emptying ourselves. If we have properly prepared for meditation by going through relaxation, centering and surrounding ourselves with the protective Light of Christ, then as we become empty we can be filled with the Energy, Power and Love of God.

This sounds easy; just to become "empty." But if you have tried it you know that our minds and bodies often rebel against that which feels like annihilation. I have felt a range of emotions from panic to boredom. I have broken into a cold sweat and have blocked the entire process with headaches and colds. Try not to let this natural resistance stop something that can be one of the most important steps you will take in your spiritual pilgrimage. I have found that the harder it becomes to meditate then the closer I am to a new breakthrough.

There are many tools that can help you develop fruitful meditation. I include only a few suggestions here. Please see the bibliography for other resources.

Mantras

A mantra, or repetition of a sound, a phrase, or a line of scripture, is one of the most effective devices to enhance meditation. The very effort involved in trying to still the mind can actually occupy or fill the mind, thus disrupting our meditation. The mind wants to be active. It loathes inactivity. The mantra is something on which the conscious mind can focus, and thus freeing the inner mind to move into meditative stillness, emptying and opening.

One description of the effect of a mantra says it is like being a mother working in a kitchen. She sees her small child has is holding in his fist a sharp knife by the blade. She knows she cannot pull the knife from his hand, so she tries to find a way to distract his attention from the knife. She offers a brightly colored object so the child drops the knife as he opens his hand to receive the safe object.

Likewise, the mantra helps us loosen our grip on rational thought, memory review, and emotional ruminations.[24]

An ancient mantra is what is known as the holy sound, "Ohm." This sound is repeated aloud on each exhalation. The mind focuses on and becomes filled with this sound, thus freeing the soul for meditation.

My favorite mantra is simply the word "One." This was suggested by The Community of Cross and Nails, an Anglican Holy Order, and was popularized by Dr. Herbert Benson's book, *The Relaxation Response*. Dr. Benson, working at Harvard's Thorndike Memorial Laboratory, studied the meditative practices of many mystics and developed a refined process of relaxation.

I was interested to see that his findings paralleled my own practices. Having a scientific background, I especially liked his research data that supports the intuitive learning of spiritual pilgrims for thousands of years. As he said in that book, "We claim no innovation but simply a scientific validation of age-old wisdom."

A later book by Dr. Benson, *Beyond the Relaxation Response*, points out the potentiating effect of a faith component in meditation.

Again his studies validate my experience that the inclusion of personal faith in a meditative exercise increases the benefits. For example, as I say the word "One" during meditation, that word represents more than a mathematical quantity. "One" stands for the unity of all things and of all people; of the One God, who is encountered in the Trinity of Christian faith, but also the One God found in the diversity of all other faiths.

As you use the word "One" you can allow that word to take on totally different meanings, and at the same time be part of that mysterious unity of everything—open to the sparkling splendor of the universe!

---

[24] Pandit Usharbudh Ara, *Mantra & Meditation* (Honesdale, PA: Himalayan International Institute of Yoga Science & Philosophy of the USA, 1981).

EXERCISE 6.1 – The Jesus Prayer

Another ancient mantra in Christian tradition is what is known as the "Jesus Prayer." This mantra originated during the first century of Christianity as the simple prayer or exclamation, *"Lord Jesus Christ."* Next was added the phrase, *"Son of God."* And later the mantra was completed to include the petition, *"Have mercy on me a sinner."* It has been said that this mantra contains all the basic tenants of Christian faith:

"Lord" - that which is central and most important in my life.

"Jesus" - the holy name of the man who walked on earth about 2000 years ago. This name comes from the Hebrew name, Joshua, which means "one who will save," or "one who will bring health and wholeness." It was a popular name during that time of Israel's history. Christians believe that this man was more than an ordinary person, and in some, mysterious way was the embodiment of, the incarnation of, the Son of God. That faith does not exclude the possibility that others have also walked on this earth as special embodiments of that mystery of God, and that in reality we all are children of God.

"Christ" or *"Christos"* - the living presence or Spirit of our God. Some call this the "Holy Spirit" while others talk of "Christ consciousness." In Christian theology we usually speak of the Christ as the "risen presence of Jesus." As always, when we speak of things infinite, our words can block our encounter with that reality. Just the word "Christ" or "Christos" has a holy sound that can invoke deep memories and deep meditation. I especially like Matthew Fox's excellent work, *The Coming of the Cosmic Christ*, which helps us understand the infinite dimensions of this name.

"Son" - born into human life through the power of God; one who has a special relationship with a parent and may sometimes be called on to speak in the name of that parent.

"Have mercy" - picking up the Hebrew meaning of the word "mercy" which was "to hover over," as God was thought to hover over the Arc of the Covenant. When we say this man-

tra we are not asking God to withhold punishment, but rather to hover over us, to surround us with love, light, healing, forgiveness, and hope.

"On me a sinner" - A sinner is not one who has been "bad" or broken God's laws, but rather one who has "missed the mark," who has broken relationships with fellow life on this planet and with the Great Spirit. A sinner is also one who has accepted illusions for truth, and thus tends to be dis-jointed and broken. As we "remember" who we are before God, as we hear the stories of our people, then we are put back together, or re-membered, and made whole again.

Thirty-five years ago I met someone who was a popular Christian author and became a good friend, Agnes Sanford. Agnes wrote many insightful books on spiritual healing and several Christian novels. At a workshop on healing prayer, she suggested that we add the following phrase at the end of the above "Jesus Prayer": *"and fill me with your light."* I have since incorporated those words into my use of the Jesus Prayer and find that after repeating the entire prayer, over and over, I do begin to sense a greater awareness of the pres-ence of Christ and of the Light of Christ flowing through me.

As we repeat this mantra it becomes part of our being, and we are thus more open to the infinite power of The Christ. The excellent fourteenth century book which first introduced me to the power of this mantra, *The Way of the Pilgrim* (New York: Image Books, 1978), had a warning for those just starting to use it. The monk who was teaching the pilgrim about this said that because it was such a powerful mantra one must be careful not to say it too often. He suggested that on the first day, one should say it no more that ten thousand times!

About thirty years ago, while in seminary, I purchased a set of handcrafted wooden beads on a string, with a wooden cross at one section. There are one hundred little wooden balls, each with the clear ring marks of the tree from which it came. I suggest that you try to find your own set of beads or a rosary. You will know when you find the right one for you. Such a rosary or set of "Jesus beads" can be a useful tool in meditation. As the mantra occupies the mind, the beads can occupy the hands. I say the Jesus prayer as I grasp a bead; "Lord, Jesus Christ, Son of God, have mercy on me a sinner and fill me with your Light." When finished, I move on to the next bead and repeat this mantra. After I have gone around this set of one hundred beads one time, I am usually deep in meditation. After years of use, sometimes I can just pick up these beads, which have become worn and have a personal warmth, and the feel of them moves me quickly into meditative space.

A Buddhist prayer wheel functions in much the same way. There are many other such devices that help focus the mind and body, or distract our minds from the knife of random thoughts, as the spirit is set free to move deep into our spiritual dimensions.

I have combined wisdom from several sources to share what I call the "One Meditation" which follows. This simple meditation is quite powerful and yet is very easy to learn and to master; and is one which I strongly recommend to both those who are beginners and those who have mastered meditative processes.

EXERCISE 6.2 - The ONE Meditation[25]

1) **Establish Your Environment** - be sure the phone is off the hook so you will not be interrupted, the pets are out of the room (cats especially love to jump on us when we move into deep meditation, and this can be quite a shock), the lights are dimmed, quiet music is playing, i.e., create space that is most relaxing and comfortable for you.

2) **Get Comfortable** - either sitting or lying down. Sitting is often better because we tend to go to sleep if we are lying down. However, this process can help us go to sleep if that is a need.

---

[25] This exercise should not be used by anyone suffering from an anxiety disorder. If you are under the care of a mental health professional, please consult with that professional prior to doing any deep relaxation/trance type exercises. Also, please see WARNING at the end of Appendix B for when you complete your time of meditation.

3) **Do a Full Body Relaxation** - start your with feet allowing relaxation to move deep into the bones and muscles; then
slowly move up your legs with relaxation. Some people find
it helpful to imagine that a warm beacon of healing light is
shining on that portion of your body where you are focused,
bringing with it warmth and relaxation. Now move this relaxation around and within your abdomen, up your back and
around your chest, on up to your neck; be sure to relax your
shoulders where we carry a lot of our daily stress; move relaxation down your arms - especially notice sensations of relaxation in your hands … sometimes you may even feel a
throbbing in your hands as they relax (you may find you can
control the level of relaxation: increase and decrease and increase); now take the relaxation up to the back of your neck,
over the top of your head and around your face. [Note: if you
are especially tense, sometimes it is helpful to take a breath,
hold the breath as you tighten an area of your body, and then
breathe out quickly as that part of your body is relaxed.]
After you have completed the full body relaxation and feel
more relaxed, go to #4.

4) **Watch Breathing** - for several breaths, simply watch
your breath as it goes IN and OUT, allowing your breath to
become slower as you become more relaxed.

5) **As You Breathe Out Say the Word "ONE"** - initially
say "ONE" aloud, and then say it in your mind. When you
say the word "one" say it in a drawn out fashion such as:
"Onnnnnnnnnnnnnne." Continue for 5 to 20+ minutes. Note
the importance of attaching faith significance to the word
"one" as mentioned above. You can also imagine light surrounding areas of pain or tension. And finally, have a slight
smile if distractions occur, or to help you become more
peaceful and centered.

6) **When Distractions Occur, Return to Saying "ONE"** -
be passive; non-judgmental. Please do not be hard on yourself when your mind wanders or you become distracted by a
sound or thought. This is quite natural. The mind abhors a
vacuum. As Eastern mystics have said, the mind is like a
chattering monkey. So when you become distracted, just notice that fact and simply return to saying "One" as you
breathe out. I recommend that you not stop to write down

some thought that comes to you, unless that is part of what you had planned to do in Step #7.

7) **Optional Step: When deeply relaxed do a pre-planned process** - for example: repeat positive affirmations; mentally go to the beach; practice a task or sporting movement; explore your inner spiritual life; focus on a biblical phrase or story; see yourself reaching a weight goal; see yourself as a permanent non-smoker; allow the healing Light of Christ to surround an area of your body that is in pain or needing healing; talk with your Guardian Angel; imagine another person for whom you wish to pray as being totally surrounded by the Light of Christ; etc.

8) **Take Time to "Awaken"** - count 1 to 5, and when you get to 5, be wide awake and refreshed, perhaps feeling like you have had an hour nap, bringing back any new insights or wisdom. Move your body some and take a few moments before standing, because blood pressure normally drops during this time of relaxation.

9) **Optional: Write in Journal** - notice what was most helpful and what was less helpful; record any special insights or experiences. I usually have my journal in my lap or right next to me. In this way, I don't need to totally awaken to write my observations, which makes them richer and more detailed.

Once you have practiced this "One Meditation" for a while, it may become easier to take a moment in the day to stop, take a deep breath and as you breathe out say "one" in your mind, especially with a slight smile. I call that "A Moment Meditation," as in the phrase, "Let me just take 'a moment' to reflect on that."

Going to sleep is also a good time to practice. I have had clients and parishioners who were having problems of waking up in the middle of the night and not being able to go back to sleep. I suggested that would be a wonderful time to practice meditation. Almost without exception the problem went away because meditation helped them change their focus from worrying about not sleeping to using the time for something beneficial to their physical and spiritual lives.

This is a valuable meditation. It has become part of my day-to-day life. Prior to every counseling session, worship service or lecture, I stop, take a deep breath, smile slightly, and then breathe out slowly as I say "One" in my mind (or aloud if there is no one in the area). As you will see later, I believe this training actually helped save my life.

It is useful to have a basic understanding of the anatomy of a brain, and how this exercise affects it[26]. If we were to look at a cross section of the brain we would see something like Figure 6.1 below.

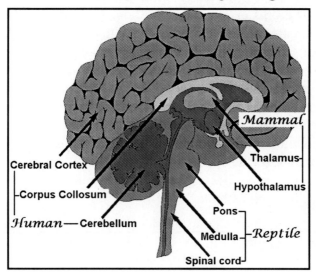

Figure 6.1

As a fetus matures in the mother's womb the brain of the developing child goes through the stages of evolution. It starts out with primarily the parts that you would find in a reptile's brain, then as the fetus grows the brain develops further and adds the elements of a mammal's brain, and then, with further growth, the cortex expands until it finally has all of the components of the human brain, as seen above. But the human brain retains the components of each stage of development.

---

[26] I first heard this way of thinking about human brain development from the late Rabbi Edwin H. Friedman, author of *Generation to Generation* and an authority on family processes in churches and synagogues.

It seems clear that reptiles are very severe animals that are primarily concerned about fight or flight, eating or being eaten, or sometimes just doing nothing as it sits in the sun. So the reptile portion of our brain has a large part to do with reactions of anger and anxiety, fight or flight. Truly, reptiles are very serious animals. And brain scans have shown that when we humans are overly serious, angry or frightened, i.e., in a fight or flight mode, then the reptilian portions of our brains are flooded with blood so these sections are ready to respond.

But as our brains evolved over millions of years, they gradually added the mammalian sections (along with precursors to the human sections, such as a gradually enlarging cerebral cortex). We know that mammals were the first animals to play and to nurture their young. Perhaps we have been to the zoo and seen otters having great fun sliding down a hill into a pond or romping along a shore and then tumbling into the water, clearly at play. Or we have seen young puppies rolling around on the floor while at play. Again, brain scans show that when mammals (and that includes us humans) are at play or nurturing their young the mammalian sections of their brains are flooded with blood.

And finally, the human brain developed the sections that allow us to use symbols, language, and logic, to store enough complex memories that allow us to have a concept of the self and of the past, present and future, to develop complex social interactions and communication patterns, and to carry on such discussions as this about who we are and how we function.

It has been shown that if a person is overly serious, angry or anxious, with the concomitant flooding of blood to the reptilian portions of their brain, this distribution of blood can be altered quite easily. This is accomplished by having the individual maintain a slight, gentle smile on the face as he or she takes a few deep, relaxing breaths. (A large grin is not as good since such a grin can be confused with a snarl.) If you accompany this soft smile with deeper breathing, then the mental relaxation becomes complete and a calm blood flow is totally restored to the brain. This literally forces blood to flow into the mammalian parts of the brain! So, if we wish to feel moments of playfulness and relaxation during the day, even if we don't feel like smiling – take a nice deep breath; then slowly breathe out and just go ahead and smile. The more such relaxation exercises are practiced the more we are conditioned to move out of a fight or flight mental state when it is not needed.

Chakras

As we increase our meditation skills we may sense our physical bodies in new ways and have a greater awareness of the energies flowing around us and within us. Several years ago I read about a physician, Dr. W. Brugh Joy, who was learning to move into much deeper meditation. One day he started feeling a strange sensation in his hand as he moved it above a patient lying prone on an examining table. He began to test this with other patients and discovered that this sensation was focused over six areas of each person's body. Then, gradually, over a year of observation, he found other minor areas of such sensations. He thought he had made a major medical discovery. Actually, this phenomenon is something Chinese and Indian medicine has utilized for thousands of years.

What Dr. Joy had "discovered" were chakras. Chakras are subtle energy centers that vitalize and control the physical body. Anyone who has received acupuncture treatment has probably learned about the flow of energy through the body along channels. These are outside of what Western medicine has recognized as the various systems of the body such as the nervous, lymphatic and circulatory systems. It appears that the chakras are centers of energy within the human body where those energy channels intersect or are concentrated. The Sanskrit word "chakra" means wheel, indicating that these energy centers are like wheels of energy. First, I will go over the colors of each chakra, the physical location in the body, and the functions associated with each chakra.

7th or Crown Chakra - *color*: purple or violet; *location*: the top of the head; *function*: the place of ultimate integration with God and consciousness of divine purpose.

6th or Third Eye Chakra - *color*: indigo (red/blue); *location*: the energy emerges at or just below the center of the forehead, but the core of energy is located at the pituitary gland (just below the hypothalamus, see Figure 6.1); *function*: the place of idealism and imagination and inner vision.

5th or Throat Chakra - *color*: blue; *location*: throat; *function:* center of communication and expression, also good judgment (darkness or blockage here makes us judgmental).

4th or Heart Chakra - *color*: green; *location*: center of chest, in area of the heart; *function*: Eastern mystics say this is the core of the soul which defines our personalities; here we fall in love and have our hearts broken.

3rd or Solar Plexus Chakra - *color*: yellow; *location*: immediately below the rib cage, at the center of the body; *function*: this is the seat of emotional living and where we balance our positive & negative energies, yin & yang, female & male.

2nd or Sexual Chakra - *color*: orange; *location*: just below the naval or umbilicus; *function*: our center of creativity, sexuality and reproduction. (also known as the Sacral Chakra)

1st or Root Chakra - *color*: red (when acting with any vigor it may become a more fiery orange-red); *location*: at the perineum or space between the testes & rectum or vaginal opening & rectum; *function*: the root or base of the human chakra system; this chakra provides our grounding with the Earth, our foundation, which relates to our understanding of the physical dimensions.

Try to visualize the chakras as colored balls or disks of swirling energy located in the center of the body (not on the surface as many drawings seem to indicate). Each chakra is connected by a spiraling flow of energy upward from one chakra to the next.

I have also experienced a ball of pure white energy up above my head about twelve inches from my scalp. Some have called this a "transpersonal chakra," i.e., outside of or beyond the personal realm. As will be discussed more completely in the meditation below, this 8th chakra or transpersonal chakra seems to be a connection with the Infinite Mystery of God, which I experience as pure white light, the Christos, or the loving and healing energy of Christ.

You can go to the Internet to see images of how the seven primary chakras connect and get a clearer picture of their location within the human body. Search for "chakras" via *google.com* or *ask.com* and you will find a vast wealth of information about chakras plus many excellent colored diagrams.[27]

The following chakra meditation can be done either sitting or lying down. I prefer to be lying on my bed or on the floor. Others prefer to be sitting in a yoga type position, cross-legged, with the back straight and perpendicular to the floor and earth beneath. An entire field of spiritual healing has developed around working to open "blocked chakras." This meditation accomplishes that type of cleansing or "opening" the chakras without going into long term chakra therapy.

EXERCISE 6.3 - A Chakra Meditation

Get comfortable, either sitting or lying down. Use a relaxation or centering exercise found in Appendix B.

1) Focus your attention on the **1st or Root Chakra** and begin to sense its color of red. I like to think of the red color of a fire truck. Now allow your consciousness to move from that Root Chakra into the surface below you, down into the earth, down through the dirt, down through the rocks and deeper bedrock, down to the red-hot center of the earth. Bring some of that clear, pure red energy of the earth back up along the same path to your Root Chakra, energizing that 1st chakra. Take some of that swirling, rotating, red energy back out to an area about twelve inches from your body (below your feet) and let it begin to surround your body, as though surrounded by a red cocoon or giant egg with a thin shell of red energy. Be sure the red energy totally surrounds your body.

2) Bring your attention back to the Root Chakra and the red ball of energy. Allow some of that energy to move upward

---

[27] Some books and Internet sites on the subject of chakras contain observations that are quite strange for a western mind, even stranger than what you find in this book. I have tried to simplify here the discussion of chakras so even the true beginner in spiritual exploration may have a chance of understanding this ancient topic.

in a spiraling movement up to the **2ⁿᵈ, Sacral, or Sexual Chakra**, where the red changes into a beautiful orange color. I like to think of the color of a fresh Florida or California orange. This time let some of the energy emerge from your body just below your umbilicus and let it move out to the red cocoon of energy, but now let the orange energy form a second layer on top of the red energy, again totally surrounding your body.

3) Return to the 2nd chakra, and allow some of that orange energy to spiral upward to the **3rd or Solar Plexus Chakra**, with the energy taking on the color of yellow. I like to think of the color of a beautiful, fresh lemon. Increase the energy of this chakra and allow some of the yellow energy to move out of the front of your body to cover over the orange layer of the cocoon with a layer of yellow energy.

4) Return to the 3rd chakra and allow some of the yellow energy to spiral upward to the **4th or Heart Chakra**, with the color becoming green. I like to think of the rich green of leaves on a tree. Green is a healing color, so surround your heart with healing green and let the green 3rd chakra become fully energized. Now take some of that green energy out through the front of your chest to the cocoon of energy, covering over the yellow layer of energy with this green energy, totally surrounding your body with the green. (If there is some part of your body needing special healing, you can also take some of that green energy and allow it to flow into that area.)

5) Return to the Heart Chakra and allow some of the green energy to spiral upward to the **5th or Throat Chakra**, with the color becoming blue. I like to think of deep blue sky on a clear day. Increase the blue energy of the Throat Chakra, and then take some of that energy out to the energy cocoon, totally covering over the surface with a layer of blue energy.

6) Return to the Throat Chakra and allow some of the blue energy to move deep into the center of the brain to the area of the pituitary gland and the **6th or Third Eye Chakra** with the color of indigo. I like to mix pure blue and red to arrive at a beautiful, rich indigo color. Increase the energy of the Third Eye Chakra and then take some of the indigo energy

out through the forehead at the place of the third eye and move out to the energy cocoon, covering it over with another layer of energy, this time colored indigo.

7) Return your consciousness to the Third Eye Chakra and the ball of indigo energy there. Allow some of that energy to spiral upward to the **7th or Crown Chakra** at the top of your head, with the color becoming purple or violet. I like to think of the color of a Bishop's shirt or a purple colored pansy. Here I can sense my connection to the Infinite Mystery, and I allow the purple energy to move upward to the surface of the energy cocoon, now covering over the surface with purple energy. As this energy completely spreads over the surface it begins a process of blending all of the colors so the cocoon now become a vibrating surface of pure white energy.

8) This then opens my Crown Chakra to a **Transpersonal Chakra** or energy center about one foot above my head. I think of this as the Light of Christ, which now begins to flow downward over the surface of the energy cocoon and pour down into my body, filling my entire body and all of its energy systems with this pure white, cleansing Light of Christ. This pure white energy flows through my body and down into the earth, with my body forming a connecting point between heaven and earth and the energy flowing back and forth between these two polarities, cleansing, healing, renewing, energizing my chakras, my body, my soul, my entire being --- now totally filled with and surrounded by the Light of Christ.

Truly, as I complete this meditation, I feel that "my cup is overflowing" with the Light, Energy, Love and Healing of Christ. I stay in this cocoon of flowing energy until I feel it is time for the meditation to come to an end. Sometimes this takes a short while; sometimes I remain in this wonderful space for 30 minutes or more.

9) Finally, I check each of the chakras to be sure each of the colors are clear, rich, and vibrant. For me that means the chakras are not blocked but open, and the energies of my body and soul are freely flowing.

10) Then I thank the presence of Christ and my Higher Self for this time of healing. Next I gradually move back into ordinary reality, usually by counting slowly from one to five. When I get to five I take a deep, cleansing breath, briefly re-call the colors of energy flowing through my body and open my eyes, back in my day-to-day world. For your conven-ience, this Chakra Meditation is duplicated in Appendix B.

After you have done this meditation a few times you may abbreviate it by not building the cocoon of energy. Just go through the process of re-energizing the chakras with energy from the earth and then moving quickly up through each chakra, ending with the energy of the Light of Christ flowing from above and back down through your body and through each of the chakras.

Occasionally I alter my centering process by taking just a few mo-ments to focus my consciousness on each chakra and its colors. By the time I have gotten to the Crown Chakra I am centered in my space, my body, and my soul.

EXERCISE 6.4 – An Energy Cleansing Process

While we are discussing energy flow and energy systems in our physical and spiritual bodies, I will share an "energy cleansing process" which I have found quite valuable. I like to do this while lying on a bed or floor.

Imagine that below you, under the surface on which you are reclining, is a white sheet of pure energy. I think of this as the Light of Christ, but you can imagine this in such a way that fits your own framework of faith. At each of the four corners of this white sheet is a golden thread. Slowly pull this sheet of energy upward through your body, by pulling the threads. As this sheet of energy reaches your body it be-gins to collect dark energy. These are things that have con-taminated your spirit or soul, and are now being cleansed from your being by this white energy or Light of Christ. As the large white energy sheet collects this "stuff," the sheet begins to droop in the center, so now the dark substance cannot spill out and move back into your body. When the sheet clears your body continue to pull it far above to a place where you can safely tie together the four corners with the golden threads. Then mentally transfer that bundle of dark energy into the dimensions of Christ to be transformed by his infinite Light and Love, never to move back into the dimensions of human existence.

When finished with this cleansing process, I usually feel that my entire being is crystal clear and each of my chakras are now shining with pure colors.

I have learned to use this process" to spiritually clean physical spaces, such as my home, my office, my car, etc. I suggest that you start with a small area. When I first cleansed my office in this way my intuitive mind seemed to hear a sigh of relief from the chair in which counseling clients and grieving parishioners would sit as they told their stories and shared their pain. I realize that logically it is quite impossible for my chair to "sigh," and that it was probably my own soul that formed that sigh of relief. On the other hand, Native American spirituality suggests that all things have a soul or spirit, even inanimate objects.

Several times each year I go into each of the church buildings where I serve and clear that space of negative energy. This is a private process I use, not a public liturgy …that would be strongly frowned upon by the hierarchy of my Episcopal denomination. The Episcopal Church is known for the dignity and order of its liturgy, and I want to reemphasize that much of this book is not orthodox Episcopal doctrine or discipline. On the other hand, meditation is recognized by almost all major religions as an important spiritual discipline and a valuable tool that can deepen our relationship with God. And I have found that my personal spiritual explorations have not only led to a new kind of *limitless living* but also to a deepening of my Christian faith.

As we continue these spiritual explorations, it is very important to remain grounded in our faith and, at the same time, to maintain harmony and balance in other parts of our lives. Mindfulness is a critical component of such harmony and balance. All spiritual masters I have encountered discuss the importance of mindfulness.

When walking, be conscious that you are walking.
When sitting, be conscious that you are sitting.
When lying down, be conscious that you are lying down.
No matter what the position, be conscious of the body's position.
Also be conscious of each breath, each movement, each thought.
Adapted from: The Sutra of Mindfulness

Chapter 7

MINDFULNESS & T'AI CHI

Since my earliest moments of self-reflection, I have been blessed with an awareness that there is something very special about seeing. Perhaps this was because, as a child, I began to suffer from myopia or nearsightedness, which means things that are far away were blurred or less clear. There are very strong, early memories for me of lying on the ground and watching ants work or worms crawl. I would pull leaves from trees and look at the small lines within their flesh, not realizing then that these lines were like blood vessels for the leaf. Myopia helped me learn to focus and be mindful of the things that I could see clearly that were close up.

I remember the joy of books and of learning that all those little marks formed words. The books with drawings or photos were such a treasure because I could look closely at a photo and see the details of buildings, of fields and trees, of birds and wild animals, that my distance vision would not reveal. So there was another gift that was given to me by myopia: a love of books, especially books that contained detailed art and photos. I vividly remember when our family purchased a set of World Book Encyclopedias. I then discovered a vast new treasure, page after page, volume after volume, filled with wonderful photos and drawings.

It wasn't until I was in the second grade that a teacher saw me squinting at the blackboard, trying to read an assignment, and suspected that I was nearsighted. She sent home a note to my parents. I remember my father, an orthopedic surgeon, saying, "Oh, there's nothing wrong with the boy's eyes!" Fortunately, my mother, who was a nurse and realized that a physician's family was often the last to receive proper medical care, made an appointment for me to see an ophthalmologist (a medical doctor who treats eyes). He told me, "You do need glasses. They will open up a whole new world for you."

Although I had some fear about wearing glasses, there was no fear of appearing to be a "geek" in the late 1940s because then no one had ever heard of a geek. I was to learn that being a "four eyes" was almost as bad as being a "geek."

But that was not my concern at all when I finally walked out of the optometry store with my first pair of glasses. I looked up and suddenly was aware of not just limbs on trees but also twigs on branches and even the smallest leaves on trees. I could see the flight of birds ... not just a blur moving through the sky. The tough boys at school could call me "four eyes" all they wanted. I just didn't care because now I was seeing a "whole new world." I was now "mindful" of so much more than I had ever dreamed. Although photos and paintings had given me hints of the larger world, it was not until I could actually see the three-dimensional details of that world with complete depth and color that I could fully appreciate its beauty and awesomeness.

Another source of mindfulness for me as a child was the gift of growing up on my grandparents' farm (some of which was discussed in Chapter Two). This was while my father was in North Africa and Europe during World War II.

We lived next to the earth. That farm had helped my grandparents, my mother and her eight brothers and sisters survive the Great Depression. We were not financially wealthy, but were rich in family strength and a knowledge of how to live off of the land and how to "make do" with what we had. I grew to love the chickens, cows and pigs on our farm. They were friends for a boy who was alone for much of each day during his first six years. My mother drove into Charlottesville to work as a nurse, my sister was in school, my grandfather worked the farm, drove a bread truck and sold patent medicines, and my grandmother had the chores of cooking and cleaning and washing and keeping the family in clothes that were not filled with holes and tears.

So I would wander about our farm to see what I could see, which was a great deal even with myopic eyes. The farm was a place of exploration and learning, my own private school. I remember I almost burned down our farmhouse conducting a "scientific experiment." I had wanted to see what happened when a lighted match touched cotton. The cotton was too close to the curtains, and you can guess what happened. I think it was my uncle Jessie who taught me about experiments, having recently finished engineering school at the University of Virginia. He asked me what would happen if we mixed vinegar with baking soda and I replied it would probably just be some white liquid. He said, "Well, let's do an experiment and find out if your hypothesis is correct." Hypothesis was another word I learned early in life. Well we found out what would happen, and he even helped me build a small, toy boat that was powered by vinegar and baking soda. I don't think I ever heard the phrase, "curiosity kills the cat," until I read it in a book many years later. All in our family encouraged curiosity, so it came to me quite easily.

My grandfather, "Daddy Whit," mentioned earlier, taught me many important lessons about what I now call mindfulness. I think back to how he talked about being aware, of noticing things. One day he had been hoeing the garden, as I pulled up weeds closer to the plants. I was trying to hurry and get to the end of the row so I could run off and play. Daddy Whit came over and sat on the ground next to me. I knew he was getting ready to say something important so I stopped pulling weeds and listened. He said, "Sonny (my childhood nickname), I want you to remember that there are two ways to work in our garden. One way is to work so you can be finished with the work and then go do something else. The second is to work in the garden to work in the garden."

That didn't seem to make much sense, so I replied, "They sound like the same thing. How are they different?" He pulled a ripe tomato off a nearby vine and wiped the dirt from its warm skin and held it up for me to look at, and then continued. "Well Sonny, it's like this. When I am working just to get the work done I seem to get tired quicker, and I don't really see things ... like the colors of this tomato. Can you see that the skin is not just one red color, but there are many different shades of red? And notice where I broke the tomato from the vine, how the green stem has little things on it that look almost like hairs and there are actually several different kinds of green around that piece of the stem. If I'm just working to get finished and then do something else, I will miss seeing so much. But when I'm working in the garden and really notice I'm working in the garden, then I am right here ... feeling the breeze on my face, feeling my back hurt, listening to that mockingbird over in the tree, knowing this ground will feed our family, and how good these vegetables will taste when we sit down to lunch or dinner at some time in the future. And, as I am doing this, I remember my father and grandfather working in their gardens and how they probably remembered their fathers and grandfathers working in their gardens. So by being here right now, I mean really being here, then somehow all this gets connected up in my mind." Today, looking back on those words of my grandfather, I realize it is one of the best definitions of mindfulness that I've ever heard. And Daddy Whit helped me learn that this kind of mindfulness can be applied to anything we are doing, to anything we are working on, to any task or activity, and to simply being alive... appreciative of each moment of life.

I remember once being with some cousins at someone else's farm. After supper they had said, "Hey, why don't we go watch Old Joe eat supper." I didn't know "Old Joe" and was not sure why they would want to watch him eat, but I wasn't going to be left out of anything that sounded like it might be fun. So, in the growing dusk of a summer evening, we traipsed off through the woods to an old cabin set far back from the road. We crept quietly to his kitchen window and peeped in, and sure enough Old Joe was sitting at his table eating supper. The other cousins giggled as though they were doing something very exciting, and I just sort of wondered why it was funny to watch Old Joe eating ... not realizing that they must have thought they were really getting away with something. My cousins then ran back through the woods, but I stayed at the window for a short while longer. I could now see Old Joe better and I could see the deep wrinkles in his face, plus there was a slight smile on his face ... obviously very aware of the spying that had been going on and seeming to enjoy it. But as I watched this old man eat, I think I became truly mindful of the fact that here was another human being just like me ... although he had lived many more years than I had. I also felt that he looked a little like an Indian. His hair was tied back into a kind of pigtail, and I saw a rawhide bag hung on the wall with feathers attached to it, like I had seen in some book that showed pictures of Indians. And in that moment of awareness and mindfulness, I also felt a deep attachment or closeness to Old Joe, like he was part of my family. Many years later I learned that I do have Native American blood in my family tree. Perhaps we really were related in some distant way.

Some might say that my being alone so much during my first five years had made me too serious. However, I wasn't really that serious in the sense of being grave or somber. Much of what I did during those years was play or made up games. I would challenge myself to see how far I could go into the dark woods back up in the mountain behind our farm before I would start to get scared. I gradually learned that there is a big difference between being anxious or scared and simply being focused and attentive, or mindful.

In those early 1940's, all of our work on the farm was very important and critical to our survival. However, there were two activities that seemed to attract a special kind of mindfulness. One was listening to our only radio for news of what was happening to our troops in North Africa, where my father was, and for any word about the war in the South Pacific, where three of my uncles were. I remember the faces of my mother and grandparents as we all were looking at the radio sitting on a special table in the living room, the way we look at a TV today. But listening to the radio back then made what we were hearing even more real than today seeing the pictures on a TV screen. What we saw in our minds was much more real than what is created in some distant TV studio today.

The second especially mindful thing happened when we got letters from my father or one of my uncles who were off in the war. We would read and re-read the letters, carefully paying attention to each phrase, to each word. Because military sensors would mark out anything in the letters that told the location of where they were, there was a playful effort by my father and uncles to give hidden hints of their current locations. For example, my father once said in his letter, "Tell Aunt Cassie that it is very hot over here. I know how much she likes the warm weather." We immediately ran to the world map pinned on the wall and looked for what he might be referring to. We found Casablanca in North Africa and put a pin there. It gave us a warm feeling to know at least the approximate location of members of our family who were in harm's way. I also noticed on these occasions that there was a lot of blotting of red eyes with handkerchiefs. To this day, when I hear about our troops in Iraq and Afghanistan, tears well up in my eyes, and I feel very connected to them and their families.

When many of my aunts, uncles and cousins gathered for Sunday dinner or other special occasions there would be great joke telling and laughter, often far into the night. Many a night my sister and I would go to sleep with our faces resting on the heat register in the floor of our upstairs bedroom, because we were listening to the stories being shared by family in the living room below. For those too young to know about such things, often the wood stove or fireplace in a room provided heat for the room above through an opening in the ceiling that was covered with a metal grate or register on the floor above, so you wouldn't put your foot through the hole. After sleeping with our faces on the register, we would awake to find our cheeks had waffle patterns that were clearly visible to everyone for several hours. We were never asked how those patterns on our faces got there. I realize now that our family knew exactly what we were doing and it was OK.

This early exposure to stories is something that helps give most families their own personal identity, and it is a valuable exercise to go back in your memories and recall some of those stories. I suggest that we ask questions of parents, grandparents and other family members to fill in the gaps in our memories. As we learn more about where we came from we become more mindful of the importance of our family history and how that history connects us to all of humanity.

So, as I think about all the things that have helped me open to *limitless living*, I realize that mindfulness stands out as being absolutely essential. It is so simple and yet so difficult to accomplish, i.e., being awake and aware – being mindful.

The following is a simple and yet very powerful method of deepening our mindfulness. Elements of this are included in the "One Meditation" found in the previous chapter on meditation. Actually, all effective meditation begins with this process. I also strongly recommend this particular exercise for basically increasing our mindfulness.

This exercise can be done sitting or lying down, but I find that initially it is best to recline on the floor or on a bed. In this way you can watch your breathing patterns more easily.

EXERCISE 7.1 - A Mindfulness Exercise

1) Begin by noticing your breath as it goes in and out. The breath can be silent and gentle as it flows in through the nose and down into the chest. The breath is almost like a small, flowing stream of water or a gentle breeze. It is not necessary to force the breath to go deeper in your lungs and down below the diaphragm now. Just breathe naturally as you notice the air going in and out, and then you can allow your breath to be deeper and longer, and notice the difference.

2) After you have become mindful of your breath, gently going in and out, there are two additional things you can do to increase your mindfulness. The first was described more fully as part of the "One Meditation" (Exercise 6.2), i.e., simply saying the word "One" as you breathe out, and when distractions occur, notice the distraction and then return to saying the word "One."

The **second technique** is similar but also somewhat different. You count each breath. I find it necessary to count on both the IN breath and the OUT breath in the following way:

as the breath comes in, say in your mind "One," and as you breathe out, say in your mind "One." As you breathe in again, say in your mind "Two," and as you breathe out, say in your mind, "Two," etc. If I count only the out breath, by leaving that space of silence on the in breath, a place is created for thoughts and distractions to enter the mind. I like to occasionally see how high I can count before a distraction takes me away from counting. When a distraction does occur, I return to "One" without judging myself for becoming distracted. On other occasions I only count up to the number "Ten" and then return to "One," regardless of whether or not distractions occur. And please do not get discouraged when distractions happen. (Notice I didn't say, "*if* distractions occur.") You will become distracted. That is natural. That being the case, I like to also keep a slight smile on my face as I do this exercise, which is a reminder to not take this exercise or myself too seriously. Simply be in the moment, awake, aware and mindful. I will usually do this exercise for anywhere from five to twenty minutes.

Some mindfulness masters say that you can eventually abandon the counting when you arrive at a state of total mindfulness with no distractions. I have never advanced to that level of perfection. I am still a beginner after fifty years of practice! (Also please note that this method of counting from "One" to "Ten" is the opposite of a technique I use to go into a deep trance by counting from "Ten" down to "One," going deeper into the trance state with each descending number. I find that counting from one to ten is better for waking up, noticing, and being mindful.)

Another of the tools that helps me be mindful is actually a form of physical exercise that can produce great spiritual benefit, i.e., T'ai Chi. There are also profound physiological benefits from doing T'ai Chi ranging from improvements in the nervous system, glands, muscles, cardiovascular system, to increased mental clarity, perception and stability, and enlightenment of one's entire life and being.

I have found that T'ai Chi assists my physical body find harmony and balance and increases my sense of *limitless living*. The full name in Chinese is actually T'ai Chi Chuan (pronounced Tie – as in a bow tie, Chee – as in a cheetah, and Chwan – with the long a as in want.) This is often translated as "supreme ultimate fist" while others call it "moving harmony."

T'ai Chi evolved through the ages as an arrangement of exercise and martial arts training using carefully structured sequences of movements. These gradually build up physical strength, suppleness and stamina. You do not need any special equipment or clothing, and you can perform the basic exercises or "forms" in even a fairly small space.

Although T'ai Chi is considered a "martial art," or a tool of battle, actually it is a tool of peace, a tool of self-defense. A story is told that one of the greatest masters of Karate challenged a great T'ai Chi master to a contest to determine which of these martial arts was the best. The great Karate master attacked swiftly, with great power and skill. However, with each strike the T'ai Chi master moved gently out of the way, using the T'ai Chi motions to easily deflect the violence and glide that energy into a new, safe direction away from the master. Frustrated, the Karate master attacked with even greater force, and again the T'ai Chi master was able to gently and gracefully move aside from the energy of attack and direct it to a safe place. Finally the Karate master stopped his attack and humbly bowed before the T'ai Chi master who humbly returned the bow, each totally mindful of the skill of the other.

A nice thing about T'ai Chi is that all movements are done in slow motion, some have called it "meditation in motion." It is a very peaceful process. The slower you move the better. A calm, relaxed attitude is promoted as you prepare for the day in the morning or as the tensions of the day are eased away in the evening. T'ai Chi is a great antidote to stress.

But we are still doing valuable exercise. During a 15 - 20 minute session of T'ai Chi with its continuously flowing movement, you will: a) boost your heart rate to moderately aerobic levels; b) promote circulation to your extremities; c) positively affect your autonomic or unconscious nervous system; d) decrease your blood pressure; and, e) free the diaphragm, for more efficient oxygen intake.

How can T'ai Chi make a difference in your life? Surprisingly, studies have found that T'ai Chi may have a greater effect than aerobics in cardio-respiratory fitness. Regular T'ai Chi practice can boost muscle strength by 15 to 20%, and may help ward off osteoporosis. One study found that T'ai Chi reduced falls among the elderly by almost 50%; another study found T'ai Chi lowers blood pressure almost as much as aerobic exercise; and a different study discovered that T'ai Chi improved the range of motion for sufferers of rheumatoid arthritis. Parkinson's disease, fibromyalgia, cerebral palsy, stroke, heart disease and emphysema have also been shown to respond positively to T'ai Chi.

In regular T'ai Chi there is a sequence to the movements that must be learned in a specific order. Taoist T'ai Chi has 108 movements, which take about 20 minutes to perform.

Many years ago I learned a simpler form of T'ai Chi. Our instructor said this kind of T'ai Chi is somewhat like dancing during which you rotate gradually around in a circle. Although it is somewhat difficult to learn without an instructor, I will provide here the outline of this form that you can play with, i.e., don't take this too seriously.

My suggestion is to simply move slowly and have fun!

The drawings that follow show the sequence of movements for instructional purposes. However, remember that you do not stop between each sequence. Each movement flows gently into the next, with no stopping of the motions.

EXERCISE 7.2 - A Short Form of T'ai Chi

As I have said, T'ai Chi is a system of slow, flowing motions. The style presented here departs from more traditional styles in the freedom and flow of movement. Less emphasis is put on the precise position of hands, feet, etc., and more on the joy and play of the movements as we "dance with" the relaxing and toning energy. I do provide direction as to position of hands and feet, which helps with the movements, but do not get frustrated if you don't remember the exact details of the form. I suggest that you tape or digitally record this written information, reading slowly the description of the movements and the inner dialogue that accompanies the movements. As you listen to your recording, you can gently follow the instructions as best you can, perhaps stopping occasionally to check one of the drawings if you don't understand the verbal direction.

T'ai Chi is more than a popular form of physical exercise. It can be a legitimate adjunct to psychotherapy and spiritual growth, as well as physical health and healing. Since all parts of the body become involved in the movements, both hemispheres of the brain are forced to activate. The need for coordination increases the flow of signals through the corpus callosum[28], thus joining the rational, mathematical, structured operations of the left cerebral hemisphere with the flowing, imaginative, artistic, intuitive functions of the right (the usual dominant operations of the left brain and right brain). As harmony of mind, body and spirit increase, old ingrained habits may be unlearned and new behaviors are easier to form. T'ai Chi has been successfully used in drug rehabilitation centers, and "cases attesting to T'ai Chi successes in curbing and curing physical and mental malfunctioning, and as an aid to longevity, are numerous."[29]

Many other advocates of alternative healing methods, such as Andrew Weil, MD, have recommended T'ai Chi as a tool in promoting mind/body healing. However, I do not promise any miraculous cures or spiritual visions. I offer this as a wonderful way to more fully enjoy our bodies and the world around us, and to tap the energies of nature.

As we practice this form, it may be helpful to lighten the mind and allow ourselves to have the perspective of a child quietly at play in a sand box: curious, creative, spontaneous, hopeful, gentle, and calm.

---

[28] The bundle of nerve fibers that connects the two sides of the brain. See Figure 6.1 on page 100.

[29] Da Liu, *Taoist Health Exercise Book* (New York: Putnam Publishing Group, 1983), p.73.

This can also be a time to allow our Guardian Angels to dance, as we open to the peaceful wisdom and vitality of the wise person within us all.

However, as with all forms of physical exercise, please check with your health care provider prior to beginning any T'ai Chi practice.

The Story or Flow of the Form

The figure numbers below are artificial divisions for the purpose of instruction only, since there is no real separation of the movements. The numbers relate to the series of drawings. All movements are to be completed in a flowing way, with one movement moving slowly and gracefully into the next. There should be no jerky stops and starts. However, as the form is being learned, you may stop and do each part several times, to help you learn the more subtle portions of each movement. As my hands move they are moving through air and energy that has substance. So there will be slight resistance to the movement, at first causing the hands to lag behind the wrists and then slowly catch up with the motion as they move into the proper position; this is especially true when there is a change of direction.

Outline of the Form

This form consists of a basic cycle of movements. You can begin by facing East and acknowledging the life, energy and spiritual forces of that direction (or you may just want to face East).

During the First Series, as each cycle is performed, you will move 90 degrees in a clockwise direction, to the South, to the West, to the North, and finally returning to the East.

During the Second Series, as each cycle is performed, you will move 90 degrees in a counter-clockwise direction, to the North, to the West, to the South, and finally returning to the East. If you are short of time, you can do one cycle. I usually do this in the morning. It is a wonderful way to greet the new day and the rising sun. I often do this in my PJs and bare feet, upon arising in the morning. I start by facing a window, if possible.

The Start of the Form:

Figure 7.01

Stand comfortably with your feet about 12" to 14" apart, depending on your height. You want to feel a centered, solid connection with the earth, so no shoes is best (but it is OK to wear shoes if you have any foot problem, or if the ground is wet or cold), knees slightly bent. Feet are pointing straight ahead. Hands hang easily to your sides with palms facing toward your legs and slightly backward.

Figure 7.02

Slowly lift your arms away from your sides with the hands at first lagging behind the wrists and then the palms rotate so they are facing forward, when your arms reach the level of your shoulders. There can be a sense of moving the arms through air that has true substance, thus causing the hands to move slower than the arms.

Figure 7.03

Once your arms are horizontal with the ground, straight out from your shoulders, then slowly swing arms forward as you reach out (Fig. 7.03) and take in as much energy as possible from this direction. The hands gradually move slightly ahead of the wrists in a cupping position to gather in the energy of that direction.

Figure 7.04

When your hands almost meet in front of you, bring that energy back toward your heart chakra.

Draw the energy into yourself until the hands are at your chest (Fig. 7.04).

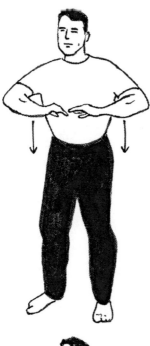

Figure 7.05

Then push the energy down (Fig. 7.05) to the lower chakras, with palms facing down, building the fire in the root chakra.

Figure 7.06

Take some of that energy in your hands and bring it back up and out.

Figure 7.07

When your hands become level with your throat, rotate your hands so the palms are facing out.

Then push out (Fig. 7.07), offering that energy to the spirit keepers of the direction you are facing.

Figure 7.08

Move your hands out as far as they will reach to the front and then move them away from the center, as though you are opening a curtain.

Open the curtain of that direction and (Fig. 7.08) become fully mindful of all that direction has to offer.

Figure 7.09

Being totally mindful of what you see, you realize it is so beautiful and so wonderful that you must step back in awe with your left foot (Fig. 7.09), toe pointed out at 45 degrees, left knee bent, right foot still pointing forward...arms now at shoulder level with the hands pointing to the left and right, palms facing down...

Figure 7.10

You then touch the horizon on the right as you slightly lift the opposite hand.

Figure 7.11

And then touch the horizon on the left as you slightly lift the opposite hand and slightly shift your upper body weight in each direction and glancing in that direction as you do so.

Figure 7.12

Slowly bring the right palm down and rotate to a point so the palm is facing up at a point just below the sixth chakra (which is below the umbilicus), as the left palm swings in still facing down, until it is just above the throat or fifth chakra .

Figure 7.13

By continuing the motion allow the palms to move up and down, rotating between the chakras, circulating the energy through the chakras from above to below, and below to above, and above to below, and below to above, etc. Repeat about 4 or 5 times, as the fire in the root chakra builds and builds.

Figure 7.14

Then slowly repeat the motion of Fig. 7.03, Fig. 7.04, and 7.05, moving your arms out to bring in more energy from this direction.

Figure 7.15

This time, as you push this additional energy down, the fire in the root chakra has become so intense that the right foot must come up as the hands move down.

Figure 7.16

Take some of that excess energy or fire from the area in front of the root chakra (in front of your sexual organs) and move the energy back up and out to the horizon as the foot goes back down to the same place it was in.

Figure 7.17

As the hands and fire reach the horizon, the fire hits the water which become steam and mist which goes up ... as the hands also drift up with the mist ... the mist forms clouds above ... and then the rain begins to fall from the clouds ... as the hands drift back down ... out in front toward the horizon.

Figure 7.18

As the rainwater reaches the horizon it forms streams that flow into rivers as the hands, with palms down, begin to move in a counterclockwise direction as the body rotates around (Fig. 7.17 & Fig. 7.18). As the body rotates (from Fig. 7.17 to Fig. 7.18) the weight is shifted to the left foot and the right foot is lifted so only the right heal is touching the ground.

The right foot is now rotated on the heel so the toes then point directly at each other at 45-degree angles.

Please note: This move involves a more precise shifting of weight and directions, and will need to be practiced until it can happen in an almost unconscious flow of movements.

Don't worry if this takes a little while. These are different kinds of movements than most of us are used to. However, these kinds of coordinated movements are an important part of the therapeutic activity of T'ai Chi.

As you continue to rotate, imagine that the waters are flowing around you, moving down the streams and rivers out to the ocean.

Figure 7.19

For a moment, both feet are pointed at 45-degree angles toward each other, as the water continues to flow in the river around the body. When the right foot has gotten to this new position the weight is shifted to the right foot... as the left foot lifts so only the left heel is touching the ground... and the left foot rotates also counterclockwise as the body continues to rotate, until the left foot is now pointing straight in the opposite direction the body had been facing (Fig. 7.19), i.e., say if you started facing East, now you are facing West, with the left foot pointing straight toward the West, and the right foot now pointing at a 45-degree angle toward the North-West.

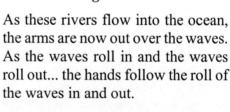

Figure 7.20

As these rivers flow into the ocean, the arms are now out over the waves. As the waves roll in and the waves roll out... the hands follow the roll of the waves in and out.

Your hands may move up and down one or two times to mimic the motion of the waves.

Figure 7.21

The wind blows across the ocean and into the branches of a tree, as the tree begins to twist (Fig. 7.21), absorbing the energy of the wind, twisting more and more.

Here we reverse the action we just did, but take it another 90 degrees so we end up facing South (first repetition).

The left foot is rotated on the heel in a clockwise direction so the toes then point directly at a 45-degree angle.

Again, for a moment, both feet are pointed at 45-degree angles toward each other.

When the left foot has gotten to this new position the weight is shifted to the left foot... as the right foot lifts so only the right heel is touching the ground... and the right foot rotates also clockwise as the body continues to rotate, until the right foot is now pointing straight in the original direction the body had been facing.

But this time you continue rotating the right foot clockwise on past that direction for another 90 degrees of rotation, as seen in the next Figure 7.22.

Figure 7.22

The body rotates as the wind continues to twist the tree (moving from Fig. 7.21, 7.22 & 7.23). As mentioned above, the weight is shifted to the left foot, as the right foot comes up, with only the right heel still on the ground, as the right foot rotates a full 180 degrees so it is now pointing directly East, as the tree twists and twists; and once the right foot is in position, shift the weight totally to the right foot and lift the left foot so only the right foot is touching the ground. You then rotate the body and left foot around until the body and left foot are facing directly South. As the wood is twisted more and more it becomes a heavy ball of metal.

Figure 7.23

The left foot is now parallel to the right foot, about 14" apart, with the weight centered over both feet, the knees slightly bent; the body is facing toward the south (or the next quadrant as you repeat each cycle). The palms are now resting below the umbilicus as they hold up the heavy ball of metal.

This next set of moves is difficult to show with drawings. What you will do is soften the heavy ball of metal to the right by moving the right hand out to the right side and up as you bring in softening energy from the right (Fig. 7.23a), slightly shifting your weight to the left foot as you do so. You then soften the metal to the left by moving the left hand out to the left and up as you bring in softening energy from the left (Fig. 7.23b), slightly shifting your weight to the right as you do so. These two photos may help you visualize this movement. (Photos are from the deck of one of my favorite and most relaxing places, looking out over the water at Chincoteague Island.)

Figure 7.23a

Figure 7.23b

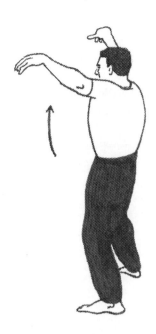

Figure 7.24

Now the metal has become liquid, like mercury, and is so heavy that you drop it down to the earth, by letting your palms move down and out; and you then continue to swing both arms out and up (Fig. 7.24), and, having dropped all of that weight, you now fly through the air.... palms now facing down, but then as the arms move back down in a flying motion, the palms drift behind the wrists. As the arms reach the lowest point you move into the next action.

Figure 7.25

You now slowly reach down and gather energy from the earth by circling your arms down and scooping up energy with your palms, and lifting that energy up in front of you (Fig. 7.25).

Figure 7.26

Moving your arms on up, you offer the energy to the heavens. Each time I do this, I try to have a sense of gratitude in my heart for all that I have received from that infinite mystery we call God.

Figure 7.27

Again reaching down you gather more energy from the earth.

Figure 7.28

This time you bring the energy up in front of you and back to the top of your head and down outside your body, cleansing your aura. (Note: An "aura" is the area immediately surrounding an object or physical body. It may be some kind of emanation, radiation, or energy.)

Figure 7.29

Finally, you gently return to the starting position (Fig. 7.01), but now you are facing South [direction changes after each cycle]. You do not pause but flow right on into repeating each of the above steps, starting again at Fig. 7.01 (same as Fig. 7.29) and moving immediately into Fig. 7.02:

When you return all the way around, completing four repetitions of these movements, you will have completed one cycle, and again will face east.

After you have completed four cycles, you then repeat the cycles four more times, but this time at Figure 7.09 you will step back in awe with the *right* foot (instead of *left* foot as in Fig. 7.09). Also, the direction of the water going to the ocean (in 7.18) will be clockwise, with motions of the feet and hands opposite that of Figure 7.18. Also, the direction of the wind, in 7.21 & 7.22, will be counterclockwise, with similar motions of the feet and hands.

This may sound complex as you read it. However, as you practice, the experience becomes more and more like a dance, especially if you practice in a playful, non-serious way. (For those who want to master this short form of T'ai Chi, I have created a video DVD in which I demonstrate the entire form and provide detailed instruction, step-by-step, through each of the figures indicated above. I also have a produced a spiral bound booklet that can lie flat, making it easier to follow the instructions. To order that video DVD and booklet go to the web site: www.ancientotter.com.)

Throughout all of our T'ai Chi practice, it is good to remember to breathe calmly and gently, with slow deep breaths. The word for "spirit" in most languages is the same as "breath." If you wish, this can also be a wonderful way to allow more and more of the "Breath of God" to move through your life, cleansing and healing.

Chapter 8

CHANNELING THE SPIRIT

In Holy Scripture we read, "The Lord spoke to Moses: 'See, I have called by name Bezalel...and I have filled him with divine spirit.'"(Exodus 31.1-3) In many places in the Bible we learn that we are to be "filled with the Holy Spirit" (Acts 9:17), that the Spirit will speak through us, that the Spirit expresses our plea in a way that could never be put into words, that "love has been poured into our hearts through the Holy Spirit which has been given to us." (Romans 5:5)

In these and other passages, we are told that the Spirit of God dwells in us, moves through us, and that we are channels for the power, energy and love of that same Spirit. This is perhaps our highest calling, to be channels of God's Spirit.

I have talked with so many people who have experienced that power and energy of God moving through them that I cannot remember all of their stories. However, one thing stands out in my recollection. Each person was convinced they had been given a special gift that enabled them to do things and say things they normally would not be able to do or say.

As I was growing up, one of the issues that bothered me a great deal was related to the question of God's spirit but it was usually phrased, "Have you been born again?" During high school I had a friend who was the daughter of a Baptist minister. I discovered that the Baptists I knew put a lot of emphasis on whether or not a person had gone through some kind of formal acceptance process that qualified them to declare that they had been "born again."

I was curious. I also wanted to score a few points with the Baptist minister's daughter. That summer I went with her family to a church camp. One evening there was a big bonfire and gathering by the river to talk about faith, and then they offered an opportunity for anyone who had not done so to "accept Jesus." Well I was one of the first to be on my feet and moving forward. I "made my confession of faith," but much to my disappointment I felt nothing. I understood with my mind that I had said "yes" to Christ, but quite frankly I felt a lot more when holding the hand of the minister's daughter than in "accepting Jesus."

The following year a group of us had heard about the evangelist Billy Graham and his powerful preaching. This was in 1955, I guess before the days of his TV crusades, or at least we had not seen them. We decided to drive down to Lake Junaluska in North Carolina, where Mr. Graham had his headquarters and a giant outdoor stadium for services. We went to one of those evening meetings and, when he invited us to come forward, again I was among the first to walk down to the field below. It was a long walk because we were sitting way up near the top so we could have a better view of all that happened. Again, I "accepted Jesus as my savior," after going through each of the steps prescribed for "salvation." And again, I think I felt more awe and wonder at the view of the nearby mountains than I did at the "experience of salvation."

A year or so later, during my senior year in high school, I did decide to become a Methodist minister. I had been walking alone in the woods of our farm and talking to God. That seemed to work much better for me than making public professions. Actually, I think it would be more appropriate to say that I had been wrestling with God. I felt that "hound of heaven" was breathing down the back of my neck, following me everywhere I went, pushing me to do something, and yet I knew not what. Finally, I said I would become a minister, and that seemed to ease the pressure some. I even preached a sermon on "Senior Youth Sunday" at my church in Danville, Virginia. That was a meaningful experience; especially since it seemed that more of the girls came up to me afterwards and said what a wonderful job I had done! Why girls liked preaching, I didn't understand. I was sort of bored listening to sermons, but found it was a lot more interesting and exciting if I were doing the preaching.

Several months later I went on a summer mission trip sponsored by the Methodist Church called a "European Travel Seminar and Work Camp." It was supposed to be only for college students, but I had just graduated from high school and was also a "pre-ministerial student," so I was allowed to go.

While on this trip we had many group meetings and many, many discussions, in the midst of travel in Europe and then when living in a refugee camp in Austria where we helped start the construction of a church. Conversations during this experience would often revolve around questions of faith, which again stimulated my mind.

I remember in London going to the chapel where, in the 1700s, John Wesley had served as a priest for the Church of England, and I purchased a gavel made from the wood of the original altar rail of that chapel. We heard a talk about his "conversion," and then walked to Aldersgate Street where it had taken place. What had happened to Wesley seemed somehow related to what was happening to me as I struggled to take a step of faith but was not exactly sure of where or even of how to take that step.

On one mission trip to America Wesley's ship was caught in a great storm and in danger of sinking. He was terrified. But he noticed that among his fellow passengers there was a group of Moravians[30] who were all very calm and peaceful as the storm raged. Later, when they arrived at the Georgia colony and were departing the ship, Wesley questioned one of the Moravian passengers about their being so calm in the midst of such terrible danger. The Moravian replied that he felt in his heart that he was a child of God and had nothing to fear. And then he asked Wesley a disturbing question, "Does the Spirit of God bear witness with your spirit, that you are a child of God?"[31] John was surprised at the question, but also dis-

---

[30] Moravians accept Christ as Lord and follow the motto: "In essentials, unity; in nonessentials, liberty; and in all things, love."

[31] This is a paraphrase of a portion of St. Paul's letter to the Romans, 8:14 ff: "All who are led by the Spirit of God are children of God.... When we cry, 'Abba! Father!' it is that very Spirit bearing witness with our spirit that we

turbed. Although he was a brilliant theologian and powerful preacher, he could not say "yes."

After completing his mission work, John Wesley returned to England. He later said that he had been almost in despair because of this uncertainty about his faith. But then at a small religious meeting in Aldersgate Street, London, on May 24, 1738, John Wesley had an experience in which his "heart was strangely warmed." He felt overwhelmed by the presence of God. He was finally able to feel an assurance that God had accepted him and that he was truly a child of God.

John shared this experience with his brother Charles, who, a few days later had a similar experience. Charles Wesley went on to write many great hymns that testified to the presence of God in his life. Unfortunately, for a while John Wesley preached that a person *must* have this experience of one's heart being warmed by God or they were "under the wrath and curse of God." Fifty years later, he wrote that it was a wonder that the people of England hadn't stoned him for preaching such a thing. By then he had come to see that different people have different psychological make-ups, that some may have an emotional inner assurance, as did John and Charles, while others may have a inner knowing ... like knowing when we are loved; and still others come to an intellectual awareness that is different and yet the same.

During my college years I moved in a very different direction, but still along the same path. I became a devout agnostic, one deeply committed to the "doubting" style of faith. And then, ten years later, after avoiding organized religion as much as my wife would allow, I began a six-month process that could be called a "conversion."

Traditionally, a conversion is considered a change from one belief or religious doctrine to another. I like to think of it as first moving in one direction but then turning around and moving in a different direction, and often needing help from outside of ourselves to make the change. Please note that conversions are not limited to one

---

are children of God, and if children, then heirs, heirs of God and joint heirs with Christ...."

religion or faith but are encountered in all faiths and usually involve some outside force or agent. C. S. Lewis suggested that conversion involves an alteration of the will, and occurs only with supernatural intervention.[32] My experience has had a distinctly Christian flavor. However, please realize that I am not suggesting that everyone must experience God or encounter conversion in the same way. Each individual must follow his or her own path. Just as God is infinite, so also the paths we follow to God are infinite.

I was walking along the Appalachian Trail in the Blue Ridge Mountains near Waynesboro, Virginia. Several months earlier I had ended my efforts in medical school, realizing that medicine was not to be my vocation. I had briefly tried the insurance business and was totally unhappy with that. There seemed to be no clear path, no clear calling. What was I going to do with my life? Was I going to be a total failure, unable to find any purpose in life? Was this all I had to pass on to my sons, 'PK' and Mark? (Please note that I had not the slightest inkling that we would have a daughter eleven years later. So much for my being a "seer," or one who sees the future.) These thoughts and many more were swirling in my mind as I walked the trail, oblivious to the great beauty of the mountains.

Finally, I decided to rest and found an area covered with moss, up a side trail away from other hikers. I lay on the moss looking up through the limbs of trees at the deep blue sky far above leaves gently swaying in a warm breeze. The questions and despair continued to fill my mind. I knew I needed help from outside myself. And then, for the first time in many years, I said a prayer. I spoke this prayer into the doubt and uncertainty of my life and into my lack of faith, "Are you there?" "Is there really a God?" And across the infinite expanse of the universe I felt a clear and certain answer, "Yes! I am here." It was more than just hearing these words in the deep recesses of my soul. It was as though these words were becoming part of the very fabric of my being. "Yes! I am here, and you are my child." This was my Aldersgate.

---

[32] *God in the Dock*, "The Decline of Religion," by C.S. Lewis (1946), p. 221.

This was a profound encounter with the numinous, an epiphany, a once-in-a-lifetime event. In my case, this experience in the Blue Ridge Mountains of Virginia was like a birth into an expanded consciousness, a new awareness that there is a presence, a force, a positive reality outside of or within what we see as ordinary reality.

However, I didn't know what to do with this new awareness. When I came down off of the mountain and returned home, I felt confusion. What did this mean? How did it relate to me and my small, insignificant life? I knew this had been an experience of the divine, so I decided that perhaps a Roman Catholic priest would know what this was all about. I'm not sure why I thought an answer would be found there rather than with my pastor in the Methodist Church. I did remember going to a Catholic service during my high school years, and the only thing I could recall was that there had been a sense of mystery about the ceremony. That "Yes" speaking across the cosmos was truly a mystery for me, ergo, a Roman Catholic priest might understand.

I picked up the phone and called St. Thomas Hall, the Catholic Church adjoining the University of Virginia. If I were going to talk to a religious person, then perhaps doing so near such a place of learning was a little safer. Fortunately, the person who answered was an extraordinary Dominican priest, Father Tom Clifford, who ultimately became my spiritual director and close personal friend. I briefly explained what had happened and he immediately invited me to come to his office at the church. There we talked for more than an hour, and he reassured me that this had been a genuine encounter with the mystery of God. He also suggested I open the Bible and learn how others had also encountered God. He said he had just received in the mail that morning a study guide about the Holy Spirit, sent to him by a Nun who also happened to be his sister ... "my sister the Sister." He said that guide must have been meant for me, not him.

I worked with that study guide long into the night and through the next several days, and I found things in Holy Scripture which were never mentioned in my Sunday School classes or at our MYF[33]

---

[33] Methodist Youth Fellowship.

meetings. I learned about Chrismata, spiritual gifts, or gifts of the Holy Spirit. I discovered that, in the words of St. Paul, "there are varieties of gifts, but the same spirit; and there are varieties of services, but the same Lord; and there are varieties of activities, but it is the same God who activates all of them in everyone." (I Corinthians 12:4-6) Some of these gifts are the utterance of wisdom, the utterance of knowledge, faith, healing, miracles, prophecy, discernment of spirits, various kinds of tongues or languages, and the interpretation of tongues; but that the greatest gift of all is love. It also appears that when spiritual gifts are present we will see evidence as to whether these gifts are activated by the Holy Spirit of God or by a spirit working to bring evil and chaos. Paul pointed out that when the Holy Spirit is active we would see fruits such as love, joy, peace, patience, kindness, generosity, faithfulness, gentleness, and self-control. (Galatians 4:22) This is another important test we can apply to all spiritual phenomena.

On the other hand, when evil or dark forces are at work there will be different evidence such as "fornication, impurity, licentiousness, idolatry, sorcery, enmities, strife, jealousy, anger, quarrels, dissensions, factions, envy, drunkenness, carousing, and things like these." (Galatians 4:19) If the spiritual activity produces any of these, then it is clear that something other than the Holy Spirit is at work. Now granted, there will be normal times of anger, jealousy, quarrels, and disagreements in the affairs of imperfect humans. However, when we encounter them, we still can be sure that we need to pause and ask for guidance from God's Spirit. The more I learned, the more I knew that I wanted to open myself up as much as possible to the Holy Spirit.

That Saturday night, immediately following my experience on the mountain, my wife and I attended a cocktail party at the local country club. At that event I met a new friend, Patricia Henderson, and we got into a deep discussion about religion. During that meeting she issued an invitation to a service of "Healing and Holy Eucharist" at her Episcopal church on the following Wednesday.

This was the next part of my "conversion" which involved the Laying on of Hands by an Episcopal priest, Father Jim Cunningham, and the reception of Holy Communion in an Episcopal church.

That was the first time I had attended an Episcopal Church. Had you viewed the moment you probably would have said it was very quiet and uneventful. There was no music, no high drama, no great processions, or fancy liturgy. There were only ten people present. And yet, in that service I experienced something I had never encountered before. When Father Jim laid his hands on my head, I felt they were like a giant spiritual vacuum cleaner drawing out all of my pain and suffering, all of my doubt and uncertainty, all of my failures, blind alleys and self deceptions of my life. I knew I was being cleaned for something special but had no idea how monumental that would be. When I received communion I "knew" that I was receiving something more than bread and wine and that a process of soul healing had begun. I could feel a powerful, new force starting to move in my life. Although I did not know it at the time, I was entering a mystical style of believing. I was experiencing a new dimension of "reality." I was touching that "non-ordinary reality" mentioned in Chapter One.

I also found a new church home at Church of our Savior, and Father Jim became my priest, pastor and friend. Although I had grown up in the Methodist Church, I found in the Episcopal Church a spiritual abode where I could be intellectually honest about my questioning and searching, and where the sacraments were more than simply remembrances.

During this period I also became involved in the charismatic prayer group which met at the Roman Catholic church mentioned above, St. Thomas Hall, led by Father Tom Clifford. At my first meeting with this prayer group, after working with the study guide Father Tom had given me and reading in the Bible about the strange workings of God's Spirit, I asked for prayers that I might more fully receive the Holy Spirit into my life. Some have called this the "baptism in the Holy Spirit." I prefer not to use that phrase in a definitive way (there is only one baptism); but it is descriptive of the experience.

During that service of prayers and praise, something happened that blew away old boundaries and enabled me to become a channel of God's Spirit. Father Tom and ten other members of the group laid their hands on my head. Even though I had never heard anything like this before, I began to sing in a strange language. I felt a power surge through me and an immersion in joy that truly was beyond my logical understanding. I knew, beyond a shadow of doubt, that the Spirit of God was bearing witness with my spirit that I was in fact a child of God, an heir of God and a joint heir with Christ.

I was so fortunate to have had Father Jim and Father Tom as spiritual guides through these difficult and exciting times. One of their greatest gifts was a strong centering in the Christian tradition, through which I could interpret and try to comprehend what was happening to me. With their help, I came to see that I was, that we all are, channels for the Spirit of that Mystery we call God. At one point, not long after my "baptism in the Holy Spirit," I remember feeling somewhat guilty that I had experienced such amazing grace and joy. I called a friend in the prayer group who read to me what St. Paul said about that, "To each is given the manifestation of the Spirit for the common good." (I Corinthians 12:7) She pointed out that although it may make us feel fantastic when the Spirit of God works through us, still that is happening not only for our benefit but for the good of all. Many years later I heard the analogy that we are similar to a garden hose. When the cool water flows through the dried up and stiff hose, the hose becomes supple and refreshed while the water is flowing out to the flowers and grass. Likewise, as we allow God's Spirit to flow through us to others, we will also receive great benefit. I also remembered those times while in high school when I decided I wanted to give my life to Christ and had prayed the most fervent prayer possible that God would use me however he saw fit. I now felt that prayer being answered in new and exciting ways.

Much has been written about this kind of charismatic experience. For me it was a doorway into a deeper relationship with a living and personal God. It also showed me how God can use individuals such as Patricia, Father Tom, and Father Jim, and that what appear to be chance events and/or chance encounters are ways God's will is working in our lives.

Any renewal process, whether it be a charismatic group, a Cursillo[34] weekend, a parish retreat, a vision quest, etc., can be a place where lives are changed, conversions happen, non-ordinary reality is experienced, and God's presence is reaffirmed in unique and exciting ways. When that happens there is always the danger that the tool, the mechanism, the process, becomes that which is honored and worshiped. In the same way that some in the Episcopal Church became extremely attached to the 1928 Book of Common Prayer through which they had encountered God in the beautiful language and liturgies, so also someone encountering God through a renewal process may come to worship that process rather than God. That is a form of idolatry and draws us away from true worship of that which deserves our devotion and faith, i.e., God.

Sometimes we are effective channels. Sometimes, we, like rivers and streams, become blocked and ineffective. Some of the processes and exercises described in this book may help remove blockages.

But there is another issue here. We can also be channels for spirits other than God's Holy Spirit. With Shirley MacLaine's movies and books on her experiences with Kevin Ryerson and others, and with the many other books being published on the spiritual phenomenon of "channeling," the new rage seems to be to try to "channel" so called "higher spirits." My fundamentalist Christian brothers and sisters might say that all such activity is the work of the devil, or at least is evil and dangerous. On the other hand, my more rationalistic and scientific friends say it is all ridiculous or absurd. I have tried to keep an open mind and inquire whether or not there is anything worthwhile here, and I discuss this more fully in the next chapter.

I agree that this is a practice fraught with danger. But it is also a practice that has provided me with opportunities for spiritual growth and learning. My introduction into this area took place many years ago. When I was in high school, starting on Sunday, December 16, 1956 (I know the date because I still have the journal notes), I began a process of regularly recording my thoughts, a process I recommended in Chapter Five. For many years prior to that date I had

---

[34] A three-day Christian faith renewal program that focuses on God's love for each of us.

been writing down on scraps of papers my thoughts, ideas, poems, questions and reflections. Then I started using a bound journal.

I believe the habit of writing what came to my mind prepared me for the next step. Suddenly on January 13, 1958 there is an unusual record. It begins, *"Dear Mr. Kinser."* There are some personal comments about some concerns I had at that time and then this passage: *Face the fact that you have work to do, hard work. We can do it together. We can start one step at a time, working and fighting and thinking together. But you must take the first step. You can't put this off any longer. Sincerely....* This was signed with the math symbol for infinity ∞, which I used on the title page of this book.

That was the first of many occasional "communications" over the years. These usually follow other writings, reflections, and/or questions, followed by a pause during which I "listen." These communications have always been a source of comfort, guidance and new insight -- never judgmental, always loving. Sometimes several years go by between such entries. As mentioned earlier, it was not until 1987 that one of these entities being channeled identified itself as a Guardian Angel.

However, in December of 1980, there began a profusion of writings that were, for me, explanations of what I was being told by the Holy Spirit.

One memorable example occurred while I was being interviewed by an Episcopal parish near Richmond, Virginia, which was searching for a Rector. Mary Ann and I both had received what we understood to be strong spiritual blocks. These indicated that we were not to accept this parish's call. However, we were visiting in the parish at the time and meeting many of its wonderful members.

Then one night I was up very late listening to the silence of the guest house where we were staying. Everyone else was asleep. I wrote the following in my journal: "Lord Jesus Christ, please help us understand what is not right here. Is this place wrong for us? Are we receiving the wrong impression or wrong feelings because you are trying to block our accepting this call? May your Holy Spirit, O Jesus, surround, protect and guide us."

As I sat in that quiet house which had been supplied for our visit, my hand began to move across the page.

My son. I have called you to be a priest in my Church. You are a priest in my Church. I have called your family to be a Holy People. And you are a Holy People.

Trust me. Continue to be open to me speaking through both your intellect and your feelings. I am with you and your family. DO NOT make a decision now. You are here to listen. You are here to be My presence with these people at this moment, not just to reach a decision.... I am with you. I have surrounded you and your family with my love and my protection. You are walking in my light.

I felt that this was more than my limited mind creating helpful and hopeful sentences. The words seemed to flow from another source. I believe this was a "channeled communication," not from some strange "entity" but from the Spirit of God, another assurance that God's Spirit was bearing witness with my spirit. And I believe such communication is possible for anyone who is listening. My later contact and communications with my Guardian Angels have been very different from these that seem to come directly from the Holy Spirit.

Please note that, just one year after writing the above, I recorded the following:

"God, sometimes you seem so far away – or rather I feel so far from you. I have lost a sense of the reality of your presence in my life, which is perhaps why I am working so hard – thinking I must do it all; not trusting that you are truly involved!"

With these deep reflections in my mind I picked up my well-worn Bible and allowed it to open wherever it would. There I read from 1st Peter: *"Make a habit of obedience: be holy in all you do, since it is the Holy One who has called you....;"* and *"Each one of you has received a special grace, so, like good stewards responsible for all these different graces of God, put yourselves at the service of others. If you are a speaker, speak in words which seem to come from God; if you are a helper, help as though every action was done at God's orders; so that in everything God may receive the glory, through Jesus Christ, since to him alone belong all glory and power for ever and ever. Amen."* Another "channeled communication," this time through Holy Scripture.

That helped me rise to new levels of conversation with the Spirit. Then in 1984, during a major period of crisis and conflict in my parish, I became spiritually bogged down in those problems. I visited my friend (and author of *Encounters in Bethlehem*) Jean Anderson. Jean suggested that I try to return to some of the more feminine types of spiritual activities such as dream work. Then she gave me a book on the *I Ching*. The *I Ching*, or *Book of Changes*, has exerted a major influence in China for over three thousand years, and interest has spread to the West. Some have used it as a source of divination. I use it to tap the more unconscious parts of myself.

When working with the I Ching one can use coins or sticks. I cut my own sticks and the *I Ching* became another way for the Spirit to speak with me. Since you cannot control the draw of the sticks, this also helped me get back in touch with my feminine side, since non-control is considered to be a basic feminine trait.[35]

In 1986 I made another spiritual breakthrough. I had been using "Hemi-Sync" tapes, developed by the Monroe Institute[36]. These tapes employ sounds and changing tones to help one achieve an alpha state of consciousness[37]. According to brain researchers, as the mind becomes calm and moves into a light meditative state, the electrical impulses given off by the brain undergo striking changes. A device called an electro-encephalograph or EEG measures these impulses. The EEG records these changes on moving paper, or on a video screen, much as one might look at the electrical impulses given off by the beating heart when using an electro-cardiogram. Computers have been developed that can detect brain states.

---

[35] If you are interested in this avenue of exploration I recommend *The I Ching, or Book of Changes*, translated by Wilhelm and Baynes, Princeton University Press.

[36] For more details of this process I recommend *Far Journeys*, by the late Robert Monroe, founder of the Monroe Institute. I don't totally agree with Monroe's cosmology, but I find his work stimulating and the hemi-sync tapes quite useful.

[37] Alpha brain waves are associated with deep relaxation and meditation.

The initial changes in the EEG patterns due to light meditation show an overall reduction in activity with an increase in what are called K waves. As the meditative state becomes much deeper, the alpha waves become more pronounced. Some researchers have noted those experiencing what has been called "enlightenment" reach an even deeper state.

There are now many electronic devices on the market that advertise a quick entrance into alpha states. I have read several reviews of these devices that are not enthusiastic. I haven't used any of them and cannot speak from experience. I still believe simple meditation is the best path to such an alpha state. However, my experience with the Monroe Institute Hemi-Sync tapes to enhance my meditation practice has been positive.

I started using a "Free Flow" tape in the collection of Hemi-Sync tapes. It has limited instructions and an open-ended process, which allows one to search more freely. That tape became a regular part of my meditation and prayer process and helped open the flow of the Spirit in dramatic ways. For example, after using the introductory Hemi-Sync tape for two weeks, I started to notice quicker access to a deep meditative awareness of an ever present pure white light about two feet above my head (as mentioned in the previous discussion of chakras). Some have identified this as a "trans-personal" chakra or energy point. That area became an entrance point for the Light of Christ, which seems to pour into me during meditation.

Another surprising event occurred after two months of using the tapes. As I was jogging one morning, I found my consciousness could leave my body and go elsewhere. This does not seem to be what others have described as "out of body experiences" although it is similar. I know that I am still jogging (and on other occasions I am sitting in meditation), but I am also conscious of being in a cave in the Himalayan Mountains.

There I met with a deep part of myself, or an actual presence, that I now call the "Mountain Master." For the next six months I would return to the cave (as I was walking or jogging) and simply sit with this Master. Finally I asked, "What am I doing here?" He responded, "I am teaching you silence." Some might wonder what took me so long to ask about what was going on. However, the experience was filled with such peace and calm that I felt no need to ask. The content of those and many other lessons over several years may some day be the subject for another book.

In 1988 I knew it was time for me to look into other kinds of channeling, i.e., channeling other Beings of Light or agents of Christ. What follows are some of my own personal experiences in this area and some of the safeguards one might use in exploring these practices.

I studied numerous works on channeling (see Bibliography) and then entered into several months of questioning prayer. After discussion with and an "OK" from my Guardian Angels, I was taken through the following process.[38]

As always, I entered into a meditative state. However, I was told by my Guardian Angel not to go as deep as when in usual meditation. I surrounded myself with extra protection and sealed myself under the guidance of Christ. I then asked my Guardian Angel, in consultation with God, to determine whether or not contact with a higher spirit or being of light would help me meet my soul's objectives and further the will of God in my life.

I again received a clear affirmation, that it was OK and that this was my choice. I then asked if there were a higher Being of Light who wished to be channeled through me. I immediately received an affirmative reply.

I spiritually opened myself to that entity. Immediately I knew I was in the presence of what seemed to be an old friend. I felt a warmth of knowing and could hear the sound of ocean surf which was related to where I had known this friend. As best as I could understand, this being had been my teacher in an ancient past life which I discuss in the Chapter Twelve.

I asked the name of this friend and was told to simply use the name "Teacher" because I was "not spiritually mature enough to know the full identity of this friend," i.e., my ego would become too inflated.

---

[38] Please do not use this process unless you are working closely with a spiritual director and have received clearance to proceed!

(My Guardian Angels know me well and are my most honest critics.)

I received the impression that I was not to inconvenience "Teacher" with questions of curiosity, but that I would receive serious and meaningful teaching and knowledge related to important issues. Then, as I recorded in my journal that morning, "Teacher" will be more than willing *"to do the hard work to be with me and help me see or learn what I need to learn at that time."*

I was recording on the computer what I was experiencing as it was happening. I will share some of what I wrote.

"I am being told that this is not some kind of psychic game -- but rather this has to do with how best I can live my life and how best I can help further God's kingdom of love, joy and peace."

I was in a semi-asleep state and slowly moved too deeply into meditation so that I could no longer record what I was receiving, i.e., I went to sleep. When I woke up I was told that contact would not be made if the content would be lost. I was to be awake enough to either write, type, or talk into a tape recorder. I moved again into a meditative state.

I am now moving into light relaxation to determine if Teacher has any other instructions concerning how I can better determine God's will for me at this time. (PK3=myself)

Teacher: *I am here and I have received your request. Be sure you have made contact with me, and not with some other spirit. This is always a first test whenever you open yourself.*

PK3: *I can hear the oceans* (which gave me an inner confirmation that this was contact with my ancient friend, Teacher).

Teacher: *Yes, I can feel us swimming together in the oceans. We had fun then.... Concerning God's will for you, you are free to do what you wish. You will learn a great deal by honestly exploring any possibility. Always remember that regardless of where you are or what you are doing, you are serving the Light of Christ; your call is to be a servant of that Light. Your soul's purpose is to experience this physical existence and learn the necessary discipline through this physical plane to make your next evolutionary leap.*

PK3: *What do you mean, 'next evolutionary leap'?*

Teacher: *You are continuing your own progression as a Being of Light. However, you realized that a life on the earth plane would help you with some important learnings, the development of some very important tools, for example, exertion of will. This is a primary tool as a being of light and you have not yet mastered that tool.*

Remember, exertion of will to accomplish a chosen task or mission is a tool, just like a hammer or a saw, or an automobile. The auto helps you get where you choose to go. The will helps you accomplish what you have chosen.

You have correctly identified another problem, i.e., the clarification of goals or choices. In the struggle to develop will, one must also become clearer in identifying and verbalizing the choices that are faced. Once a clear choice is selected, then the exercise of will becomes the tool to accomplish that. This is not a game of mental gymnastics or positive thinking. Rather this concerns the hard work of will power.

I will not say that your next few years will be easy. If you are to continue to be able to use this life to its fullest advantage, you MUST learn to clarify choices and to exercise your will!

(I did not know then that I would soon face a heart attack in January, 1989, and bypass surgery in 1990.)

You have always had a wonderful interest in all of life and in all processes involving spiritual life, and in the many different manifestations of God on all levels or dimensions. You are a wonderful explorer. But now you have chosen to also be a worker, which involves will. Keep this problem/opportunity for growth always in the back of your mind. Each time you face a choice, e.g., whether or not to get seconds at lunch today, see it as an opportunity to exercise those will muscles.

The other things you are doing to achieve harmony and balance, to further develop your spiritual life, to align chakras, will give you the strength to accomplish ANYTHING you desire!

In all of this, appreciate this physical life you have chosen and the possibilities it opens to you in this lifetime. Above all, have fun!

PK3: *Can I regularly talk with you or am I limited to my Guardian Angels?*

Teacher: *You can talk with me, with GA* (my name for my primary Guardian Angel), *and even with the infinite Light of Christ and the Power of God. Since I am a Being of Light, as I told you this morning, I can be in contact with 1000s of different others who need my help, all in the same second -- light does travel at 186,000 miles per second, and we are not even limited by that. I can compress time or expand time to communicate with you.*

And as always, we are lower vibrations than God. Therefore, it is easier for us to talk with you so you can understand. Also, for you, we have been together in another life, in this same relationship of Teacher and Learner. You can continue to experience the Light of Christ, as you have been doing, in prayer, in the Sacraments, and in the world around you.

Likewise that which we call 'God,' is everywhere and within everything, and will speak directly in an infinite variety of ways. However, only if you are a 'prophet,' and told to speak for God, are you to quote directly that infinite mystery. Rather, God is to be known and experienced, not quoted by you. We are to be 'friends' with God; in communion with, in relationship with, open to and in fellowship with God. Actually, that is the way it is whether we realize it or not. Existence is just more fun when we realize our union with God.

When I finished writing the above and came out of my meditative state, I began to realize that I had gone beyond acceptable Christian boundaries by "channeling." I entered into deep prayer, asking God if I had gone beyond His/Her acceptable boundaries. I was immediately given the words of St. Frances, "Make me a instrument or channel of your peace...." and was shown that God does not have boundaries. The very nature of God is as one without boundaries, infinite, transcendent, and yet totally present.

This was my first experience of channeling a spirit other than God's Holy Spirit. I have since had many conversations with "Teacher." These discussions are in no way a substitute for my regular meditation and prayer life, or for my direct communion with God. However, they have provided a wonderful new resource for my own personal learning.

On one occasion, I was given permission during a spiritual guidance session with a person (I will call him "Bob") to ask for the counsel of Teacher on behalf of that individual seeking spiritual direction. I allowed Teacher to speak through me, using my voice. I was totally aware that I was speaking. I even remember at one point, when Bob asked a question for which I believed I had no answer, thinking that now I would see that this whole channeling thing is just an activity of my own mind. I was quite surprised that my voice began giving a very clear answer to the question asked. However, when the session ended I could not remember the actual content of anything that had been said until Bob reminded me of something -- then I would remember that portion of the conversation.

I have only done this twice because I found it to be an uncomfortable experience. It was as though too much energy were trying to move through my body. I also did not like the feeling of not being in total control of what I was saying. These drawbacks are not so great that I would refuse to use this technique again if the situation warranted or the needs were great enough.

However, I must conclude this chapter with a repetition of an earlier warning. Move into this area of spiritual life with caution and only with trained guidance. Some people get into trouble here because they are not firmly rooted in any faith tradition, did not have a safe structure within which they could work, and tried to "go it alone." Also, if a person has been diagnosed as having a dissociative disorder or an anxiety disorder, I think such channeling is contraindicated and must be avoided.

I do not think we are to live in fear of the bad things that might happen. At the same time, we must try to exercise as much wisdom as possible as we move into unchartered waters. And as Teacher had said to me, *"Above all, have fun,"* and as Jesus said in the Gospel according to John, *"I have said these things you so that my joy may be in you, and that your joy may be complete."* (John 15:11)

Chapter 9

CONVERSATIONS WITH THE MASTERS

Although this chapter follows the theme of the previous chapter, i.e., supernatural communication, I believe this material requires its own introduction. If you looked at my brief biography you know that my background is quite varied. My primary vocation is that of an Episcopal priest. That being the case, I strive to base my teachings and actions upon truth. I am also a board certified clinical hypnotherapist as well as a pastoral counselor and psychotherapist. Such training and experience has taught me to question behavioral and emotional phenomenon. At the same time, my theological training included reflection in the field of phenomenology, which is an approach that concentrates on the study of consciousness and the objects of direct experience. I am also trained as a scientist. I had a minor in the sciences in college and later taught chemistry and physics.

This being the case, I cannot help but question the objective reality of the experiences discussed in this chapter. I know they are part of my life. However, I also know that the human brain can easily be deceived or duped by its own desire to experience something. That is part of the nature of trance states or hypnotic activity, which is why evidence obtained from a witness through the use of hypnosis is not admissible in most courts of law. The evidence is simply too unreliable.

Therefore, I must warn you that the following evidence I present in this chapter may be likewise unreliable. Nevertheless, I think it has value. St. Paul in his letters to the young Christian churches, would, in some places, begin by saying, "This is from the Lord." I think that means Paul had an inner knowing which made him believe in the reliability of what he was saying as coming from God. But often Paul would say, "This is from me." In those cases, Paul was sharing his opinion, his interpretation, his own inner vision with the reader. Therefore, the content was open to question, argument and discussion. Likewise, please recognize that the following material is open to question and I hope discussion. Do not simply accept this as fact and truth, or dismiss it as fantasy and fiction.

You *can* accept as truth that these experiences did come to me while deep in meditation. They are part of my life, part of my memories, and thus part of who I am. However, meditation is a kind of trance state. Therefore, anything that happens in such a state is subject to serious evaluation and review, not blind acceptance. As St. Paul would have said, "This material is from me."

I make these preliminary comments because this chapter contains what some may consider the most controversial material of this book. The following "conversations" occurred while I was either sitting at my computer deep in meditation, allowing my fingers to type what you see below, or they were written in long hand – what some call "automatic writing" while in a deep meditative state, and later transcribed with editing for clarity only.

As best I can understand, some of these conversations are with "Ascended Masters." The term "Ascended Masters" refers to souls who supposedly, after many incarnations and life experiences, have mastered the lessons of physical existence. They appear to have chosen to assist or guide souls who are currently living on planet Earth (and perhaps elsewhere in the universe).

It has been my experience that Ascended Masters speak to us through chance events, dreams, meditations, art, music, and direct conversation utilizing the intuitive and creative aspects of the brain. Connecting with an Ascended Master allows us to go to levels of knowledge to which we normally do not have access. They are a source we tap into when we want to trigger that higher knowledge within ourselves. Ascended Masters differ from Guardian Angels in that our Guardian Angels are always with us. An Ascended Master comes to us for a short while to provide instruction or guidance and then seems to be absent for a time.

I recognize that all of the following could be purely products of my overly active creative processes, products of my imagination. However, as Dean Urban T. Holmes told us in seminary, "The imaginative faculties of the brain are the avenues through which the divine must speak." If there are such entities as Ascended Masters, then it seems logical that any conversations with them must utilize those same faculties. And since those are the same processes that create works of fiction, it becomes difficult to differentiate between authentic conversations with such teachers and fabrications of the creative mind. I have utilized the tests mentioned in *Appendix A* to measure whether or not these are genuine, and I have found them to be filled with truth. But I know of no way to verify the historicity of this material.

When I used the tests mentioned in *Appendix A*, I felt at peace about the content – although I know I could be totally mistaken. Some readers may have difficulty living with this kind of ambiguity, and that is fine. It may feel safer to deny that any such conversations could possibly occur, and that is also quite OK. Each person must follow the path they have been led to follow, and to do so with as much faith, hope and love as is possible. My path seems to lead to areas that sometimes move outside that which is considered "orthodox" (traditional, established, following established doctrine, accepted, authoritative, official, approved). And yet orthodoxy may not be all it is promoted to be. Elbert Hubbard wrote in 1914 that orthodoxy is a "corpse that does not know it is dead." George Orwell, in 1949, suggested that "orthodoxy means not thinking -- not needing to think. Orthodoxy is unconsciousness."

So I present these conversations realizing they are unorthodox, and with the warning that these are outside of what is considered normal religious or spiritual doctrine. Also, some of these conversations appear to be with individuals who once lived on this earth but who are no longer alive. Such a possibility is hard for me to believe. And yet, there was for me such a sense of authenticity to these experiences and to the content given to me that I have to trust that it contains truth.

When asked if he believed the Bible is true, my Old Testament professor in seminary said, "I believe what the Bible presents is truth. Some truth is contained in the myths or stories presented, some truth is found within the history of our forefathers in faith. Other truth is contained in the poetry, the psalms, the urgent longings of the religious heart." Likewise, I believe the following material contains truth, but I cannot tell you whether or not it is a fact that these actually came from Ascended Masters, from old friends I have known in this life and in previous lives, from Guardian Angels, etc. There is no way anyone can prove or disprove such beings exist and converse with us in this time and space. So, please take everything you find here with a grain of salt, i.e., question the authenticity and decide for yourself whether or not it has value for you.

The following is from my Journal, Friday, August 11, 1989, 10:41 a.m.: I have prepared this room, cleansing with incense and prayers. I feel I am now to await teaching from the "Ascended Masters." Not sure what this means....

PK3: GA, are you there and is Teacher? Is it possible to talk with Ascended Masters, and is that permissible, that is, will it work for the higher purposes of Christ?

GA: *We are always here... And it is OK to ask for teaching from Ascended Masters. You have already been working with two, i.e., Teacher and the Mountain Master. Now is time to expand that contact, for you are about to learn how to tap the Akashic records*[39].

---

[39] It is said that the Akashic Records contain the entire history of every soul since the dawn of Creation. Information about these Akashic Records can be found in folklore, in myth, and in the Old and New Testaments. It is traceable at least as far back as the Semitic peoples and includes the Arabs, the Assyrians, the Phoenicians, the Babylonians, and the Hebrews. Among these peoples was the belief that there was some kind of celestial tablet or book that contained the history of humankind as well as all manner of spiritual information. The first reference in Jewish scripture to such a record or "book" can be found in Exodus 32:32.

We believe you have sufficiently been prepared in this lifetime to handle the data recorded therein.

Now wait and breathe...

AM (Ascended Master): *You have taken long to approach us. We have put clues all around, and finally by our rubbing your nose in our presence, you have opened to us. Thank you for now being willing to listen, and to prepare for your next step in training as an initiate.*

I wonder to myself, what is an initiate? And, where is this going?

We hear your thoughts and questions. An initiate is one who is moving toward AM status, but still is in the preparatory stages. You have a good way to go, perhaps in this lifetime, perhaps in the next, if that is the path you choose.

We are now preparing you to be one who sees, which is the source of your name, Soaring Eagle. You will see what must be seen. But your readings last night do point correctly to your need for perseverance, purity of mind, and a clear ideal.

Be clear about your motives. You will always have a part of you that wants fame and recognition, that is part of the human condition. However, you are doing well in putting that need into proper perspective.

Now sit back, and prepare to merge your mind with a portion of the Akashic records.... [Although corrected in this text, I realize that some of the material I am recording has spelling errors.]

PK3: If I am truly talking to an AM, why aren't the communications with correct spelling?

AM: *We must work through the equipment you have in this lifetime. And you are correct; there is a defect in the left anterior portion of your frontal lobe where the spelling and name remembering functions synapse with the identification portions of your memory. You can identify an almost infinite variety of individuals, topics, elements, etc., but your ability to connect those objects with their correct name is defective. This was due to your mother drinking alcoholic beverages during a certain period of your development as a fetus. However, you have compensated well for this defect, and your higher level of intelligence is an asset that has actually been accelerated in its functioning because of this lack of contact with the naming functions of the brain.*

Again sit back, breathe and prepare to merge with a portion of the Akashic records....

So do not fake the merge, or try to guess the content. You will know when the merging takes place....[I am moving deeper into a meditative trance state.].....*There is no time, all things are here....Do not try to evaluate the data, just receive...*

There is darkness, a feeling of going down into something...

No, also of going up; it is all around me... I am connected to all of history, all of time...I sit with monks in Nepal and India, in China, in Vietnam, in Hawaii, in South America, we are all moving into communion at this very moment, but I am the only one sitting at a computer to record this happening.

A vast Ohm is being spoken into the Universe, radiating from the earth and out through space and non-space, into the inner reaches of the atoms and into the multi dimensions of spiritual reality.

I feel I am becoming one with all my brothers and sisters who are part of this reality. We are all here to further love in the Universe... LOVE, the divine nature of all things, true spirit....

I feel sadness because I can't see clearly yet, but I am comforted and assured that I will, and I must have patience with my training. Ommmm.

I can dip into a lifetime of one who lived 2000 years ago. He is plowing the fields in Asia; his shelter is good, with wife and children. He works hard, and I can feel the life within him.

The image of flying over a vast body of water is very similar to that of moving across the Akashic Records, as I am doing now. I can dip in anywhere I wish... Napoleon, Kennedy, Casey.... All individual lives are very similar in the basic human feelings that are going on from moment to moment. There are different activities, different foci of intent or purpose, but we are all joined by common genes to a similar experience of this earthly existence.

The question is, do we progress through our own learning toward AM status and do we help humanity move toward the LIGHT???? Is this truly real????

AM: *How can you ask the question, Is this real? You know what you are experiencing is unique, and real.*

Back into the silence.... Ommmmmmm....

AM: *You see when you have available the infinite resource of all past memories and experiences, the curiosity seems to die and you can sit in peace....*

Moving into the life of a person now living is a different matter. You have not been given permission to do that, except on a face-to-face basis, when you can get GA clearance at that time, but not for a person absent. You can go see them, but not move into their consciousness.... Understand?

PK3: Yes. I see Patricia playing on a field with other girls, some kind of outdoor activity... now getting ready to walk back to her cabin. It is wet, and her feet are wet...

I see a friend in an office looking at a yellow pad. Another friend is at home in her kitchen worrying about her daughter. These are verifiable....

AM: *And it is OK to test the data you begin to see, that is part of the training of one who sees. You must learn to trust what you see....*

While I sit in meditation and conversation with an Ascended Master, at the same time I travel in my mind to walk on the beach near Ramada Towers (at Virginia Beach near A.R.E.®). After walking on the beach, I zoom out across the water, around a ship with its dirty condition, then across the surface of the planet to the Himalayan mountains. I walk down the path to the Mountain Master (MM), and move into his cave. I realize I am wearing a brown monk's habit with hood.

The master begins to teach me.... [long pause in recording while I receive private teachings from the Mountain Master, then the typing continues...]

MM: *You must learn to care for your body; it is Holy and is your vehicle in this lifetime. The body must become purified, cleansed, opened up as a channel for Light.*

PK3: What of the rest of my family? I have been with them so long and do not want to leave them!

MM: *We are all your family and you will never leave any of us.... We are all part of each other and can never be apart.*

Now hear instruction concerning your body. As you finish the Cardiac Rehab program you will replace that with disciplines we provide. Your body becomes what you put into it. Do not consume anything that you do not want to be a permanent part of your Ascended Body....

Be very conscious of what you eat...reduce the volume gradually over the next month and keep it there until your weight is around 165 of your lbs.

Do not lift weights at this time. All exercise will be natural and beneficial, and bring health and harmony into your being. Later you will use light weights to supplement your exercise routine.

You will not fail because we are all going to be helping you.

[I pause to go to bathroom...and then return.]

See how once this contact has been established you can pick it up even with interruptions.... I am here with you; any of the monks that have been assigned to help are available to you.

PK3: I am concerned about my lack of success at getting up at an early time and keeping to the physical disciplines.

MM: *You do well to recognize that this will not be easy for your physical and emotional forms...they will always tend toward inactivity...which is part of the human evolutionary survival mechanism. Let us show you why....*

When there has been an over supply of food, then the body will naturally want to seek shelter and rest, keeping that reserve of food until time to go on the next hunt.

Since your current environment and thus your body is always in a mode of over supply, it is hard to keep to a rigid discipline that requires you to get up early and to move your body in exercise.

That is why the new discipline and food regime will be an initial shock to your system. We will try to guide you through this gradually.

PK3: Thank you MM, AM, GA and Teacher.

I conclude this session with a feeling that I have truly experienced an expansion of my consciousness.

Much later in my journals I found another record. I did not record the date or time of the following, but knew I was hearing from a spiritual master or Ascended Master other than those I had come to know as Ascended Master (AM), Mountain Master (MM), Guardian Angel (GA), and Teacher. The character and dimension of this communication was somewhat different than my listening to Guardian Angels or receiving guidance from the Holy Spirit. Whenever I hear from the one I call "Teacher" or from any other Ascended Master, I feel I am actually in conversation with an old friend. This particular communication seemed to have a different tone or timbre, as though it were from a university professor or great scholar. The source does not identify itself, but I have the feeling it is from a master that can be trusted. My fingers start to type what I am being given:

The symbolic story of Adam and Eve portrays the psychic breach that exists for so many human beings between themselves and the Spirit that surrounds them.

As creation proceeded on this physical level a part of the Spirit was given to each atom, each molecule, each element, and each combination of these building blocks. As earth, air, fire, water, and all other inanimate things came into being, each was given a soul or psychic link with the Creator.

Much theology and philosophy is wrong in assuming that only human creatures have souls. Each rock, each drop of water, each cloud has a soul.

The Native Americans were, and still are, correct in talking to the Thunder Beings (in the clouds), to their Rock Brothers, to Grandfather Sun and Grandmother Moon, to Mother Earth, to the Spirit Keepers of the North, South, East and West, etc.

These people lived close to the earth and moved slow enough to be able to hear the voices of inanimate objects.

And then the spark of life began the process of animation, of respiration and reproduction. The density of the soul force increased as did the level of psychic communication between the Creator and the created.

Since the basic nature of the Creator is Love, then the structure of this physical universe is one that moves it toward greater communion with the Creator. This is what the Biblical phrase refers to when we read, "Mankind was created in the image of God." But as the complexity of the creature increased so did the necessity for choice.

The Garden of Eden symbolizes the original state of all creation where the created MUST obey the Creator because the physical laws created into matter compelled obedience. The souls of the plants and animals, rocks and rivers, the oceans and the grains of sand, the winged creatures and four-legged friends, all these souls are infinitely complex. These spirits have the task of nurturing. What has been called "Devas" and "Nature Spirits" are part of these soul supporters for the inanimate and animate (non-human) creation.

Much has already been written on these entities. Their direct communication with humans has always been present. As the human being was going through its evolution, prior to the final link with advanced souls (i.e., pre-choice humanity) the devas and nature spirits were the primary caregivers and nurturers of pre-humans, enabling the survival of those species.

Finally, about one and one-half million years ago, the Creator allowed Spirits or Beings of Light to enter the advancing human form and to begin to more actively guide the growth and evolution of a particular species of humanoids. The process was much more complex than most of your modern scientists think. It involved the mingling of different early branches, and gathering traits that would enable your ancestors to survive the hardships of marginal subsistence living. These ancestors would ultimately to become what you now call Homo sapiens.

You remembered from a past life recall where you once lived in a different part of the physical universe several million years ago. There were, and still are, other beings in many different parts of this physical universe and in the multitudes of other levels of existence.

Those who choose to sacrifice their almost infinite freedom of choice to come and nurture the human experiment were able to exercise love at an advanced degree. But the pain of separation from immediate, direct communion with Creator was so great that these beings built into their evolutionary process a blocking of these psychic or soul memories.

In that way, they could continue to nurture the human evolutionary process and have somewhat anesthetized their psychic pain so they could more effectively further their work here.

This memory blockage has never been total. The moments of direct communion, of past memories, etc., have helped to spawn the religious urge to "reunite with God," e.g., in the words of St. Augustine, "my soul is restless for thee oh God and can only find rest in thee."

About 100,000 years ago a civilization developed that finally broke through these memory blocks and reestablished a high degree of communication with spirit guides and ascended teachers or masters. That civilization developed the complex cultures known as Atlantis, Lemure and several other advanced systems of human endeavor.

These civilizations were not destroyed just by the "evil of some of its members" as many myths suppose. Although it is true there were misuses of some of the great mental and physical powers that resulted from the rich psychic connection.

As has been said by others on the earth plane, "Power corrupts and absolute power corrupts absolutely." We see the terrible cruelty of even primitive animals and insects that are more powerful than its brothers and sisters. However, it is our eyes that tell us this behavior is "cruel." For these creatures it is not cruel; it just is the way they were created, i.e., to find food and survive. The very nature of the living ecosystem requires the acquisition of usable energy to fuel the life force. As a system becomes more complex the need for energy increases.

The introduction of Beings of Light into this evolutionary process was intended by the Creator to "humanize" the ecosystem of Earth. As is written in your Bible, "God gave man dominion over the fish of the sea, the beasts of the land...." That dominion was not for the purpose of domination and destruction, but to bring more love into this energy acquisition equation.

In the same way that devas, nature spirits and Guardian Angels assist the human animals to carry out their function as whole, loving creatures, so the human animal had, and still has, the task and responsibility of assisting all living organisms in their struggle to BE in this world.

One of the great tragedies that results from the psychic breach between humankind and the Holy Spirit, is the lack of ongoing connection with the natural world around you, and thus the ecological destruction of the air, water, forests and other living spaces on this earth.

Even your "Earth Mother" herself is being seared with toxic chemicals, scraped bare of her precious resources and is left in danger of being barren for future generations.

This is one of the reasons why limitless living *is not only urgently needed by most human beings, it is essential to the survival of the very life-support system of this fragile earth your island home.*

As a person heals the separation between self, soul, psyche, and the soul of the Universe, the Cosmic Christ, the Infinite Mystery of

Infinite Love, then that individual will be able to walk in harmony and balance with nature and with our Creator and move into limitless living. *Some day you will share this material with others in the form of a book, and we hope that sharing will assist in healing your planet. But humans do have freedom of choice, and this experiment which began those many years ago can still fail.*

It is now the next day. I have taken time to adjust my office chair. I am again sitting at my computer keyboard, resisting the temptation to write something just to get things started. Part of me, the Doubting Thomas part, stills questions whether or not this is genuine communication or creative writing, or perhaps just wishful thinking. I go through my preparations and wait....

Hello Sonny. This is Carole[40].

I pause immediately, feeling my breath move in and out even more slowly. My concentration deepens. Could this really be Carole, my dear friend? The writing continues...

Yes, this is Carole. You know it is me. You shouldn't be so surprised that we can be together again at this time. I have often been with you to help with specific projects. I especially enjoyed dropping by while you were in Seminary classes. I was simply not allowed to initiate the contact, until invited. Since we now have been invited to openly communicate concerning this book, here I am.

You do well to question the content and reality of this contact. However, as you were told last night, the truth of what we say will be determined by the results of what we have to offer.

Be at peace. Do not try to anticipate chapters or content. Simply have peace filling your being, and that wonderful smile.... yes, that is it!

---

[40]Carole Marion Johnson was an early love during my high school and college days. She died in a tragic automobile accident in 1962, the year after her graduation from the University of Richmond. Her father, the late Rev. Dr. Johnson, wrote a beautiful book about Carole after her death. This is the first time since her death that I feel like I am truly in conversation with her. I was known as "Sonny" as a youth, to distinguish me from my father, Prentice Kinser, Jr., M.D.

Sonny, we will be going to more ancient memories today. These will not go as far back as your first past life recall that you will report elsewhere in your book. [Chapter Twelve]

Yes, you are picking up the sensations of a jungle type of vegetation. Many giant, large leaved plants, and trees much like the giant redwoods that you love so much. This is part of why you love those redwood trees where your son, Mark, lives.

You can begin to record what you see and what you feel. These are your memories that we are assisting you to recall.... Record what you see, for this is to be part of your book.

I am walking down a worn path. The sounds of the ancient forest are all around me. I feel secure even though I know there are giant animals searching nearby. My tribe has taught me well, and I am now on my first trek alone, to the dark forests. I carry only a spear and a vine rope. Thinking of the rope I stop near a tree whose girth is not as great as the giants nearby. With a skilled flick of my arm the rope circles around the tree and I grasp the other end. With a quick hooking of what is like a wooden connector, I lean back against the vine rope, and start to walk up the side of the tree, regularly pulling myself close to the tree and yanking the rope up higher. I slowly move up above the dense undergrowth. I am cautious not to expose myself fully for I know there is danger both from the sky above and from the forest floor below. Many animals like the flesh of the two-legged ones.

Far in the direction where Grandfather Fire rises in the morning from his sleep I see a wisp of smoke. That must be the camp toward which I am to travel. I lean back against the rope and look up into the deep blue sky, above the canopy of leaves and vines still much higher above me -- up where the meat-eating birds are masters. I shudder and begin to slip quietly back down the tree.

I am on this trip to go meet the senior shaman of the forest. He no longer lives in a village, with a specific tribe or clan, but stays in the deepest parts of the dark forest. There he teaches those who wish to explore the spiritual world and learn to help their own village.

I know I must leave the well-worn path now, to go in the direction of the wisp of smoke. The way will be more dangerous, and the passage much slower.

It is now night. I next am sleeping in a tree, where I have tied myself into a cluster of branches. Nestled down in the leaves I am safe. I have awakened and it is still dark. I sense some large animal nearby. I can smell its breath, a meat-eater, not a leaf-eater. I slow my breath and imagine that I am part of the tree. Our village shaman has taught me the importance of disguising or hiding my true thoughts and taking on the slower thoughts of the trees. In that way an animal cannot sense my presence, unless he is close enough to actually smell my flesh. I was given special oils to put on my body that take away the flesh smell, so even my skin had the odor of a tree or bush.

But this animal seemed to be moving directly toward my hiding place. I could hear the crashing of its great feet through the dense underbrush below. I did not even dare to open an eye, for that could send out signals to this meat-eater ... "Here is flesh, here is flesh!" So I became a tree. The tree welcomed me, and let me move even closer into its bark. A little light appeared to dance around within my spirit vision and I thanked the tree spirit for its shelter and its love. Slowly, into my awareness came these words: "We have been in this place for so many day lights that your mind could not understand. We are the true masters of this world. But we have been told that the two-leggeds will soon become the masters. We do not understand because you seem so weak. You burn our flesh for heat, and have learned to use parts of us for shelter, weapons and tools. But don't ever forget -- our flesh and your flesh are made of the same kinds of living tissue. We are brothers and sisters."

I felt so close to this tree, and to all of the trees around me. I did not feel like a two-legged but rather like a tall one. I could feel my roots go down in the earth to drink and bring up little pieces of material that would feed my flesh. I felt the memory of sun shining on my leaves and felt that energy also move into my flesh, there to be stored and to be burned.

As I gradually left this union with the tree I knew the flesh-eater had gone. But then I realized the leaf-eaters were also flesh-eaters, eating the flesh of my tree brothers and sisters. Going back to sleep I felt even closer to the life all around me. The dark forests were not dangerous places filled with evil, but simply places filled with life and with the spirits of all that lives.

Late the next day I arrived at the small camp of the old one who was to teach me the secrets of helping and healing. I cautiously circled around the camp, watching for any sign of the old one. I had heard he liked to play tricks on his students, some of which were quite painful. So as Grandfather Fire moved toward his bed I quietly crept and merged with the bushes and the plants.

Then right next to my ear I heard, "You have been taught well. You know the plants as friends, and they receive you. The bush oil gave you away. We don't have that kind of bush in this part of the dark forest. But that is something you could not have known. Only my students learn that, and you are to never share that knowledge with anyone. I will give you another oil, and teach you how to prepare it, so that we can remain hidden from all who might come this way.

"We were together in the oceans, and now we are together again. Do you remember the oceans, the waters that go on beyond the bed of Grandfather Fire?"

I searched my memory but could recall nothing of such great waters. "No, I remember no oceans."

"The Great Ones tell me you will, when it is time."

Rather than go into the camp, the old one gently tugged on my hair and pointed to an opening in the bushes that I had not seen before. He led me into the darkness. It became so dark that I could not see where I was going, and was hurrying to keep up with the old one. Suddenly the darkened path dropped out from under me. I grabbed a vine as I slid down the dirt wall. I hung there gasping for breath. I was hanging over a giant cavern. Rocks that I had dislodged clattered onto the rocks far below. If I had not caught the vine, I would have died.

I heard a chuckling above. "Yes, you are also quick. I knew they would not have sent one who was not ready, but I must be sure. Come, and this time do not trust only me. You must always know where your foot is to fall. Sometimes you may choose to step off the edge, but let that come as your choice -- not the choice of another."

I pulled myself, hand over hand, up the strong vines. My eyes were now adjusting to the darkness and could see the dark image of the old one standing next to edge. He motioned for me to follow around the opening, which I did more slowly, feeling the earth beneath my foot before all my weight went down. How could I have forgotten that lesson? My village teacher had stressed it many times. I had let my excitement, over finally meeting the old one, and my fear of being left behind, take me out of myself.

Now I was back into my space, feeling the life forces around me. We came to two more openings to the deep cavern below. I sensed the openings long before we were even close. The cool air and bat smells were clear. At the next opening the old one showed me a vine ladder and led the way down into the cavern below. When we were both down on the cavern floor he moved toward an even darker space off to one side. He pushed through some roots and vines, and I carefully followed. Suddenly I was almost blinded by the light of a small fire.

I blinked and then could see I was in a comfortable lodge. Small trees had been cut and bent over to form the supports for this lodge. It was taller than two men; so the smoke from the fire pit went up to the high parts of the roof and then out the ends, open at the top. It was much warmer in here, away from the coolness of the cave. I immediately saw the wisdom of this place for a shelter. In the hot times, the cave helped to keep one cool. In the cold times with white rain on the ground and when the rivers were all hard, this cave would be warmer and the water would always flow. In this lodge, even a small fire would keep the shelter warm, and the smoke would dissipate into the foliage above, hiding the source. Also, only a heavy, blowing storm might bring rain back to the side of this cavern from the opening far above, and even that would be drained away by the leaves and branches that crisscrossed the arching beams above.

I look around the lodge and saw in one corner that there were many plants hanging to dry. Their pungent odors drifted throughout this wonderful space. I felt as though I were breathing health and life. When I closed my eyes, I realized that what I felt was true. There seemed to be a special spirit glow that floated around this lodge filling the air, the bedding, and the water flasks, even to the most distant lodge pole. Here was true "holy space" as my village teachers had talked about. I settled to my knees with goose pimples down my arms and legs.

I came to learn that the camp I had seen above was only a place to rest during the day, and to fool any chance visitors.

I hear Carole's voice and come back to the present.

Sonny, that was the beginning of three years of training with the old man. What I want you to especially remember now is your closeness with the trees, as you came to this place, and how you could "see" the holy space. These are two gifts we will now talk about in more detail.

First, your closeness with the trees. As you have already felt and remembered in this lifetime, the plant life around you is truly "life." These life forms are our brothers and sisters. What we want you and your readers to now do is go out and find a tree, and sit with that tree until you can communicate with it. When you have accomplished that task, come back and record here for your readers what you received, and I suggest your readers record their own experience in their journals....

I went to our backyard. There is a tree about 40 or 50 years old, perhaps older. I sat facing it, with my hands against the tree. My dog Dodger, a Golden Retriever, kept wanting to play, but finally understood that I was there for some other reason. He couldn't understand why I would want to be with the tree when I could have played with him, but he finally found a stick to chew on and was temporarily satisfied.

For a long while I could sense nothing about the tree or from the tree. Slowly I began to sense a pumping throughout my body. It was especially strong in my arms and hands that were touching the tree.

I began to sense that the tree was letting me feel the liquids being circulated through its body, just as liquids are being pumped through mine. Although osmotic pressure and chemical transfers were the primary means of "pumping" fluids in this tree, it was telling me that we are still brothers. We both must circulate fluids in our bodies.

Next, I began to feel the tree breathing. I could feel the air moving into its leaves, as I also could feel the fresh air move into my lungs. I was taking in oxygen while the tree breathed in carbon dioxide; we used these in various ways and then I breathed out carbon dioxide and the tree oxygen. The air was moving in and moving out, and we shared and supplied each other. Again our common respiration made us brothers.

I knew I was to now sit with my back against the trunk of the tree. I sat that way for a long while, hoping the tree would "talk" to me. But again I felt, rather than heard, our common need to have a strong trunk, a backbone, a structure to hold us erect. The tree has physical roots and I have sociological and family roots. We both are tied into the "ground of our being," i.e., our Creator, whose life force moves through our bodies.

I began to think that I would not be able to mentally communicate with the tree. But then I started to feel the soul of the tree. The soul was much larger than the physical tree. It spread out around the tree, and a special spiritual presence was there also. I remembered that some have called this presence a "deva" or nature spirit. I simply felt it as a higher spirit that was there to help the tree. I asked the tree spirit if I could talk with the tree and it let me know that the soul of the tree must function much slower than my brain. So if I really wished to speak with the tree, the communication must take place between souls, between my soul and the soul of the tree.

I moved deeper into meditation and tried to feel my soul, which was out beyond my body, mingling with the soul of the tree. There was a union of spirits, and an understanding of friendship. I let the tree know it was not alone, and that as long as I was here, I would care for it. I then understood that the tree also felt the presence of the other nearby trees and plants, and did not feel alone, although it did seem to appreciate my acceptance of it as a true soul and not just some object. Again I could feel the wholeness of the tree and the life forces moving freely throughout its body.

I went to a smaller tree nearby, which had a large limb that composed about one-third of the trees branches. That limb had broken in a thunderstorm the day before. I thought, here I will be able to feel the pain and approaching death of this part of the tree. Perhaps, I might learn something here about soul healing and *limitless living*.

When I went to this tree, I was surprised to smell the wonderful fragrance of freshly cut wood, and could feel a sense of joy. The branches that had broken away and were starting to sense their approaching death were actually feeling joy. I held a leaf and it let me know that it was soon returning to the earth to continue to be used by the life forces of our Creator. Death was not the end of its particles but simply a time of change and new life!

In the undamaged tree the energy seemed to move slower and the soul was quiet. In this damaged tree there was excitement and vigor. The soul of the tree seemed glad to be able to give its great limb. There was no pain and grief but a kind of graciousness and generosity of such depth that I have rarely felt in any human soul.

What a startling surprise. This was not at all what I had expected.

Carole began to speak with me again.

Sonny, don't you see that one of the first steps in soul healing and limitless living is a willingness to give, a willingness to sacrifice. If a soul is to heal, if life is to be limitless, one must be willing to let go, to share wealth, and know that life goes on.

However, to have that kind of readiness to share and give, a soul must feel its union with all of life, to know that anything given is also given to self. That is the message of the tree. That is a message all of your readers can also feel, if they will take the time to be with a tree.

Now let's move on to the second gift, being able to see "holy space." There is a texture to space that has been hallowed by the love and loving actions of the past. Tomorrow, when you go into the church, you are to spend time moving into and out of that space until you can "see" the texture of holy space. You are then to record for your readers what you have seen so they will also be able to use this ability.

The next day I went into the church where I then served as rector, or senior priest. Over the past eleven years of working in that space I felt I knew every corner, every light, every aspect of the space. So I really was not expecting to encounter anything that different. Actually, I thought I might see some of the spiritual light that I have felt there many times before. The space truly did seem to often be filled with holy angels, so I also hoped that I might see an angel.

I started walking around, expectantly. But gradually I realized I was encountering only that which I had already been experiencing there for years. I was a little disappointed. As I walked down the center aisle to leave, I suddenly walked into what felt like a thickening of the air, as though I were passing through water. I could wave my arms around in this and could feel a clear difference.

I stepped back and moved out of the thickening. I walked back into this thicker air and continued on out the other side. The dimensions of this area seemed to be about fifteen feet in diameter. I did this several times with my eyes closed to be sure I wasn't just creating the sensations of thickening in my mind. It was there. It was a positive, pleasant force, not negative or evil.

I asked myself, "Is this the holy space I was to feel, or is this some aspect of the holy space?"

For some reason I felt blocked from going back to the computer keyboard to listen for my spiritual friends.

Was this getting out of my control? I wondered, "Do I have time to be working on this book?" The last two times I sat to write these "communications" I continued for about three to four hours. I could not spend that much time writing. My vocation, which at the time was disrupted enough, didn't need me becoming involved in another project that could be so absorbing -- and fun!

I think I was fearing what might happen if I really let go and devoted myself to this work and the writing of this book. It was too unknown! I began to let my hand move a pen across the pad of paper I had with me:

We will help it all get done. Relax and listen, record and learn. This is a process that will continue for many years. You do not need to think it must be completed now, or even in a few years. However, there is nothing more important for you right now, other than the occasional emergencies. We were with your wife when she had her accident last week.[41] We tried to ease the pain and keep the blood supply going in areas that were especially damaged. We knew it was coming, we felt the ripple in the skein of time, and knew that it was an event that had to happen, because so many other things depended on that.

As you now have seen, you were not to go to Kansas City to be part of that wedding. There was a high probability that you would have been in a major accident. You might have been killed. Plus, Mary Ann will use this time of healing as a time of major spiritual growth, and expansion of her own powers.

Later in the day I am sitting at my computer. I first surround myself with the Light of Christ, move into deep meditative space, and wait....

This is Teacher. Carole will be here soon.

At this time I want you to understand a little more about what you encountered at the church.

You did sense the general aura of the holy space as you walked around the church. There is present the vibration of worship that has been going on in that area since the mid 1800s. Actually, Native Americans used this portion of the hilltop as a medicine circle. Their primary village was closer to water, down toward the shopping center in the flat lands. But up here, the holy man would come for his ceremonies.

---

[41] A heavy kitchen window in the Rectory fell on Mary Ann's thumb and tore the flesh down to the bone. We thought, at first, that the bone was also broken. Because of that accident I was not able to go to Kansas City to be part of the wedding of a very good friend.

I will take you back now and let you walk with him in that time and space.... This will not go back to the more ancient memories you recorded yesterday.

My body becomes more deeply relaxed and my mind drifts into the light as images start to flow:

I am walking along a well-worn path up a fairly steep hill and then along a ridge. This path follows almost exactly the current "Winchester Street," but now there are only woods, the smell of the forest and the sounds of animals and birds. This is a special day for our village is preparing to travel toward the great waters, along the river a day's walk to the south. This will be a trading trip. We have been growing some new grains and fruits. Our brothers near the big waters will trade us dried fish and the leaves I use in my medicine pipe. We both will also share the different healing leaves and roots that come from our own parts of the land. They have discovered a plant that grows in the big waters, which they dry and grind into a powder. It helps some of our older people with the neck swelling.

But today I must make special medicine for we are to travel, and I need to see if the path will be clear. Are there the wild ones who like to kill and torture still roaming the forests between here and the big waters? Our tribes have worked to drive them away. And I have prepared many magic totems to hold the evil out of this area. But I sense a darkness out toward the south and west.

I walk down a short way from the ridge along a much less used path (along what is now "Culpeper Street"). I step back through a thick cluster of short pines and come to my space. As I move into my circle I can feel the air change. It is thicker, and I wave my arms around to get accustomed to its density. I remembered when my teacher first brought me to this space as I was learning to be a shaman. I was frightened then and thought I could not catch my breath. But now I can feel the power flowing up from the earth, and feel its connection with what looks like a giant fish net all across the land. When I am here I can travel quickly along the strings of the net to different points. Wherever the strings of the net cross, I can stop, look around, and see if game is there or danger.

I start a small fire and then spread out on a deerskin the contents of my medicine bag. I take up my pipe and ask the Great Spirit if I may join my pipe. I hold up my arms, with the pipe bowl in my left hand and the stem in my right, I look up through the trees and remember the wondrous day when an old medicine man from a far distant tribe to the west came to me here at this spot. Only his spirit was here. He was not dressed as I am. He wore many feathers and painted his face in a much different way. I was frightened at first, but then he sat with me here in this circle. He held out his pipe and showed me the ceremony of the pipe. My mind heard the story of the White Buffalo Woman, and how she had brought the pipe to all of us, and that we are to share its medicine. His image faded from my mind as I received the clear and open feeling that let me know it was time to join the pipe.

As I placed the holy leaf from my pouch into the bowl, I also put into the pipe my requests of the Great Spirit. I tried to picture in my mind what area of the net I needed to search, and I asked the Great Spirit to let me see clearly and to do only those things that created good medicine. I also put in my pipe some other herbs and leaves for the healing of some members of my tribe, and spoke their names, so that when the leaves and herbs burned those names would go up to the Great Spirit.

Taking a twig from my fire I lit the pipe, drawing in the first smoke, offering it and all of the prayers contained in the pipe. I turned the stem out from me and moved slowly in a circle, to offer the pipe to all the spirits who I know gather each time a pipe is lit in a holy way. I emptied the pipe and placed it in my lap, as the power of the net seemed to increase. My eyes were closed and I could feel myself starting to journey down into the earth and then south. The movement was swift, much faster than a running deer, but not as fast as the streaks of light in a storm. We came to a crossing of the net strings and I came up briefly. Having been here many times before, I knew where this point was, and looked carefully for any unusual signs. There were fresh signs of deer and a few bear, but no footprints of the warrior tribes. So down again I went this time moving east along the net to the next crossing point. This was much closer to the great waters.

When I came up I immediately knew something was wrong. I could feel evil in the air. Since the evil warriors also use these power points as holy places I have in the past found evidence of their making sacrifices around such net crossings. Hanging from the limbs of a tree nearby was the naked, bloody body of a young warrior. But this body was not that of one of our fellow tribes. This was one of the evil warriors who like to torture. It appears he had been captured by a tribe that lives near the great waters and had received some of his own kind of medicine. Discarded oyster shells lay near the base of the tree. They had been used to remove much of this warrior's skin and various parts of his body. His remains had been left hanging here as a warning to any other evil warriors.

This was a good sign. Our people were getting stronger and soon we will travel as we wish without fear. I returned quickly to my place in the net and returned to my body sitting quietly with the pipe in my lap. Knowing the ceremony and travel was over, I lifted my pipe again and thanked the Great Spirit and all my spirit friends and all my other relations who help me in my work.

Opening my eyes, I looked across my circle and saw a baby fawn watching me with a smile on her face. Another good sign! Our travels would go well.

Teacher, spoke again, bringing me out of this recall from a past life.

In one of your lifetimes, as you have just seen, you served here as a medicine man. That is why you have been brought back here as a priest, to touch again this space and its power, and to learn to use again that same kind of power for healing and wisdom.

As you saw, this network of power stretches all across the land. You now know again that you can travel along its lines of power and surface anywhere there are crossover points. Something that you did not experience in this recall is the fact that there are also more major crossover points, where more than two lines of power cross. In some places there are multiple crossovers, because these nets do not follow absolute north - south, and east - west directions. These networks follow the lines of power in the earth, as well as spiritual power lines. When there are multiple crossing points of earth and spiritual power lines you will find what has been called a major "vortex" of power. The site of your old medicine circle, and where your church is now located, is a minor vortex of power.

Often, both these major and minor vortices have come to be used as holy spaces, for churches, sites for county court houses, or the location of government buildings. Occasionally a very successful country store or other business will be situated over such a vortex. Part of the success will come from people being drawn to that power without understanding why.

If you wish you can go and sit on the dirt floor under the church, in the same place you did hundreds of years ago as a Native American medicine man. That vortex of power is still there. You felt its presence as you walked above. You will be able to travel along this giant network to any place you wish to go, and then return quickly simply by thinking of this space back here. The travel is almost instantaneous. Although you currently travel in other ways, this will give you a new awareness of these power spots and how they have been used by the current civilization now occupying these spaces.

You said "current" civilization. Does that mean that this civilization will pass?

One of the lessons of history is that all civilizations come and go. Although we are not allowed to tell you exactly what the future will bring, we can help you look at the possibilities and the probabilities. That is an art, not a science. In that art you can use astrology, cards, runes, prayer, anything you wish, provided you are doing so to serve your own highest good and the highest good of all people and all life. This is part of why you have had a growing interest in Celtic runes and the I Ching. These are not forms of divination but rather sources of spiritual guidance, and are only tools in the art of limitless living.

The network of power in the earth is only one such net. There are the constantly shifting networks of planetary and cosmic power. The minute forces exerted by planets and stars in their courses, as well as the stronger forces of our sun and moon, all participate in the physical and spiritual life of each individual. None of these forces can you control. However, being aware of their presence and their movements through astrology, and the usual effects of these forces, can help a person so order their lives for greater health, happiness and wholeness -- as well as holiness. These all promote limitless living, *and thus are worthy of study.*

Carole wishes to come through at this time....

Hello Sonny. I am here. Yes, you know. Do not despair, the tasks before you are not insurmountable. There is much to learn, but this learning will continue long after you have left this parish and long after this particular lifetime has ended. You do not have to learn it all now. We will continue this process of helping you remember those things you have already learned and used in other lifetimes. In this way your learning will be accelerated, and likewise you can help others accelerate their own learning, provided all such learning is motivated by the desire to serve Love and Life, not the darkness of money and power for their own sake. Such darkness will only bring more darkness. We are here only to help bring the Light and Love of Christ.

Yes, you thought of my father. He loves it here. He was, like you, one who always wanted to be learning and growing, and that process is so accelerated here that your current mental process could not begin to grasp what wonders you will again return to after this life is finished.

But do not be eager for ending your current pilgrimage. You have much to accomplish. The people of the earth need every possible form of preparation for the changes that are soon to arrive. There will be vast physical disruptions across the entire face of this planet. Landmasses will change shape. Lowlands will be flooded as oceans rise due to climate change. Some will change gradually. But some will change suddenly, as has happened in the past. The damage of these changes can be moderated somewhat by the healing prayers of people who know how to uses these kinds of spiritual forces. That is part of what this book is about -- the healing of this planet earth, as well as individual soul healing.

Those who are readers of this book are not to take lightly their responsibilities. They are to learn to use these healing forces and to train others, so that when the changes come, large and small, there will be a human network of soul healers that can hold this planet and its life forms together, thus preventing total annihilation.

And throughout all of this, these changes will provide major shocks to the entire spiritual and ecological systems. That will enable new, healthier patterns of living. This does not have to be a time of catastrophe, but rather a time of major new life and new growth, helping all mankind establish higher priorities -- those of life, love, healing, hope, justice and truth. You and your readers will be part of that process, as will many millions of others who are learning of these ways through other teachers.

This is part of why there has been such a proliferation of books around spiritual teaching and growth, to train as many people as possible prior to these times of change. This book is part of that process. Thank you for letting us work through you. As you learned after the last two sessions, this is not an easy process. This will take much energy and spiritual concentration. That is why you and your readers must continue to care well for your physical bodies, and do all you can to enhance your energy and spiritual resources. We will also be here to help.

Later another Ascended Master came to me in the midst of deep meditation.

AM: *Peace and Power. These are to be key words for you.*

PK3: How does all of this fit with my priesthood and Christian theology?

AM: *It fits perfectly! Christ truly was and is united with, and is the Son of, that infinite Power and Love and Peace. You are a priest or servant of that Peace and Power – centered in that Light or Love. Light and Love are synonymous – use them interchangeably. They mean the same thing on this level of understanding. Peace and Power – Centered in Light and Love. REMEMBER! Peace and Power are also synonymous on this level. When Universal Power is flowing it is also true that Peace is flowing. If the Power is in tune with G_d or YHWH then it is also Peace! See yourself as immersed in the Power, part of the Power – connected to that which is pure Power – that is the truth to which your life is to bear witness.*

You are – all of life is – a part of that Universal Life, which is pure Power, pure Peace, pure Light, pure Love. Everything is part of that. We all are one in the One.

You hear me because we are already one – connected, together, and yet individual and created by the One. No one knows why we have been created within this One. As we have suggested earlier, it is as though the One was such perfect Love that a natural expression of that Love was to create, to share. And to truly share, there had to be an individuality that could receive. Every created thing has that individuality although not always that consciousness. Because the spatial world is infinite there are infinite expressions of that Love and Light, that Power and Peace.

Different entities are in different places – but all of us are created in the image of the One. That means our center is Light and Love. I have taken you to that Light at your center – try to go there more often, now that you are experiencing the Universal Power of which we are a part.

I sincerely believe that this was a message not just for me but for all of us. Our center *is* Light and Love, Peace and Power. And at our center we find *limitless living*.

One of the avenues to greater Love, Light, Peace and Power, was, for me, through Native American Spirituality, the topic of our next chapter.

Vision is the art of seeing things invisible.
Jonathan Swift

When there is no vision, people perish.
Ralph Waldo Emerson

Chapter 10

NATIVE AMERICAN SPIRITUALITY

As is clear from previous chapter, I seem to have past life memories as a Native American. When I was a young boy in this life, I always wanted to play the part of an Indian in games of "Cowboys and Indians" with my friends. I never questioned this. It was just known that 'Sonny' Kinser would be one of the Indians. Then one summer I went with my family to Cherokee, North Carolina. After we watched the Cherokee Indians perform their dances, I hung back from my family and stayed to watch the Cherokee families gather near their shelters. On some level, I felt very close to these people ... like I was a part of their tribe. I sat on the ground next to a tree and simply watched. One of the Cherokee children walked over to where I was sitting and he just sat there with me, as we watched the tourists walk by. In a short while my family must have realized that I was not with them and came back looking for me. In those days there was less concern about kidnappings and the threat of pedophiles. Children were free to wander and discover on their own. And I was discovering an ancient connection with my Native American brothers and sisters. I believe this connection exists both through past life memories and through my genetic connection to the Powhatan tribe and Pocahontas. Although my primary biological heritage is that of a white Anglo-Saxon with strong German ancestry, there is a core connection for me to all things Native American. I hope it is becoming clear how that relates to *limitless living*.

In 1987 I happened upon a book entitled *The Vision* by Tom Brown, Jr. It was one of those books that seemed to "jump off" of the bookstore shelf and right into my hands. In that book Tom describes his childhood adventures of meeting and learning from an old Native American medicine man named Stalking Wolf who was also called "Grandfather." It is still today one of my favorite books, worn and dog-eared.[42] Tom's explorations and the instructions he received from Grandfather helped me return to that core connection with my Native American relations and to renew my pilgrimage into Native American spirituality.

After reading Tom's book I telephoned him to ask about his survival-training program. He described a program that sounded far too rigorous for me at that time in my life, so Tom recommended I contact the Sun Bear Tribe that he said offered a softer and easier program started by the late Sun Bear, a Native American medicine man.

In the spring of 1988, my son, 'PK', and I participated in a wilderness survival school, sponsored by members of the "Sun Bear Tribe." Sun Bear believed he had been guided by the Great Spirit to gently share his Native American teachings and wisdom with non-Native Americans. This was a bold and courageous move on his part that was being condemned by many traditionalists in the Native American community.

At that school (an amazing experience) 'PK' and I learned that, if necessary, we could survive without grocery stores and malls. We practiced identifying edible and medicinal wild plants. We built small animal traps and emergency shelters. Without matches we started campfires and cooked our food over those flames. We

---

[42] Tom Brown has written many excellent books about these experiences and several field guides to the natural world. I highly recommended all of his books that are for anyone who loves the outdoors and good stories about the spiritual life.

learned about the tremendous number of useful items that can be made from the bodies of wild animals. We practiced ancient tanning methods for deer hides, which were used by Native Americans to produce clothes, moccasins, bowls and shelters. I still use a part of a deerskin I tanned as a reminder of my connection with our animal friends. And perhaps most important, we learned to observe the natural world around us not as outsiders but as participants.

I have come to realize that there is a direct parallel between observing nature and observing spiritual signs and wonders. And through my experiences in Native American culture and spiritual practices my own *limitless living* has been enriched. Too often we think spiritual happenings are totally separate from the natural world or from what the stoics called "the flesh." But the longer I live the more I have recognized the intimate connection between the physical and the spiritual ... and my explorations in Native American spirituality helped me see that.

An example of that connection is found in one of the great spiritual symbols for Native Americans ... the medicine pipe. While at the wilderness survival school, I experienced my first (in this lifetime) medicine pipe ceremony. The medicine pipe has been an important part of the plains Indians' spiritual life. A story, mentioned in the last chapter, has been handed down for centuries about two scouts who were out looking for bison. When they came to the top of a hill and looked toward the north, they saw something coming in a cloud of dust a long way off. At first they thought it was a white buffalo. But then, when this thing came closer, they saw that it was a woman. One of the scouts, being foolish, had bad thoughts and spoke them to his friend. But the other said, "That is a sacred woman. Throw away all bad thoughts."

When the woman came closer, they saw that she wore a fine white buckskin dress. Her hair was very long and she was young and very beautiful. She knew their thoughts and said in a voice that was like singing, "You do not know me, but if you want to do as you think, you may come to me." And the foolish one went out. But as he stood before her a white cloud came and covered them both. And the beautiful young woman came out of the cloud, and when it blew away the foolish man was a skeleton covered with worms. The beautiful woman then spoke to the other scout who was not foolish: "You shall go home and tell your people that *I am* coming and that a big tepee shall be built for me in the center of the nation."[43]

And the young man went quickly and told the people, who did at once as they had been told. And there around the great tepee they waited for the sacred woman. And in a while she came, beautiful and singing, and she went into the tepee. And as she sang a white cloud came from her mouth and it was good to smell. She then gave to the chief the medicine pipe with a buffalo calf carved on one side to signify that the earth gives us life and feeds us. The twelve eagle feathers hanging from the stem represented the sky and the twelve moons, and these were tied with grass that never breaks. The woman then said, "Behold! With this pipe you shall multiply and be a good nation. Nothing but good shall come from it." Then she sang again and left the tepee. As the people watched her go, she suddenly transformed into a great white, snorting buffalo, galloped away, and soon was gone. That is one version of how the medicine pipe was given to the Native American people by the White Buffalo Woman, which I heard at the wilderness survival program.

When I returned home from this survival training, I told my family about what had happened and what I had learned. I also talked about the medicine pipe ceremonies and what they had meant to me. So, on my birthday in 1988, my family gave me a traditional medicine pipe made from red stone (which can only be mined by Native Americans). Since it had not been "awakened" or consecrated by a medicine man, I couldn't use it in ceremonies. Nevertheless being gifted that pipe brought new life into my life and symbolized the beginning of a new phase of my *limitless living*.

---

[43] Please note that in the Jewish Bible or Christian Old Testament, or Muslim Quran, when God or Allah appears the name He/She often uses is "I Am." I really believe there is a deep spiritual unity between all religions, which makes even more tragic the current atmosphere of hostility and anxiety.

I knew I was to continue to explore my connection with Native American spirituality, and I learned about an upcoming "Vision Quest" being sponsored by the Bear Tribe and led by followers of Sun Bear. It was to be held in October in the mountains of New York State. I immediately registered and began planning for the event, reading all I could about Native American spirituality and about vision quests.

A little over a month before that vision quest, I attended a talk given by Sun Bear at a church in Charlottesville. I was told that the next day he would be at a retreat center, Seven Oaks Path Works Center, north of Charlottesville. Bright and early I was there. I spent the day with Sun Bear and others at the center. Part of what Sun Bear shared that day was his understanding of the purpose of all life, i.e., to be happy and to walk our paths in a sacred manner. To do that he suggested that we make "medicine" for everything in life, which is accomplished by putting our needs and concerns into this prayer: "O Great Spirit, this is what I want...." By creating an image of what we want or where we want to go in life, the medicine is being created to take us there. This sounds very much like "creative visualization" made so popular by others in the "new age" movement, and if we go back to the early 1960s we would find the same suggestions in the form of "psycho-cybernetics," based on Dr. Maxwell Maltz's classic self-help book. It was not surprising to find that great teachings cross cultural and religious boundaries.

Sun Bear suggested that we must move in the direction we are praying, and that we must walk as "spiritual warriors." Those words reminded me of the teachings of Chogyam Trungpa in his book, *Shambahala, The Sacred Path of the Warrior* (Random House, 1984; translation © 1978), which is founded on the sanity and gentleness of the Buddhist tradition -- yet another connection to another teaching, another culture.

During lunch, as I wandered among the other conference participants, I found a woman selling medicine pipe bags. She was a member of the Bear Tribe who had made the bags by hand. I immediately purchased a bag that I *knew* was to be the "home" of my medicine pipe. The lady asked me if I wanted the bag for myself or for someone else. I told her about being gifted a pipe by my family, but that it had not yet been consecrated by a medicine man. She suggested that I talk with Sun Bear about that.

So, later that afternoon during a break in activities, I went to Sun Bear and presented him with a bag of pipe tobacco as a token of my regard and respect for the "good medicine" he shared with others. I also asked how a medicine pipe could be awakened. He asked me if I had it with me, which I did. He then lit a smudging fire to cleanse the pipe and bag, and then he blessed both. In that ceremony he prepared the medicine pipe for me to use with my family and in small personal medicine ceremonies.

Here was another example of finding myself in the right place at the right time, and being blessed by the Spirit of God. My medicine pipe is a living reminder of my connection with our earth mother, with our Native American brothers and sisters who suffered so much at the hands of the white man, and with the universally present and loving one God or Great Spirit.

Sun Bear also talked about the use of a medicine pipe saying that it is like a very sacred altar that can be taken anywhere. He said the bowl is made of stone or clay to represent the "elemental kingdom." The stem of wood represents the plant kingdom. The pipe can be highly decorated or can be plain. When it is decorated with fur and with feathers that is done to represent the animal kingdom. As we use the pipe, all of the kingdoms are brought together in our ceremony. The bowl symbolizes that which is feminine, and the stem symbolizes the masculine. Sun Bear believed "the symbols of the pipe are never-ending; they are like the universe itself."[44] My pipe was consecrated. I had previously learned how to conduct a pipe ceremony, which I did with my family when I returned home the next day. I now felt somewhat more prepared for my upcoming vision quest.

In my reading about vision quests, I had learned that when Native Americans needed to find direction for their lives or to seek guid-

---

[44] *The Path of Power* by Sun Bear, Wabun, and Barry Weinstock, Prentice Hall Press, 1987, p. 232.

ance from the Great Spirit, they would go into a wilderness and begin a total fast, i.e., eating no food and consuming only water. There in the wilderness, in a state of spiritual sensitivity deepened by hunger and isolation they would "cry for a vision." After receiving a vision they would return to their village and an elder or medicine man would then help them interpret the meaning of their vision.

I believe we all search for vision and purpose in our lives, and the stronger our vision then the more deeply we move into *limitless living*. Often our visions come in small glimpses or in moments of clarity of purpose. Sometimes the moments come out of more modern quests for vision. Working with a career counselor or vocational consultant may be a modern way of going on a vision quest. However, the traditional Native American method of crying for a vision can provide another model for going to the core of our need to discover a vision or purpose in life.

My vision quest was to start on a Monday morning near a camp in a remote part of New York State. On the preceding Sunday morning I had conducted three worship services, then performed a wedding at 3:00 PM in the afternoon, and in the evening I drove to a motel in Port Jervis, New York. I was exhausted. I was also needing a renewed vision for my life.

On the morning of October 3rd, 1988, I arrived at the camp. After meeting the leaders and other participants, we spent several days in preparation. One of the first things we did was have another member of the group sit in front of us and ask, repeatedly, "Why are you here?" The questioner recorded each of our answers in our own journals. It is very interesting now, in 2007, to look back at the answers I gave in 1988. I strongly recommend this exercise for anyone trying to discover their own purpose or encounter a new vision. Some of my answers to that question are still relevant for me today, such as: "To get a clearer reminder of what I am to be doing in the next ten years of my life. To let parts of myself die that need to die. To see more clearly. To walk in a sacred manner. To be closer to nature. To talk with my guardian angles and spirit guides. To know what I am to do for my family, for my people and for my church. To find direction for my book about *limitless living*. To listen. To cry for a vision. To experience serious fasting. To open my third eye. To touch the mystery of God. To have a knowing of who I am and where I am going."

The next task was to answer this question, over and over, "What do I fear?" This is another valuable tool to use as we seek a vision for our lives. Some of my responses in 1988 are still part of things I fear today, e.g., "Being lost. Being left behind. Losing my wife and children. Dying before I am able to dance at my daughter's wedding. (In October of 2005 I did dance at my daughter's wedding!) Losing myself in the demands of a parish or in the needs of others. Failing. Not having a vision. Wandering aimlessly. Being too dumb to understand a vision given. Not having the courage to act on a vision given. Forgetting how to play. Waking up and finding a snake in my sleeping bag. Dying before I learn what I am to learn this time around. Dying before I have a chance to share what I have learned this time around. Finding out who I really am and not liking what I discover. Having others totally reject what I have found to be true. Not finding out what is really true. Emptiness or lack of vision. Hurting my family, my friends and my people."

We were then told to go out into the woods with a shovel and dig a hole about a foot deep, lie face down on the earth, with our heads over the hole we have dug. Into that hole we were to pour our greatest fears; we were to speak our the hate and anger and bitterness residing in our souls; we were to vent the garbage in our lives, to pull up old pains, distress, and hurts, and place them into the hole we had dug, allowing our Earth Mother to take those things into her breast and clear them away. We were then to plant a seed in the hole and cover it up, so new life could grow from all those things buried there. For me, this was very much like a Christian confessional. I felt blessed. I felt forgiven.

Next we learned that there are two kinds of possible visions; each with two possible alternatives:

1) *A Waking Vision*: Encountered while awake, for example, moving out of body and seeing something that is not there in ordinary reality, such as a spirit being or a power animal. This waking

vision may be whole and complete in itself, or a partial vision -- one piece of a larger vision; and,

2) *A Sleeping Dream*: This may be a whole and complete dream which answers the questions we have for our vision; or it may be a partial dream vision, perhaps connecting to past dreams, or it may be the beginning of a series of future dreams. We were told that our bodies will know if we are awake or in a dream.

On a vision quest there seems to be a greater awareness of nature. To start it is best to be in a state of relaxed anticipation and acceptance, being ready, so we will know when it arrives. It is good to remember that there are no stupid fears or stupid answers. There are no irrelevant events or dreams while on a vision quest. We must be open to the possibilities. We are going within to receive the gift that is there for us.

There are things that can help us cry for a vision. The desire for a vision must come from our hearts and not be in the form of canned prayers. The best visions involve not only ourselves, but in some way have the potential to give life to people who are important to us, people we may have temporarily left behind while on our vision quest. It is also important to remember that we do have the ability to have a vision. Many before us have done this and have received visions. There is no set way to cry for a vision. We can do so however we want, within any religious system or belief system, or we can simply pray to our higher self or connection with the Holy Spirit or Great Spirit. Ceremony is helpful for some people. For me, having my medicine pipe with me was important, as was a small copy of the New Testament and Psalms. These are sacred items that became part of my holy space.

On the morning of beginning our vision quest, long before dawn, we entered a sweat lodge to be cleansed and made ready. Large stones had been heated in a fire. These were brought into a totally enclosed low shelter covered with multiple layers of animal skins and pieces of canvas, with a single opening in the shape of a small tunnel. On the outside, the sweat lodge appeared to be a great turtle, which is symbolic of Mother Earth. More stones were added to the pit at the center of our lodge. The space became hotter and hotter, and I began to sweat more profusely, especially after herbs and water were splashed on the hot stones. It was similar to being in a sauna, but with much greater spiritual significance. I remember the heat being almost unbearable.

We sang ancient songs and beat upon drums. At one point I found myself on all fours roaring like a wild animal, as one of the songs about the great bear of the west consumed my consciousness and the rhythm of the drums increased a spiritual awareness in my soul.

When the sweat lodge ceremony was completed we went out into the cold air as the glimmer of a new dawn was showing on the horizon. We used sage branches to wipe the sweat from our cold bodies. The grass was frozen with ice crystals that hurt my bare feet as I walked to where my clothes and backpack were waiting. (The frozen grass reminded me of C. S. Lewis' book *The Great Divorce*[45] in which a person takes a bus trip to heaven. Upon arriving there he finds that, as he starts to walk up the mountain toward heaven, the reality is so great that the grass pierces his feet. He continues his journey up the mountain into greater reality as others return to the safety of the bus.) I felt I was moving into a more potent reality that could easily pierce my soul. There was a moment of thinking I wanted to return to the safety of my tent and car, and to go home. But some inner strength or courage (or Grace?) enabled me to continue.

We were taken into a nearby wilderness, one at a time, and assigned a place in the dense woods. Each was out of sight of any other person and was completely alone in that space. We had no food. A circle was made around each person's area with corn meal, and we were told to stay inside that circle until we received a vision. We could leave to dig a hole in the woods for body waste, and to go to a tree about 100 yards away to retrieve a gallon of water each day. We were to set up a triangle of sticks next to this water site to indi-

---

[45] I strongly recommend all books by C. S. Lewis. He is one of my favorite authors and should be included in your studies if you are serious about your spiritual journey. I especially like his fiction, which contains some of the greatest spiritual truths to be found in literature. See Bibliography for some listings or go to Amazon.com for a full listing of his books.

cate that we were still alive. All the rest of our time was to be spent in that circle, about 20 yards across.

We were allowed a sleeping bag and tent because the nights were below freezing. The first night I slept in my sleeping bag under the trees rather than in my tent. I wanted to be as close to nature as possible. I could see millions of stars through the clear mountain air. I remember awaking in the night to feel warmth coming through the bushes next to me. I smelled a musky odor that was not unpleasant. In the morning I discovered that several deer had slept less than two yards from me. Perhaps we were sharing warmth for a while. I was certainly living close to nature, and I felt welcome in my part of the wilderness because of it.

As the first day continued my hunger began, and then deepened; but then on the second day all hunger seemed to disappear. I still had hypoglycemic types of severe headaches for another day, but late on the third day even those disappeared. I became more aware of every thing around me and there was an elimination of distractions that are associated with food, eating, and being hungry. Some have said that this heightened sensory awareness has survival components that enabled our pre-historic ancestors to find food and shelter. Drinking lots of water during a fast helps! We had been told to put our foreheads directly on the earth to relieve light-headedness, and to drink a minimum of one-half gallon of water per day, and to abandon our quest if we stopped having urine output (a sign of kidney shutdown) or encountered uncontrollable shivering or numbing (which could be signs of hypothermia). Otherwise we were to remain in our areas until we received a vision or until the fourth sunrise (the beginning of our fifth day of fasting). It all sounded so easy, so clinical. Although we had spent three days getting ready, I was not prepared for the difficulty. The following are parts of what I recorded in my journal during those four days. The content gives some insight into how such a vision is encountered.

Day One of Vision Quest Arrived at my site. Very special place, full of energy. Two old pine trees. Set up tent - head to West, feet to East -- so even if it is raining I can face out of my tent toward the East.

Sitting now with back to Grandfather Pine (which is in the North part of my circle) facing South. When I arrived here deer were in the laurel thicket. Many signs of deer around. I feel great anticipation. I am going to be given a vision, I can feel it! When I arrived in this circle a crow had greeted me.

Later Day One Got very cold so went in tent and warmed up in sleeping bag. My feet get cold and my hands.

Back at North Pine with medicine pipe, sitting on blue tarp. Will I receive my vision?

Went to get water and someone had left "green magma"[46] for me if I need it due to hypoglycemia. Thanks Great Spirit. I am prepared and ready. No headaches, very little hunger. A small squirrel quietly ran counter clockwise around my circle, but stayed on the outside. I think it is checking me out.

Lying on my back at North Pine -- patches of blue sky can be seen through thick trees. Just noticed beautiful colors, yellows and reds, light green and dark green. My little squirrel just ran from SW to E around outside of my circle for 3rd time. She glides silently. I must be in her space (I think it is a she). The sun is getting ready to set. I have my sleeping bag out on a tarp under North Pine. I'll try to stay here for part of night to cry for a vision!

The sun has gone down and it is starting to get dark in these trees. Sky is still blue. Cold, strong wind blowing out of the North. I still have no headaches. A hint of one now and then but the North pine removes it.

Just a little hungry, amazingly warm in my down sleeping bag. When I move my hands out to write, like now, I am surprised by how cold it is. Started thinking about the possibility of a snake wanting to get in this tarp with me for warmth. Even though snakes are big medicine, I hope none try.

---

[46] A chlorophyll-rich powdered food substance that is made from barley grass.

I am next to a bog and creek to my left. Am slightly up hill to right or west. Woods getting much darker... my squirrel continues to scamper back and forth along the southern line.

Woods now very dark and animals are starting to move. I hear a deer to my left. I am not expecting my vision tonight. I think this is part of the preparation. I'll stop writing now and observe -- BEHOLD... The sacred voices are calling.

<u>*Day Two*</u> *Spent entire night out under North Pine. These woods are very dark at night -- could see almost nothing. I remember feeling so much a part of these woods. The trees, the earth, the bog, the animals making sounds, the silence, I am not an alien -- I feel at home.*

The air was very cold but I was warm in my sleeping bag. Very cold this morning. My squirrel is upset I am still here; did some squawking, but now silent. Have been in tent in sleeping bag since sunrise. Only way I can keep warm with wind and cold. I can feel my body slow down.

Something else I remember of the night. When the moon got high enough for me to see it through the trees -- I could actually feel its gravity pulling at my body fluids as it pulls at the oceans and forms the tides. The fasting has heightened either my sensitivity or my imagination!

Geese flying over to the East, going from N to S. Stuck head out of tent and my squirrel started chattering and running along line again. I keep asking if she has something to tell me ... no reply.

Today I started talking to an Irish elf who lives in these woods, who said that directly below me is a giant emerald. I ask if he was just fantasy, being made up by my mind and I got no reply. I ask E pine to drop something on tent if I should really listen to him -- no reply. Hallucinations?

Looking out of tent I watch my squirrel run around circle -- finally stops on log 20 feet in front of me and eats something while I talk to her. She sits on hind legs and watches me and listens. Still is saying nothing. She is cute and busy eating. Some kind of bird is directly above me in E pine -- making a funny sound. It is too cloudy to know what time of day it is. No shadows. Time moves strangely in these woods.

<u>Late Afternoon</u> The sun finally came out -- thank you Grandfather sun. It felt good to stand with my face in the sun. Very little gets thru these trees.

It is so cold. The wind is blowing. I ask the wind to talk to me:

"I am the wind of death. I bring you death. Feel the cold and know some day you will feel that cold death. Now I bring death to past fears, past pain, past hate, past loss, past attachments that block you."

I feel terrible. Slight headache -- not enough for green magma, but my body does not like fasting and being so cold.

This is part of my testing, to see if I am worthy of a vision.

Earlier I made tobacco offerings to all the trees in my circle -- asking them to help me, to give me strength that I may endure as they endure... and that I may be given a vision.

The sun is out from behind clouds -- the last sun I will see until morning, the last sun I will see with these parts of me that must die.

Is a vision worth all of this? I can't stay out here much longer -- must go back in tent, in sleeping bag; am starting to shiver. Many geese flying over today, flying south to warmth -- smart geese! They have no problem with vision, it is built into them. Back to tent.

The sun has gone down -- much activity of squirrels and birds. Finished 1st gal. of H2O, kidneys working well flushing my system.

Another large flock of geese flew over. It was as though they were saying, "Go in the direction we are going. Go home; be with your family; be with your people. You are not to be some great medicine man. Live simply, and follow the vision you have already been given by our Creator. Don't aspire to be great. Live, be comfortable, have fun, help the people you are given to help." I hear the geese honking, but these words are given to my heart. I think this may be part of my vision -- but I know I am not to leave yet.

Another flock of gees fly over and say to me: "Not yet, there's more. Not yet, there's more," over and over. I know I am losing track of time. Is this the second or third day? I think this is the third day, but I have been too weak and too centered in this space to write.

My guts don't feel as bad as they did earlier. My body seems to be adjusting to the ketosis and toxicity of my blood. I wish it weren't so cold -- but then I would have mosquitoes. I think I prefer the cold. Even sitting here in my tent, under piles of coats and clothes -- I am cold!!! Not shivering, but a bone-chilling cold.

Time to get back in sleeping bag and warm up. I'm glad I'm not an arctic explorer. I remembered something else about last night. Once in the middle of the night I was awake and knew there were deer sleeping nearby again. I could smell them, an almost sweet, rich scent. It felt good knowing they were there.

End of Day Three or beginning Day Four Awake in middle of night feeling very nauseous. I am throwing up, but there is almost nothing in my stomach. Haven't eaten in days. A wind started and I asked it to speak to me. It said, "I am the wind of your life. You have died. Now I bring you new life. The sickness you feel was death squeezing out the last part of you. Now I bring you a new beginning, a new life." And then the wind stopped.

Later in the night I become violently ill and vomit a yellow liquid that contained the dead me. I was extremely sick and felt like I couldn't take much more. I could hear deer walking right outside my tent and they gave me energy to keep going.

I start to see a wheel with a cross in the middle, with lights swirling around the rim and across the spokes. Am I starting to hallucinate? A little later, still dark. I start singing, "O Lord hear my prayer..."over and over. I am crying and singing for a long while. I am truly crying for a vision.

I hear a loud roaring in my ears - as though someone has left a radio on with the volume up but not on a station. With my eyes closed I see round blobs of light moving from the North, from my right. My heart is beating very loudly directly in my 3rd eye. I am told: " I hear your prayer. I am with you. I am removing the protec-

tive cap placed over this area and you will be a see-er of visions. You will bear their pain and joy. You will also be a leaven where ever you go with my people. Your name, to be known by only you is _____, not to kill but to be aware of your strength and power, looking for people and creatures to help and to heal. As _____ you come from the North country -- a place of darkness and death and you fear not. Your name for others to know is Soaring Eagle, who sees visions, and can show the way to his people. As Soaring Eagle you come from the East always bringing new life and hope.

"Your family has been together as far back as time itself and I will never destroy that unit. You will be together for eons to come. This is the end of your Vision Quest but not the end of your vision, which will continue for the rest of your life. You may write books. But what is most important is that you be _____ and Soaring Eagle. When it gets light go back and receive nourishment; this is not a good thing for your body. However, I know you needed this suffering. I never require suffering." Then a light moved off to the East toward new beginnings, shaped like an arrow head and then a round circle... zooming away! I have received my vision. Now I must go to sleep....

It has been light now a good while. Very cold. I still feel dizzy. Earlier I just wanted to cry. A bird came to my tent and told me to cheer up. A little while ago my squirrel ran around my tent right next to the edge -- telling me it is time to go. A moment ago she came up from the South and chattered at me -- "Time to go... time to go... time to go." I've had some green magma to try to get enough strength to pack up and leave. May take another cup.

Still feel terrible. A crow just flew over to give me a greeting and strength. Not since day one has any crow come near my circle. I have heard them far away, elsewhere in these deep woods. But not here.

[Note: Crows have been friends at the field where I had been jogging each morning near my home. When I returned home and told my wife about that crow she said that one morning she had looked out the window and seen a crow. She asked the crow to send me some love in New York. I believe that was the message I received as I ended my Vision Quest.]

After I pack I don't have strength to take down my tent. Had to rest often as I packed. I knew it was time to go, but also knew there was no hurry. I lie down to rest. Finally ready to try to go. Very hard getting pack on back. I rest often walking out of wilderness. Finally get to base camp, put pack in my car and go sit next to a fire. Others get me stuff to drink. Can't sit too close to fire; too warm. Hard being around people talking, but also good to be there. We have survived! We are told not to talk about our vision.

I meet with the group leaders to review my vision and get help with interpretation. That was very valuable. Then I have some chicken broth.

Finally late in afternoon I go back into woods to get my tent and tarps. Am surprised by how tired I still am. Why surprised? I remembered that, in the A.M. when I got up, I had buried what I had thrown up during the night; it felt like I was burying parts of me.

Last Night at Base Camp Very cold outside, way below freezing. We all bring our sleeping bags into the meeting cabin to sleep there, totally covering the floor with our bodies. I awaken in the night and hear the sounds of my tribe sleeping and breathing nearby.

I imagine I am living long ago in a Native American village, sleeping in a large lodge house, and am surrounded by those of that ancient tribe. It is a powerful feeling to be aware of such close ties to people who a week ago had been total strangers.

Wake up again during the night with terrible pain in middle of forehead, at third eye -- worst headache yet! I am told, "Do not be surprised by this pain. Last night you went through psychic surgery, and this is now part of the healing of that area."

I get up in the morning and take an ice cold bath at an outdoor shower (no hot water), and dress quickly. After a light breakfast I start my drive home, with my vision still swirling in my mind and soul. This has been more, much more, than I expected!

The next thing I was not prepared for was the range of emotions I would feel after returning home. It was very hard to feel concern for petty parts of parish politics. I found myself feeling anger that people could not see what I see, and they could not hear what I was trying to tell them. I tried to share some of the story of my vision quest with a small group of interested parishioners, but got only amazed looks of disbelief. Their eyes seemed to say, "Why would anyone ever want to do something like that?" Since then I have been careful to share only parts of my vision. Sun Bear once said to me, "Don't let others piss on your vision, which may happen if you try to tell too much it."

Some have asked me how such "non-Christian spirituality" could be appropriate for me as a Christian priest. My response is, as I have said earlier, that I believe Christ has been, is now and forever will be present in my spiritual life and in the life of all humanity. If that is true, then that infinite presence of God in Christ has been present in the spiritual lives of Native Americans. As Sun Bear told me one day, "Us Indians didn't sit on a hillside for 50,000 years waiting for the white man to tell us about God. We have been experiencing God for thousands of years, although we may describe those experiences in different ways than you do as western, Anglo-Saxon Christians."

These experiences have not drawn me away from my faith as a Christian but have enabled me to move even deeper into my faith and my own encounter with our risen Lord. And to this day, almost twenty years later, I still continue to feel the impact of my vision quest.

One of the things I experience each time I do T'ai Chi (Chapter Seven) is to feel a connection with the sacred directions, as understood by Native Americans. The following exercise honors the seven sacred directions. This is also related to the Native American Medicine Wheel. I have read that at one time there were over 20,000 Native American Medicine Wheels in North America, all being used by the various tribes across our land. This exercise comes out of some of those ancient practices and can deepen our *limitless living*.

I try to find a time each day or at least each week to do this meditation, usually as part of the T'ai Chi form I use. As discussed in
Chapter Seven, that form moves in a circle, always facing one of the
four earth directions. So this exercise also fits into that process.

Some find it helpful to do this at the same time each day because
such regularity deepens the experience. Others prefer to have a
special time, once each week to do this meditation.

Exercise 10.1 - Honoring the Sacred Directions

First, find a comfortable and undisturbed place to stand.
When you can, it is good to take off your shoes and do this
outside, with your bare feet directly in contact with Earth
Mother.

Breathe deeply a few times, allowing yourself to move into a
meditative space, exhaling tensions, problems, worries, and
other distractions.

I usually place my hands pressed together over my heart in a
posture of prayer, as in the image of the praying hands. It
has been said that the hands held in this way represent the
oneness of an apparently dual cosmos, the bringing together
of spirit and matter, or the *individual self* meeting the *Infinite
Self.*

As you feel your connection to the Earth through your feet,
remember the Circle is holy and represents our Creator who
is the source of all directions and of all connections.

One of the ways I honor a direction is to prayerfully or gently bow to that direction as I quietly say, "Namaste."[47]

---

[47]"Namaste" is pronounced as "Namastay" with the first two a's as the
first a in "America" and the "ay" as in "stay", but with the "t" pronounced soft
with the area just behind the tip of the tongue pressing against the upper-front
teeth with no air passing. In Sanskrit "Namaste" means, "I bow to you," or "I
honor you." For many it means, "I salute the Divine in you." A deeper veneration
is sometimes expressed by bringing the fingers of the clasped palms to the forehead, where they touch the brow, the site of the Third Eye. A third form of
Namaste brings the palms completely above the head, a gesture said to focus
consciousness in the subtle space just above the Crown Chakra. This form is so
full of reverence it is reserved for God.

Namaste, in a religious context, can be taken to mean any of these:
—The Spirit in me meets the same Spirit in you;
—I greet that place where you and I are one;
—I salute the divine in you;
—I salute the Light of God in you;
—I bring together my body and soul, focusing my divine potential, and bow to the same potential within you;
—I bow to the divine in you. I recognize that within each of us is a place where Divinity dwells, and when we are in that place, we are One.

Now face each of the Sacred Directions, one at a time:

1) Face the East. Be present with the energies of the East, the place of awakening, of birth, of spring, the place representing new beginnings, new days. The Eagle is in the East. Stand quietly ... receptively ... sensing the energies. Allow yourself to simply be in the experience. You may see images or colors, hear sounds, have sensations in your body, or have an inner knowing. Or you may face the East and simply be aware of that spatial direction. There is no right or wrong experience. Turn your attention to the East and be present. Move your consciousness into the East. Traditionally the color of the east is yellow or gold, the color of the rising sun. The path of the east is the gate of the Spirit. When you feel ready, honor the Spirit Keepers of the East and thank the East.

Maintain your connection to the East, while turning to the South.

2) Face the South. Be with the energies of the South, the time of mid-day and of summer, the years of fruitfulness and of rapid growth. The South is the place of the Coyote, the trickster, so it can be a place of humor and surprises. Stand quietly, receptively. Sense the energies of the South, move your consciousness into the South. Allow yourself to be in the experience, without expectation. When you feel ready, honor the Spirit Keepers of the South and thank the South. Continue your connection to the South, while turning to the West.

3) <u>Face the West</u>. Be with the energies of the West, the place of evening and autumn, the time we reap our harvest, when we have found the knowledge we need to move to our center. The Grizzly Bear is in the West. Sun Bear said that the "West is the home of the West Wind, Father of all the Winds."[48] Stand quietly, receptively. Sense the energies of the West, move your consciousness into the West. Allow yourself to engage the experience, without expectation. When you feel ready, honor the Spirit Keepers of the West. Maintain your connection to the West, while turning to the North.

4) <u>Face the North</u>. Be with the energies of the North. Stand quietly, receptively. Sense the energies of the North. The North is the place of Night and winter. It is the place of the White Buffalo. The North is a time of resting for us and for the Earth Mother. Sun Bear said that the North is "the place that represents the time when we have the white hairs of snow upon our heads, when we prepare to change both worlds and forms."[49] Allow yourself to engage the experience, without expectation. Honor the Spirit Keepers of the North.

Experience yourself at the center of these four directions, in the middle of this temporary Medicine Wheel, with lines forming a sacred cross from North to South, East to West, and radiating from this place into infinity.

5) Next, <u>lift your face to the Sky</u>. Be with the energies of the Sky. Allow your consciousness to move upward, extending into the heavens. This is the home of the Sun, Moon and Stars. Allow their energies to flow into you. Honor Father Sky, Grandfather Sun, Grandmother Moon, and all the Star people of the universe, and especially our Heavenly Father, our Creator ... the Great Spirit, the Infinite Mystery.

6) Now allow yourself to <u>rest deeply upon the Earth</u>. Feel the Earth beneath your feet. Imagine your weight being supported by the ground under you, all the way down to the center of the Earth. Be aware of the Earth holding you, totally

---

[48]Sun Bear, Wabun and Barry Weinstock, *The Path of Power* (New York: Prentice Hall Press, 1987), p. 182.
[49]Ibid, p. 181.

supporting you. Be open to the energies of the Earth Mother, waiting to flow into you, through you ... kissing Father Sky. Feel the heartbeat of the Mother, cradling you, sustaining you. Honor your connection to the Mother Earth.

7) Finally, move inward. Become cognizant of yourself at the center of six directions between Earth & Sky, amid East & West, North & South. Find that point within you where the six directions join (North, East, South, West, The Heavens, The Earth). Here is your sacred Center. From this Center, experience your place in the divine order of the cosmos. Honor the energies of Self and Place. This is a place where we can acknowledge our connection with the Creator—that we are not separate from our Creator or from each other.

Whenever you feel scattered or disconnected, I suggest that you pause for a moment and honor these sacred directions. If you are not able to physically turn toward the directions, do so in your mind or reflect back to an earlier experience of honoring the directions. This will put you in touch with your own center and help you connect to the Mystery we call God.

Throughout the world, different cultures honor the sacred directions in different ways, with their own symbols and significances for each direction. If you find this exercise useful, you may wish to explore some of those other traditions.

There are also many other practices or rituals that may assist you in your spiritual journey.

One of these Native American practices that I have found useful is that of smudging. Smudging helps us center ourselves with any of the four herbs: tobacco, sweetgrass, sage, and cedar. I prefer sweetgrass or sage. If those are not available, I find a cedar tree and break off a small portion of the leaves, thanking the tree for this gift. I use a seashell or bowl to hold the herb and a large feather to serve as a fan. With these things, I stand for a while and become centered in that space. I smudge the room, slowly walking clockwise around the perimeter of the room, fanning the smudge pot, keeping it lit and wafting the smoke about. I smudge any medicine tools I will be using such as my medicine pipe, and other objects in my medicine bag. If there are others present, it is a good practice to smudge each person in the group, circle, ceremony, and lodge. Starting in the East and moving clockwise around the circle, hold the smudge pot so each person may bathe himself or herself in the smoke, using their cupped hands to draw the smoke toward themselves and over their heads. Many people smudge the heart area first, next the head area, and then the arms, then downward toward the legs. This isn't the only way. It isn't wrong to smudge another way. Some medicine men recommend that we purify and cleanse ourselves fairly regularly in this day and age with so much sickness and violence around.

This chapter introduces only a few of the great spiritual practices found in Native American traditions. During my studies of Native American spirituality, I have experienced power objects and the medicine pouch, power animals, sweat lodges, vision quests, sacred circles or medicine wheels, the use of the medicine pipe, and sacred stories. Not long after my vision quest, I was given a medicine pouch by a dear friend in Kansas City. It still holds objects that I have collected over the years and which are part of my own medicine pipe ceremony.

Some years before I began my personal journey into and deeper study of Native American spirituality, I learned of "power animals." I believe my first encounter with this topic was through the writings of Carlos Castaneda (1925 – 1998). Castaneda was the author of a series of books that claimed to describe his training in traditional Native American shamanism. He claimed to have met and been trained by a Yaqui shaman named Don Juan Matus in 1960. Castaneda's works contain some amazing descriptions of paranormal experiences, psychological techniques, Toltec magic rituals, shamanism and experiences with psychoactive drugs (e.g. peyote). I found his writings entertaining and in places quite insightful. However, his major use of peyote as a primary means of having these spiritual experiences is something that left me quite cold. As can be seen in this book and in many other resources, it is not necessary to subject ourselves to the dangers of drugs in order to experience spiritual adventure and exploration. Also, drugs tend to take control of the experience, sometimes with very damaging and life threatening effects. I strongly discourage the use of LSD, peyote and other psychoactive drugs to enhance spiritual experiences.

On the other hand, it has been my experience that power animals are our spiritual friends, much like Guardian Angels, but functioning on a more primitive and intuitive level.

I first met my power animal while in deep meditation. One of my preferred meditations is to recall a place my sons and I used to go spelunking in the mountains of Tennessee during the years I was in seminary in Sewanee, Tennessee. This particular cave required that we walk up a stream of water to where a waterfall came out of a rock face about twenty feet above the stream. Long ago hand and foot holds had been carved in the rock face next to the waterfall, which was our means of getting up to the cave opening. After entering the cave we were in a room about 20 by 20 feet and only four feet high, so we had to crawl over to another opening into the deeper recesses of the caves that tunneled many miles into the mountain. In my meditation I go into this cave and explore the deep recesses of my unconscious self ... sort of like a shamanistic journey into my self. On one occasion, prior to beginning this meditative process, I said a short prayer asking that I might meet my power animal. When I got to the second opening of the cave, I saw a large gray wolf. He was looking at me, and I knew he was my power animal!

Although the wolf was once a greatly feared and hated animal, it has lately become more appreciated. Above my computer screen is a large, framed poster of a beautiful wolf, with the words below, "In wildness is the preservation of the world." I believe the wolf as my power animal reminds me of the importance of wilderness. All spiritual journeys seem to begin with a journey into a wilderness or wild place, such as the forty-day journey of Jesus after his baptism by John.

For me, my power animal, Wolf, has become a close friend. His ministry to me is one of a presence that brings strength and courage. That presence, on one level, encourages me to be less "civilized" and to allow the animal or wild spirit to be present in my life. He doesn't talk with me although I talk with him, and I feel he understands what I say. I have read that in both Celtic and Native American traditions the spirit of the wolf stands for the path of discovering the deepest levels of self, of inner knowing and intuition, as symbolized by the image of the wolf baying at the moon. In some ways this is a solitary path. To come to truly understand oneself one must take time to be alone, undistracted by the opinions of others. One must learn to listen to the voice within which speaks in the silence of the wolf. At the same time, the wolf is a very social animal, reminding me of the importance of life mates, family and parish, of community and nation. Also, it is known that adult wolves participate in the teaching and training of the young of its pack, which is part of my function as a parish priest, as a father and as a grandfather. In the wolf I find my solitary and social paths merging. And finally, it is partly through the encouragement of Wolf, as my power animal, that I have come to see I have a responsibility to share with my tribe, with the human race, that which I have learned about *limitless living*.

And this may sound strange or delusional to some, but when I had my heart attack in 1989 (next chapter), I felt Wolf beside me from the very beginning. I could reach out my hand from my hospital bed and rest it upon the fur of Wolf. He was my day-to-day spiritual companion during a very painful and stressful time, and he helped me relax and heal.

If you wish to discover your own power animal, I suggest you relax, as suggested in Appendix B, and then in your imagination go to a place in nature where you have especially felt peace and harmony. When you are there, look around and see if an animal appears. Some have been disappointed when they discover their power animal is, for example, a snake or a mouse. However, before you reject the animal who comes to you, take time to learn from him or her. Look up "power animals" on the Internet and find the meaning of your animal when it appears as a power animal. Often the most humble of animals brings the greatest wisdom, strength and power.

All of these aspects of Native American spirituality have deepened my spiritual journey and have given me a greater sense of *limitless living*.

Chapter 11

SPIRITUAL & MIND-BODY HEALING

O n January 4, 1989, after my October, 1988, vision quest, I had a serious heart attack while skiing in the mountains of Virginia. It was an extremely cold day. For my third run down the mountain, I had taken a lift to the highest level. As I started to ski down a trail where snowmaking equipment was re-plenishing the slope, I breathed in some of that super-cooled air. Immediately I felt great pain in my chest and down my left arm. It didn't take a cardiologist to know that I was having a heart attack. I told Mary Ann, who was skiing with me, what was happening. I then skied down the mountain to the lodge, went into the Ski Patrol office and asked them to call the rescue squad.

I lay on my back on the floor of the office and moved my con-sciousness inside. Fortunately, for years I had been regularly using deep meditation techniques to relax my body and deepen my spiri-tual awareness. (These were discussed earlier in Chapter Six.) As I took a deep breath I watched the air move through my nostrils and into my chest, then, after holding the breath for a moment, I started to slowly breathe out, again watching the movement of the air; and in my mind I said the word "One." However, I didn't say "one" the way you would repeat a number, but rather I said, "Oooooonnnnnnnnnnnne," allowing the sound to continue in my mind as the breath was slowly going out. On the next breath, I repeated the same process, but this time as I breathed out I also tried to allow a slight smile to come to my face although I was still feel-ing tremendous pain. I kept repeating this process until the rescue squad arrived 45 minutes later. After briefly describing my symptoms to a crewmember, telling our daughter Patricia that everything would be OK, and being loaded into the rescue vehicle with Mary Ann, I returned to that same meditative process. It felt like a giant weight was crushing my chest and the pain was almost unbearable. At one point the oxygen tank on the truck was depleted and the pain became even worse, so bad that I signed myself with the cross and felt that perhaps the end of this life was near. Still I continued with this process.

After a 40-minute drive, I was taken to a small community hospital in Woodstock, Virginia, where no cardiologist was on staff. The doctor on duty in the ER was convinced that I couldn't be having a heart attack because I was so relaxed and because my EKG was not too distorted from normal. I was kept in the Intensive Care Unit, and it wasn't until the next morning that blood tests were returned which showed a major increase of an enzyme in the blood which indicates the presence of heart muscle damage …I had had a serious heart attack! After consultation with Dr. Carlos Ayers, then Chairman of the Cardiology Department at the University of Virginia Medical Center, my family decided it would be best to have me transferred to the University of Virginia hospital (about three hours away).

In talking with Dr. Ayers later, and describing what had happened after the pain had begun, he suggested that my use of those meditation techniques probably saved my life. He said the first reaction for most people, when they realize they are having a heart attack, is panic. That fear reaction causes even greater constriction of the coronary arteries and even greater damage to the heart muscles. In my case, such a panic reaction would probably have been too much for my damaged heart.

I truly believe that my faith in our living God, my awareness that death is not the end of life, my recent vision quest, the meditative process I described above, and my loving family, all contributed to my being here today to write these words.

In the hours and first days of recovery, I added another part to my prayers and meditation. Once I was deeply relaxed, I would visualize the Light of Christ entering through the top of my head and moving down to my heart. There the Light would slowly work its way through each artery, clearing out the plaque and any other debris found there. I then envisioned the Light totally filling and surrounding my heart, healing as much of the damage as possible. Although there was a large area on the backside of my heart that had received permanent damage, I could feel this meditative process working to heal my heart. On the fourth day after my heart attack an angiogram was performed, which involves inserting a thin tube into the femoral artery. The tube is passed up into the heart where dye is injected and x-rays are taken to visualize any blockage of the arteries. This test found that all of my arteries were clear, except where the infarction had occurred. Had this meditative process utilizing Light actually helped to clear out my other arteries? There is no certain way of knowing. Regardless of whether it did or not, the feeling that I might be doing something positive to help with my healing had value for me and my emotional state, which in itself has healing value.

Spiritual Healing

I must confess that after almost 30 years of Christian ministry as a priest and pastor, I still do not understand spiritual healing. I have read hundreds of books on the subject. I pray with and lay hands on most people I visit in hospitals and nursing homes. Each week I conduct two healing services that involve anointing each person with oil blessed by my Bishop and prayerfully laying hands upon each person, and also includes the celebration of Holy Eucharist.

I do not understand why some people are healed and some are not. I have seen what I would consider miracles, and I have read accounts of many others. When I hear such stories I feel great compassion for those individuals who have prayed for a miracle but do not experience an obvious healing. I can imagine that some must wonder why God has ignored their plea and yet answered others. Are they loved less by their Creator? I think not.

I believe God loves each and every one of his children with a love that far exceeds our ability to imagine. Our human minds can conceive only of love that is partial and incomplete. There must always be some element of selfishness, some slight holding back, some concern for self-preservation, as we struggle to love others. That is not so with God. The word used to describe the love that God has for His/Her children is "Agape," which is total, absolute, unconditional love. Most major religions recognize that the nature of this infinite mystery we call God includes such absolute love. That being the case, I cannot believe our loving God would chose to heal one person and withhold healing from another.

At the same time, a deep part of my faith is that God is doing more than we can ever ask for or imagine. I will share a story that may help illustrate this point.

I mentioned earlier about being part of a charismatic prayer group in Charlottesville, prior to going to seminary. One element of the gatherings of that prayer group was a time to have prayers for healing. These could be prayers for our own healing, for a family member or friend, or any person for whom one prayed.

At that time, a good friend of mine, Frank (not his name), had been diagnosed with terminal leukemia. He was in the final stages of dying when Mary Ann and I went to visit him one evening prior to going to that prayer group. Frank was in a coma, was bleeding from his pores, and the nurse said he would probably not last through the night. This was especially sad because he was then estranged from his wife and children and his business was about to go into bankruptcy. As we left the hospital and drove to the Catholic church near the University, I knew I wanted our group to have prayers for my friend. I was thinking that these would be prayers for his ultimate healing, that is, an easy passage into death and into the arms of our Savior.

On that same night, another friend, Ed (not his name), decided for the first time to respond to our invitation to join us there at this prayer group. Ed, a Navy pilot, was then an ROTC instructor at the University of Virginia, and later was to become commander of his own squadron and finally went on to be a very high ranking Admiral for the U.S. Navy.

Once our prayer group had gathered we had some initial time of silence and then some vocal prayers. I stood, pulled a chair to the center of the circle, and asked any who were so inclined to lay hands on me as an intercessor for my friend, who was in the final stages of dying less than two miles away. Many in the group gathered around me and placed their hands on my head, shoulders and back. Ed had joined with them and was standing immediately behind me and had placed his hands on my back. Please keep in mind that this was the first time Ed had ever attended such a prayer session.

He later reported that as the prayers began, some in clear English and some in unknown languages or "tongues," his hands began to get hot. Gradually they become so hot that he thought to himself, "Prentice must be wearing some kind of heated back brace." Finally his hands became so hot that he had to remove them. Looking at them he could see they were red but not burned. He returned his hands to my back, in another area. Again his hands became extremely hot, but he held them there until the prayers were ended. As this was going on, I felt nothing other than the pressure of hands on my body, which was very relaxing.

Five days later my friend walked out of the hospital, the leukemia in total remission. Over the next twelve months he was able to reunite with his wife and children and get his business back into such good shape that it could be sold to provide his family with some modest support. Approximately a year after that amazing prayer meeting I was with him again in the hospital. His leukemia had returned, but he was not fearful. On TV was some evangelist shouting that we must come to Richmond to encounter God. My friend said, "We don't have to go to Richmond to see God. He is right here in this room, right now!" Amen! My friend died early the next morning, slipping peacefully into that Infinite Mystery and total Love.

I cannot begin to explain why this healing occurred the way it did. I consider both the temporary remission and the final peaceful death to be forms of healing. I only trust that God, in His/Her infinite wisdom, was working out a purpose for my friend and for each of us who witnessed this healing. I know that event touched my life in ways that still impact the way I pray for healings with an openness to anything being possible. My guess is that it probably also made a difference in the way Ed continued to serve his country as a Navy pilot, a commander of many other pilots, and ultimately as an Admiral concerned with the lives of other U.S. Navy personnel. God touches our lives in so many great and small ways.

One of my favorite Psalms is the 23rd. I especially like the image of God being our Shepherd. As an Episcopal priest, I must have read this Psalm to hundreds of parishioners who were suffering great pain, were critically ill, or nearing death. I have gone through my own dark valleys of illness and pain, and this Psalm has been one of reassurance and comfort.

And as I have re-read these verses and studied this Psalm, I've had some insights that seem quite relevant for those wanting to move toward *limitless living*.

First, we encounter the truth that the Lord is our shepherd. On the wall of my office is a drawing of Jesus holding close to his chest a small lamb. The expression on the face of that little lamb is one of total trust and profound peace. Such peace is experienced when we trust that the ground of our being, the support for our lives—now and forever, is the Great Shepherd.

Second, "I shall not want." Our Shepherd knows what we need better than we do. He sees to our innermost being, and he provides great spiritual riches.

Third, "He makes me to lie down in green pastures; he leads me beside the still waters." Sometimes we need to be forced to lie down, to find rest for our souls. When I was having my heart attack on the ski slope, I was surprised by one thought that flashed through my mind. I recall thinking, "Now maybe I can stop work for a while." Clearly, God had to *make* me lie down and rest.

Fourth, it is a known fact that sheep are frightened by moving water, so the Good Shepherd finds "still waters." Our Lord will provide a source of refreshment and renewal that does not generate fear, but true restoration for our souls.

Fifth, as we follow the spiritual guidance of the Great Shepherd then we will be led in paths of righteousness. And we will do this for the sake of the name of our Lord, i.e., to further Love.

Sixth, and although we frequently will walk or drive through dark valleys in the shadow of death (just look at the danger we face daily on our highways or from a virus and perhaps even from a terrorist) we need fear no evil because the Great Shepherd is with us.

Seventh, the rod and staff of the shepherd are used to drive away wild beasts, which may threaten our existence, so we are comforted by the powerful presence of the Shepherd.

Eighth, we are given a feast before our enemies. This can mean many things, but the one I like best comes from an ancient Jewish understanding of holy meals. There is the belief that when you eat such a meal with others, you not only consume the food but you also consume each other's presence; which would certainly remove them as our enemies. And when the thorns of life pierce our souls, our Shepherd will anoint our heads with his healing oils.

And finally, we are assured that goodness and mercy will follow us all the days of this lives and that we will dwell in the house of the Lord forever.

Just hearing these words and repeating them over and over can bring great peace. If we are going through a time of great pain or stress, if we have just learned bad news about our health or the health of a loved one, if we seem to be surrounded by darkness, I suggest that we read this psalm several times each day. However, please do not just read it rapidly to get through to the end. Read each verse slowly, intentionally, allowing the meaning to soak into our souls. Keep this up for several days or several weeks, and I think we will discover things are different. Life is not quite so dark.

Ralph Waldo Emerson said, "A man is what he thinks about all day long." Norman Vincent Peale said, "Change your thoughts and you change your world." The Twenty-third Psalm is a pattern of thinking, and, when the mind becomes saturated with it, a new way of thinking and new life results. The twenty-third psalm represents a positive, hopeful, faithful approach to life and another path toward *limitless living*.

There is such a rich selection of books related to spiritual healing, holistic health, and mind-body healing that I cannot begin to, nor would I want to, repeat their wisdom here. What I have done in the Bibliography is provide a good cross section of such texts. For those dealing with serious illness or health issues, I strongly recommend a three-fold approach.

1) Continue to work closely with your healthcare professional. Do not discontinue any medicines or therapies while you explore the spiritual dimensions of health and healing.

2) Select two or three of the most respected authors in the field. I recommend: Andrew Weil, M.D.; Herbert Benson, M.D.; and Deepak Chopra, M.D. Then also some of the others such as: Bernie S. Siegel, M.D.; Melvin Morse, M.D.; Sandra A. McLanahan, M.D.; and, Judith Orloff, M.D. All of these authors share their wealth of knowledge and experience both as physicians and as individuals who have an awareness of the spiritual dimensions of healing and health.

3) Participate in regular worship within your community of faith. If you are not a part of a church, synagogue, or temple, start to explore. Visit a variety of places of worship and see what form of ritual and liturgy resonates with your soul. I recommend that you avoid groups that say they are the only way, that their path is the only path. Many paths lead to God. I also suggest that you find a place that feels open and welcoming, not closed and condemning.

If there is a prayer group meeting in your church, synagogue, or temple, go and ask for prayers. If there is not now such a group, see if there are others who would be willing to join with you to pray for your healing and for the healing of others in the parish. As mentioned earlier, for many years I was part of a charismatic prayer group in a Roman Catholic Church. That was a great source of inspiration and healing. Unfortunately, some charismatic groups have adopted very rigid faith perspectives and very narrow interpretations of Holy Scripture, often tending toward extreme fundamentalism (a belief that the Bible was verbally dictated by God and thus without error). Most people who have seriously studied the Bible find such positions untenable, undesirable, and unhealthy. However, some people need to adopt such an absolutistic style of faith. If that is your preference, go for it, although I find it is your preference, go for it, although I find it hard to believe that anyone of that persuasion would have read thus far in this book.

In many Episcopal churches we have weekly services, as mentioned above, of healing and Holy Eucharist during which we anoint with oil blessed by a Bishop and have laying on of hands for the healing of mind, body and soul. I would assume that similar types of liturgies are available in many other mainline Christian denominations. Having a church home can be a great source of peace. Having a pastor and fellow church members who can visit you in the hospital or when you are shut-in at home is also a source of healing and hope. Some of the greatest ministry I have seen in churches has not been carried out by the ordained ministers but by the lay ministers (those not ordained), by those who feel a call to carry the love of God to those in distress or hurting in any way. And often the people who have the greatest gifts for such a healing ministry are those who have themselves experienced great pain and suffering. I have found that the best healing is done by "wounded healers." They help us move toward *limitless living*.

Chapter 12

REINCARNATION
&
PAST LIFE RECALL

It is appropriate that the final chapters of this book about unconventional spiritual adventures focus on topics which are not
only related to endings, i.e., to death, but which are also unorthodox and unaccepted by most western cultures and religions ...
reincarnation, past life recall, and near-death experiences.

Twenty two years ago, having just arrived at a week long "MATC
Lab" or training conference[50] in Elizabethtown, Pennsylvania, the
thirty participants had gathered in a circle for an orientation session.
As the leaders talked about the upcoming meetings, I looked around
at the faces of the other members of this group. I had earlier
scanned a list of names of those present, and recognized none. But
suddenly I saw someone, directly across the circle from me, who
was very familiar. I knew she was an old friend from somewhere
but couldn't place her. I saw that she was also looking directly at
me, and we both smiled. When that session stopped for a break, that
woman and I immediately walked toward each other. I introduced
myself and she gave me her name, "Elaine _____ " which I didn't
recognize. I said, "I'm sure I know you from somewhere but can't
remember where." And then I started asking a series of questions
such as, "Are you from Danville, Virginia? Did you ever live in
Charlottesville? Did you go to Randolph-Macon? How about
graduate business school at the University of Virginia? Are you an

---

[50] A Mid-Atlantic Training Consortium (MATC) "Basic Human Interac-
tion Conference" in 1985.

Episcopal priest?" etc., etc. To each question she just smiled and said, "No."

Finally I said, "But I'm sure I know you." She replied, "Yes, you do. We were husband and wife in a previous life." As soon as she said this, I *knew* she was correct, although reincarnation was not a part of my belief system. The truth of her statement resonated within me in a powerful way. I was aware that the majority of people on Planet Earth believe in reincarnation, and I had read several books that discussed the topic. But, for me, the jury was still out.

And yet here was a person who was so familiar to me, on a soul level, that I was sure what she said was correct. My brain was struggling to absorb this truth. One moment I thought, "No, this is impossible." The next moment I thought, "Yes, I know this woman was my wife in a previous life."

The group was called back together and our workshop continued. Elaine and I, and several others, became part of a smaller sub-group. And later I realized that another member of that sub-group may also have been a soul from a previous, but different, lifetime lived as part of an Amish family. It was as though we had all decided to somehow meet in this life, at that place and time ... or perhaps it was simply an amazing coincidence. When I got home and told my wife, in this present life, about this, she asked, "Did you take up where you left off in that previous marriage?" I explained that this "soul recognition and connection" was much different. It seemed that the physical component had not survived, although the recognition, the soul familiarity and closeness did seem to survive. One of these two past-life links still continues to be a close friend.

That experience was good preparation for my next "mind-blowing" experience. While attending a post-Easter conference for clergy at A.R.E.®[51] in Virginia Beach, I met a delightful lady, Ms. Carole Young (this is not the Carole, mentioned earlier, who was a High School love). During a coffee break we had exchanged comments

---

[51]See footnote # 1 on page two.

about different parts of the conference, and I had asked her about the primary focus of her ministry.

Carole's response intrigued me. She said she was a counselor and often helped clients do "past life recall." As mentioned earlier, I have always been a spiritual explorer who likes to "push the envelope" of mystical and esoteric experience. Based on a strong faith in a loving God, I have been ready (my wife says I'm too ready) to jump into whatever new or exciting spiritual adventure may appear.

So my ears quickly became attentive when I heard, "past life recall." "Hum," I said, "I'd love to do something like that!"

The next day, after the mid-day meditation at A.R.E.®, we went out on the beach. I reclined on a towel and Carole placed a tape recorder near my head to record any possible recall material. For some reason, none of the first side of the tape--which included the deep recall material, recorded anything. So what follows is based on my journal records made immediately after this session and from the second side of the tape that included reflections on the earlier recall.

Throughout this experience I was completely conscious though in a deep meditative state. I was reflecting upon what I was recalling as it occurred. It was a beautiful spring afternoon, unusually warm for early April. Hearing the ocean as I lay there on the beach and feeling the sand and sea breeze perhaps helped to evoke these memories which started with the feeling of "home" or of "going home."

Being accustomed to regularly going into deep meditation as part of my spiritual disciplines, it was not difficult to follow this first impression. I allowed myself to deepen my state of relaxation and of inner awareness. With the promptings of some gentle questions from Carole, I began to see more clearly where this feeling of home was leading me.

I was in a dwelling that had glass/transparent walls with the ocean against the glass. I could go to an upper level where clear domes gave views of the blue sky. One side of the home was attached to land.

When I looked down I couldn't see my feet, which seemed strange, but I could see a floor of solid wood or some similar organic substance. My clothing was of a soft natural, off-white substance like cotton.

My family unit, who lived in this place, was roughly the same family unit I now have in this life. However, my spouse was "away." At first thought he/she was exploring our planet, but later meditation seemed to suggest there was some kind of extra-planetary exploration going on, i.e., distant planets in other solar systems were being investigated. Also, all of my family members seemed to be feeling a kind of temporary grief because this significant part of our lives was so far away.

We communicated almost totally through a kind of mental or spiritual telepathy. When anyone entered the dwelling we would all reach out spiritually and "touch" each other. There was a kind of physical touching that also took place even though we were in totally different parts of our home. Communication was truly a special kind of communion.

Life was being lived in unique harmony with the natural and spiritual forces around and within us. There was a balance, and we assisted in maintaining the balance by regularly swimming with the higher forms of sea creatures in the surrounding ocean waters. Our association with these sea animals helped cleanse us of discord and harmonic imbalance.

Early education for children was in the form of playful exploration of the sea with adult teachers. These teachers would use moments of play to help imbue lessons of harmony, balance and communion. As I remembered these times of joy and harmony I began to openly weep--while there next to the Atlantic Ocean and swimming in some ancient ocean.

Carole asked me to recall dinner. I was at a meal, sitting with my family at a round table, consuming food we had all helped to gather. But there was something very different about the food that my rational mind couldn't identify. I remember wondering, "Is this Atlantis? If this is Atlantis, why are things so different?"

At the time of this recall, I had not read much about the Atlantis "myth," except briefly in my college studies of Plato as a philosophy major. That material discounted any possibility that there might have been a historically real place called Atlantis.

As we were eating I knew there was an empty place left for my wife or spouse. I think I was male (as I am now), but there was a kind of androgyny and gender seemed different somehow. I could not tell who in our family unit were male and who were female.

Carole asked me to move several years into the future, which I did. Then I didn't want to be there. I wanted to leave that time, but she encouraged me to look around to determine the cause of my distress. I felt pain and grief. Many people were dying. Each time someone died, even if they were a hundred miles away, I felt the shock and pain of the death.

These were tragic, unexpected deaths. Death had been a natural part of our living. But this was different. We had never experienced anything like these multiple deaths. There was nothing in our memories of a similar event.

Great minds were being brought together to try to determine what was happening and how to restore the balance and harmony. Carole asked if I were one of the great minds. I responded that I was not. Rather, I was helping the process, as one of the leaders or coordinators, but not as one who knows the details and inner workings of the natural processes that had become disrupted.

I think I was helping with the dead and dying, and with their families (much as I do now as an Episcopal priest). At least a thousand of us had died.

I moved on to a later time when the balance had been restored. Even the pain and grief had become part of our new learning that was generating new wisdom.

Then I moved to the end of my life in that lifetime, to the time of my death. Family had gathered. There was no sadness, but a loving atmosphere for saying goodbyes. Slowly the family helped me move on. There were spirits on the other side to greet me. Death was a moment of joy and release, not sadness and grief. The previous deaths had been filled with pain and grief because they were tragic, often involving children.

In a later meditation on these memories, I was shown that those tragic deaths were caused by contamination brought back by space explorations. When I prayerfully asked, while deep in meditation, from how many thousands of years ago had these memories come, I received the clear response, "Think not in terms of thousands of years but of millions!"

How could such ancient memories hold this great attraction for me? As I recalled these images, tears flowed freely down my face. I had the feeling, "I want to be there, that is my home."

Were these "memories" only archetypal images from my deep unconscious? Psychologists have talked of a kind of primitive "oceanic" consciousness. Did I dip into that part of my subconscious life or did I touch some part of the "collective unconscious" about which Carl Jung wrote?

I must also ask--realizing it is contrary to orthodox Christian doctrine--is it possible I did recall a past life, from millions of years ago? The way we reached out to touch those entering our home suggests bodies with different energy configurations. I remember thinking it strange that I could not see my "feet" when I looked at the floor, although I could clearly see the floor. Also, when we swam with the sea creatures and played in the ocean, we did not need breathing apparatus.

My two sons, in this current life, resided at that time in Norfolk, Virginia. Later, on the day of this recall, I picked up from work my oldest son, 'P.K.', so we could go buy some shrimp for supper. As we drove to a marina, I shared with 'P.K.' this recall experience. When I finished, 'P.K.', who is now 45 and a down-to-earth graduate in computer engineering and specialist in information technology and computer security architecture, said, "Oh.... Dad, you aren't going to believe this. When I was about seven years old I went to a movie at the public library in Charlottesville. It was about a boy and a dolphin.

"The boy and the dolphin could communicate with each other through their minds. As the movie ended the two of them swam off into the ocean, almost becoming one. I remember I started to cry and felt like I was supposed to be there. I looked down at my body and said to myself, 'I don't belong here... that is where I belong.'

"When I got home I started to cry again. You and Mom kept trying to console me. I just didn't know how to tell you that I didn't belong here...that I was supposed to be at a place like that boy and the dolphin in the movie."

We both sat in silence, absorbing the impact of these memories and feeling a new kind of closeness that was more than just father and son in this life. Was this perhaps part of a relationship going back millions of years and through untold other lifetimes?

When talking later with my other son, Mark, then in college at Old Dominion University, he remembered having many dreams of being able to swim under the ocean without breathing apparatus -- and then suddenly thinking "I can't do that" and going back into a more normal dream where he needed to go to the surface for air. As he told me about those dreams, I also recalled my own past dreams of swimming in the ocean and being able to breathe under the water.

As I have reflected on these memories, I have wondered what I might learn from them.

Part of what I sensed in these memories was a time when all of life, and every experience, was important. Everything that happened was significant. Every object had its own energy and function. There was life even within non-living objects. All participated in the balance and harmony which helped produce a wonderful sense of joy and happiness.

As adult beings in that ancient place we would sometimes begin to feel out of sorts from having been on land too long or from some unusual stress or concern. As I mentioned above, we would then return to the sea where the sea creatures would help cleanse us of the disharmony so we could move back into balance and full life.

That past life seems to have been an especially "real" and "alive" existence. My current human life seems like a less substantial substitute. The contrast reinforces my vocation as a priest, which I believe is to assist myself and others to live abundant and joyful lives, a vocation I think all people share with life on this planet.

That primary vocation, as Christ said, is to have life and have it in abundance. And I quote again what Jesus also said, "I came that you might have joy, and that your joy be complete."

Isn't that what we are about? Aren't we to strive for, and to help others find that joy and abundant life that I found so beautifully portrayed in this "past life" recall? The movement to care for our ecology, to love our earth and all of its creatures, as well as to love each other, can promote the kind of harmony and balance, reconciliation and peace, which does bring joy and happiness and *limitless living*.

On further reflection, I realize what I desire is not to return to that past life, but to help this life and this earth fully experience the richness of God's abundant love for all creation and all creatures. This experience reaffirms that calling and the possibility of opening up new areas of spiritual adventure.

This "past life recall" is another example of how life or God or synchronicity can put us in the right place at the right time to meet the teachers we need. I think it was not just chance that brought me to A.R.E.® and to this meeting with Carole.

Carole was also gracious enough to spend several hours helping me learn past life recall techniques. Subsequent training, study and personal explorations have led me to seriously consider the entire subject of reincarnation and of remembering past lives. I now offer this as a possible pastoral counseling modality, with astonishing results.

Attendance at an A.R.E.® conference with Dr. Brian Weiss[52], Dr. Robert Jarmon, and Dr. Raymond Moody helped to authenticate my

---

[52]Brian Weiss, M.D., has written several books. For those new to this field, I especially recommend *Many Lives Many Masters, Through Time Into Healing, Mirrors of Time: Using Regression for Physical, Emotional and Spiritual Healing*, and his latest book: *Same Soul, Many Bodies*. Dr. Weiss provides the most professional treatment I have found of the subjects of past-life-recall and

own past life experiences and has opened new and exciting avenues of spiritual and past life explorations.

So, what about you? Would you like to try to recall some content of a past life? Or, if you can't yet accept the idea that you may have lived some other life, how about moving deeper into the unconscious areas of this life to see if something there needs to be expressed? Such content may come to the surface disguised as a "past life recall".

Below is a "Past Life Recall" exercise with steps you can follow. This does not deeper trance states that might be used in a counseling session. Rather it allows your intuitive faculties to move you in the right direction. I would suggest that you have a friend with you when you try this exercise. Sometimes it is helpful to have your friend ask guiding questions, once you are deeply relaxed. Remember to respond verbally, so your friend can shape the next questions to your ongoing experience. If possible, find a therapist who is skilled in conducting past life recall sessions.

Do not use this exercise if you have been diagnosed as having a Dissociative Disorder, Borderline Personality Disorder, Schizophrenia, or have psychotic episodes or hallucinations. If you have any other emotional disorder, talk with your mental health professional before using this exercise.

EXERCISE 12.1 - Past Life Recall

1) As I have described in Appendix B, move into meditative space. As always, surround yourself with the protective Light of Christ. See that light as a sphere all around you.

2) Once you are deeply relaxed, ask your Guardian Angel or the Holy Spirit to help you remember whatever you need to remember at this time; or just relax and open your mind.

---

regression therapy. His courageous publications in this field have given many physicians, psychotherapists, and pastoral counselors, the courage to utilize such insights in the treatment of their patients and parishioners. I have participated in two of his workshops and in a brief training by him for mental health professionals. I strongly recommend any books written by Brian and any of his workshops. His web site is: http://www.brianweiss.com/.

3) "Listen" for a feeling or thought or a glimpse of a scene. You may smell something, or hear something. Be patient, in the silence. Know that your Guardian Angel is there and will guide you.

4) Once you have picked up what I call the "beacon" signal, follow that beacon. Allow yourself to move in the direction of that signal, deeper and deeper into your memories, into your past, into the profundity that is there.

5) Soon you may begin to sense that you are somewhere else. You can mentally observe and describe what you see. Again I recommend you do this with a friend who can take notes about what you see, or that you have on a tape recorder. You must remember to talk out loud. I have done this quite a few times and occasionally get so involved in the explorations, and am having so much fun, that I forget to describe what I am seeing. I now try to do this in front of my computer keyboard and record any recall sensations or experiences this way. A laptop is especially handy.

6) Once you have a sense of being in a past life, or into some inner experience, ask your Guardian Angel to take you to a moment in that life which you need to see at this time. Usually, I am taken to a past life during which I learned an important lesson that is needed now in this life. I can bring that learning back from the past and again use it in current situations.

7) Describe aloud what you are learning from that past life. If it is not clear, ask yourself, "What did I learn here?"

8) If this is an especially meaningful past life, or if this is the first time you have tried this, you may want to go back to your childhood in that life and see what it was like; or look at your family members there; or go to the time of your death. You can let your Guardian Angel or an assisting friend be your primary guide here.

9) When you have finished, come back into ordinary reality. Give yourself time to move slowly into your regular space and time. Do not stand up too soon.

10) I recommend that you immediately take the notes your friend has written, the tape recording, or the notes you have

made on your computer, and go over them while the memories are fresh. Fill in the gaps of what was recorded. I usually remember a great deal more of what I saw or experienced than what actually got recorded.

11) Finally, spend some quality time reflecting on the content of your recall. What did you see that you can use now in this life? What learning did you gain? What fears can you let go? Record your observations in your journal. Discuss them with your priest, pastor, or rabbi. If you are in counseling or therapy, go over your journal notes with your therapist. Sharing your reflections with another person is a powerful way to expand the learning and to gain a more objective point of view on the content of your recall experience.

If you are interested in exploring the Christian perspective on reincarnation, here are two recommended books: *Reincarnation in Christianity* by Gedees MacGregor (The Theosophical Publishing House, Wheaton, Ill, 1986) and *Reincarnation for the Christian* by Quincy Howe, Jr. (The Theosophical Publishing House, Wheaton, Ill, 1974).

Many other books have been written on reincarnation. Sadly, I find too often that authors have either an anti-Christian or anti-religion bias, sometimes distorting the basic and primary Christian or Jewish message, or they bring no faith perspective at all.

A wonderful exception is Edgar Cayce who was a devout Christian. He read the Bible through in its entirety one time for each year of his life, and he taught Sunday School in his local Presbyterian Church. One book that picks up on the Cayce work but is not favorably inclined toward Casey's Christian viewpoint is: *Many Mansions, The Edgar Cayce Story on Reincarnation*, by Gina Germinara (Nal Penguin, Inc, New York, 1950, 1967). Another good Cayce book is: *Edgar Cayce on Reincarnation*, by Noel Langley (Warner Books). I also like this one by a best selling author: *Here and Hereafter* by Ruth Montgomery (Fawcett Crest, N.Y., 1968).

Many have asked me, "But do you really believe in reincarnation?" I must respond that my Christian faith is in no way dependent on any "belief" in reincarnation. At the same time I find the theory of reincarnation to be one way of explaining some very unusual phenomenon.

The late Dr. Ian Stevenson, a psychiatrist and researcher at the University of Virginia Health System Department of Psychiatric Medicine, explored many cases suggestive of reincarnation[53], and I find that his study is a good starting point. As part of his research into reincarnation, Dr. Stevenson had sent word out to associates around the world requesting that if any child began reporting memories that appeared to come from a past life that he be notified prior to any attempt by family to investigate the memories.

One of Dr. Stevenson's most convincing accounts[54] of such children with past-life memories came out of India, where there is no prejudice against such a possibility. A physician in a town in India where a young boy was reporting such memories contacted Dr. Stevenson. He immediately flew to India and traveled to the town, a long grueling trip. He said the roads were almost impassable, and only their two 4-wheel drive Range Rovers enabled them to get to the remote village. The family said they had not done anything to verify the child's memories of another life.

As Dr. Stevenson listened, through a translator, to the boy talk about things he remembered from a previous life, the translator said that he thought he recognized the village the boy was remembering. So the boy and his parents were loaded into the Range Rovers and traveled for many hours to another remote village, a trip that such a poor family would never have taken in their lifetime. When they arrived at this village Dr. Stevenson suggested the boy be allowed to wander around to determine if he could remember anything about the village. Almost immediately he went down one of the dirt streets, like he knew exactly where he was going. He turned right on one street and then left on another and walked to a house that was boarded up. The neighbors said the house had been vacant since the

---

[51] Ian Stevenson, M.D., *Twenty Cases Suggestive of Reincarnation, 2nd Edition, Revised,* 1974

[54] This account is taken from notes I recorded while hearing Dr. Stevenson speak at the University of Virginia School of Medicine.

old man who lived there had died about five years earlier. Boards were removed from the door and they entered. Dr. Stevenson reported that clearly the house had not been entered for many years as evidenced by the spider webs and dust over everything.

The young boy walked across the main living room to the fireplace. In front of the fireplace he began working to lift a loose board in the floor. When he finally pulled up the board he reached down into the space below the floor where he retrieved a bag with coins and other valuables. The boy held up the bag and said, "Mine!" Although the saying goes, "You can't take it with you," it appears this little five-year-old boy had discovered a way to do so.

It seems that some memories can be retained from one life to another. I cannot help but wonder if some experiences of déjà vu are due to actual memories from a previous life. I find it quite interesting that before a new Dalai Lama can be proclaimed, a child candidate, who is presumed to be the reincarnation of previous Dalai Lamas, must be able to identify possessions of past Dalai Lamas, selecting items from a table covered with many different objects of which only a few are such possessions.

Dr. Brian Weiss, in his books, has many other reports of past-life memories, which have come from his practice as a psychiatrist. Dr. Weiss risked his reputation as a noted physician, psychiatrist and scientist to report these cases. Unfortunately, in the United States and the Americas, and in much of Europe, where Christianity is the dominant faith perspective, there has been widespread prejudice against the hypothesis that humans may live multiple lives and move from one life to the next through a process called reincarnation. This is true both within scientific as well as religious communities. Dr. Weiss was one of the first medical professionals to break out of this prejudicial belief system and report actual cases of patients with memories of past lives. Since his first book on this topic, *Many Lives, Many Masters* (Simon & Schuster, 1988), there has been a great outpouring of reports of past-life memories from patients of other medical and mental health professionals. As mentioned earlier, Dr. Weiss has written several other books, as has another noted psychiatrist, Raymond A. Moody, Jr., MD. For those who wish to study this area in more depth, I strongly recommend any and all of their books, along with the writings of Ian Stevenson, M.D.

I think it is beneficial to note that a vast majority of humanity accepts reincarnation as an ordinary part of life and death. A case can be made that even Jesus accepted reincarnation as part of his own theology. When he was asked if he were Elijah or Moses (implying that the soul of Elijah or Moses now had reincarnated in Jesus), he did not refute that possibility by saying that such a theory is unacceptable. He simply ignored the question.

In the early church, and in writings by some early Church fathers such as Origen[55], reincarnation was an accepted doctrine. It was not until after the council of Nicaea, in 325 A.D., when the teachings of Origen were declared unacceptable, that reincarnation was also shunned, by inference but not by direct reference. Some say this rebuff of reincarnation was more a political move than a theological one.

If there is a desire to control people, such as may have been the desire of early church leaders when the Church in Rome became part of the Holy Roman Empire, would it not be effective to threaten hell and damnation for all eternity by withholding one's last chance for forgiveness? The Church became the sole proprietor of forgiveness and could thereby more easily control the masses. This power was all the greater in light of the Church's rejection of the experience of reincarnation.

Our understanding of reincarnation, on the other hand, gives us the hope of possible future lives and future learning, either on this earth or elsewhere. We are not bound by the earthly control of worldly leaders. They may be able to control and even destroy our earthly existence, but they never have ultimate control over our souls.

---

[55] Origen (185-254) was an early Christian scholar, theologian, and distinguished "Church father." In his writings he endeavored to offer an intellectual description of Christianity. He also sought to present scientific thought of the time from a Christian point of view.

For me, reincarnation is not a matter of belief or faith. Rather it is a matter of experience. I recall having lived many other lives. I agree these "memories" could be the product of a very active imagination, or it could be that I somehow tap into a collective storehouse or well of memories of those who have lived before. I accept these as possibilities. Nevertheless, I keep an open mind and enjoy the growth I have experienced through these explorations. I think it is also significant that my memories of past lives do not involve me as some great ruler or major public figure with great power, which would put such "memories" into the probable category of wish fulfillment. Rather, most of the past life memories I have retrieved are of individuals who lived somewhat normal, although occasionally tragic, lives.

In one case I was a Native American living as a Plains Indian. In that past life recall, I remembered my tent, hunting for buffalo, some of the tools I made, and the way I died. When I returned from the recall process that helped bring these memories to the surface, it made even more sense to me that as child in this life, playing Cowboys and Indians with my friends (as mentioned in Chapter Ten), I always wanted to be the Indian.

In another life recall I was a white woman, living in squalid surroundings, I think near the Chesapeake Bay, in a time of the early settlements of Colonial Virginia. My husband had purchased me from a ship captain and treated me like a bonded slave. I remembered sleeping on the dirt floor of our small cabin, working a small garden until my hands were bleeding, and finally dying alone next to the water after a terrible beating by the man who called himself my husband. I remembered the moment of my death as my soul moved into the presence of light and love and healing -- which was a tremendous relief after that horrible life. I gained from that life a great compassion for those who are powerless to change their life circumstances and for those who suffer physical and verbal abuse.

In one rather unusual past life recall I was a monk in England, when the entire realm was Roman Catholic. Later, during the period of 1529 to 1533 the king and English Parliament broke from Rome and made the Church of England protestant. Henry VIII required all of us monks to acknowledge the king as head of the church on threat of death (part of what was known as the "Submission of the Clergy"). One of my friends, another monk, refused to switch his allegiance and was burned at the stake. I immediately switched, with no hesitation – it appears I've never been one to hold too tightly to dogma.

This recall came to me during an A.R.E.® workshop when Dr. Brian Weiss was leading a group past life regression. Earlier I had talked with another participant. We had eaten a meal together and both felt like we had known each other for years, although we had just met. We were sitting next to each other during this recall session and were asked to turn to the person next to us and share our recall. He started first and said that he remembered being a monk in what may have been England during the time of Henry VIII. He had been required to renounce his religious affiliation with the Catholic Church in Rome, which he refused to do. He died a painful death by fire as a result. He shared this with me before I had said anything about my own recall. When I shared mine, we both sat in total amazement that time and fate had brought us together again, in this lifetime, to meet briefly.

Again, it was almost as though we had planned this chance encounter prior to our coming into this life. However, neither of us felt the need to further renew our ancient friendship. That previous life had ended and we were now more focused on living this life. And yet that particular experience gave me more to think about and further reinforced my acceptance of past life memories, and how those past lives are part of my *limitless living*.

A somewhat related area of inquiry is that of near-death experiences or NDEs, which we discuss in our last chapter.

236 ∞ Near Death Experiences

Chapter 13

NEAR-DEATH EXPERIENCES

Much research has been done on this topic of near-death experiences. Modern medicine has been able to bring more people "back to life" after they've entered into a state that, in the past, has been called "death." As a result, many of these people have returned from death to report on life on the other side. My first encounter with this phenomenon was in 1970 when my wife was a medical secretary for a psychiatrist in Charlottesville, Virginia, George G. Ritchie, Jr., M.D.

Dr. Ritchie invited me to lunch one day and shared his incredible story of what had happened to him when he was twenty years old, which I immediately recorded in my journal when I got home. This report comes from those notes.

As Dr. Ritchie and I were eating lunch he told me what had happened to him in 1943, during World War II. He was serving in the Army after college and was stationed in Texas. The Army had decided to send him to medical school and he was about to leave Texas to attend the Medical College of Virginia in Richmond, now Virginia Commonwealth University School of Medicine. Just prior to his departure he contracted double lobar pneumonia and died. He said, according to his medical records, he had been pronounced dead by a physician at a hospital on the Army base, a tag had been placed on his toe, a sheet pulled over his face, and the morgue called to pick up his body. About ten minutes later, the orderly from the morgue was starting to transfer his body to a gurney when he noticed Ritchie's foot twitch. The movement was different from that of rigor mortis, or the stiffening of muscles that sets in several hours after death due to the coagulation of muscle protein. The orderly called a nurse who immediately started a Code Blue crash and he was "brought back to life." He had officially been dead for nine minutes. That was what most would have seen had they been in his room.

Dr. Ritchie told me that something quite different was happening within his awareness. He knew he was very sick and somewhat delirious, but he felt a compulsion to get to a train going to Richmond so he could start his medical training. And he was concerned he might be declared A.W.O.L. if he didn't show up in Richmond as ordered.

He remembers moving toward unconsciousness and then was suddenly walking down the hall of the hospital, still with the urgent need to get to Richmond. An orderly was approaching and he said something to the man, who proceeded not to notice him, and then walked right through him. He told of several other things happening and then came a shift of his attention. He suddenly realized he was in the presence of someone and was surrounded by and filled with bright light. He said that he believed it to be the "presence of the Christ" or the "Light of Universal Love." That presence then escorted him through what he described as the "many mansions of heaven." First he saw some spirits that seemed to have been trapped around the Earth by their concerns about earthly events, or people, or businesses, etc. On the next level there were spirits gathered to continue learning, in an atmosphere much like universities. He then went through more levels or mansions of heaven until he finally arrived at the highest or ultimate level, which was filled with a blinding light of total and absolute love. Dr. Ritchie said that his experience of that which he could only assume must be God was so life changing that he has never since feared death. He felt that if such love is present at the time of our deaths then there is nothing to fear.

He said that once he was at this highest level, he heard a voice say, or he came to an awareness or understanding, that his time to die was not now, that he had much more to accomplish. Immediately he was back in the hospital looking for his body. He passed a room where a body was covered with a sheet and he could see a hand protruding from under the sheet. That hand was wearing his college ring.

With that awareness of his ring, Dr. Ritchie reported that he must have moved back in his body but was now unconscious. He said the memory of this experience has never left him. Dr. Ritchie has since written, in much greater detail, several books on this experience and on the great insights into life and death that have come to him due to that experience.[56] Please note that I have not altered my journal notes above to match Dr. Ritchie's much more complete report in his books. This account from my journal notes is much abbreviated.

I *strongly* recommend all of Dr. Ritchie's books because they give not only more detail about this life changing event in his life, but he also shares many other amazing stories and how this encounter with the Light of Universal Love continues to impact his life and his faith. In recent conversations with Dr. Ritchie, I learned that he has another book soon to be published, which I eagerly await.

Because of my encounter with Dr. Ritchie, and my reading in the field of NDEs (or Near-Death Experiences), I was very open to this possibility when I met a man who had a somewhat different NDE, but one which also had a lasting impact on his life.

I was attending another conference in Pennsylvania and an individual came to visit our group. It was late in the evening after all scheduled events had ended for the day. Many of the conference leaders had met this man before and vouched for his credibility. This is a brief retelling of his story, which he shared over several hours, and which I also recorded in my journal (please note again the importance of my journal). I will call him "John."

John said he had been a truck driver for a steel company and was home one weekend working on his pick-up truck that was up on jacks. He was under the truck trying to tighten a bolt when the jacks

---

[56] *Return From Tomorrow*; *My Life After Dying, Becoming Alive to Universal Love*; and, *Ordered to Return, My Life after Dying* by George G. Ritchie, Jr., M.D.

collapsed and the truck transmission housing came crushing down on his chest. He said he could hear and feel the ribs breaking on both sides of his chest as the air was pushed from his lungs and then all went black. Suddenly, he realized he was in a long dark tunnel, through which he was moving very rapidly. All he could see was darkness for a long while, until finally he could see a dot of light far ahead. Gradually the dot became larger as he drew closer. Then he moved out of the tunnel into total pure light that was pulsating with complete love. He was told he could choose to return to his current life or he could join that total love. He chose to merge with the Absolute Love. As he was moving into the knowledge, light and life of what he understood to be God, suddenly he felt himself being pulled back down the dark tunnel, back toward his body. And then he was back in his body feeling terrible pain.

He later learned that after his truck had crushed his chest, someone called the rescue squad. When it arrived, the crewmember who crawled under the truck was John's best friend. Several months earlier this crewmember had been in Vietnam and had held another friend as he died from having part of his brain blown from his body.

When the crewmember saw under the truck his other best friend, now dead from this accident, he was so overcome with rage that he started striking his dead friend in the head. John's only explanation was that somehow the blows or perhaps his friend's love brought him back to life in this world. John had chosen to not come back and had begun to merge with God. He believes he had also started to absorb great knowledge from the merger.

Several amazing things happened after he was pulled from under the truck and taken to the local hospital. X-rays were taken of his chest which clearly showed that all of his ribs had been broken but they now were healed, a medical impossibility. Also, he could now answer almost any question about any topic, although he said he had been a "not so bright high school drop out." Before the accident he could barely do basic math. Now he could do calculus. Prior to that death he knew nothing about world geography. Now he could name the capitals of any country in the world, describe their primary natural resource, even the nature of their national flag. He answered questions almost all night long. He would talk about any subject with a level of knowledge that was astounding.

Another part of his story was also quite interesting. He said that, several years prior to our gathering in Pennsylvania, a team of researchers into NDEs came to interview him. As he described in great detail all that happened after he died, he recalled that prior to or as he was merging with God, he had a total life recall. However, this recall involved experiencing each event of his life from three different perspectives: first, as he originally experienced it, second as viewed or experienced by significant others in that event, and finally from above, as from the perspective of God. In that recall he re-experienced an event while hauling steel into downtown Philadelphia. He was driving down a street and was cut off by a small car so that his truck almost jackknifed. He was so angry that when he came to a stoplight behind that car, he got out of his truck, pulled the man from his vehicle and hit him in the face breaking his jaw. He returned to his truck and drove off.

In his total life recall he re-experienced this event from the perspective of the man whose jaw was broken and who had to go through terribly painful surgery and repair of his jaw, which remained wired shut for over six months. The guilt of having hurt someone so badly for such a minor offense was part of the judgment he experienced as the life recall continued. But then he saw this same event from above. He noticed that on the roof of a building near the stoplight, where he assaulted the man, was piled some old building materials, laid out at peculiar angles. The researchers went to Philadelphia and found from police records the street corner where this had occurred. They then located the nearby building and the property manager who said the door to the roof was locked, and no one had been up there since the building was constructed many years ago. He eventually found a key and took them to the roof. There they found the building materials laid out exactly the way John had described it, and it was clear that those objects had been in that position for many, many years.

Recently, as I was talking with a member of one of the churches where I currently serve, I was told of an incident that happened to her when she was a much younger mother of three beautiful children. She had contracted polio and was hospitalized. She could feel herself becoming worse and worse and finally was starting to lose consciousness. She vividly recalls that she could see a long tunnel, with a light at the end, and that she was starting to slip toward that tunnel. But then she saw Jesus sitting in the chair next to her bed. He gently told her that now was not the time for her to leave, that she had three young children who needed her very much. She said that this image of Jesus sitting there with her was so vivid that she can see it just as clearly now as she did that day many years ago.

I have found that to often be a by-product of such experiences, i.e., the associated images are so burned into our memory that they stand out as having been a very special experience. That was the case for her because she drifted away from the tunnel and then back into her hospital room, where, over many months, she finally recovered.

Another NDE story happened to one of my psychotherapy clients who I will name Jane. Jane had lost a child not long after his birth and she had never totally recovered from the grief. Many years later, five years prior to my meeting her, she had cancer surgery during which she died due to an allergic reaction to the anesthesia. She reported that, while dead, she encountered this departed child, heard his laughter, and felt his life and his love. Later she went through eight additional surgeries for reoccurrences of other cancers, and during all eight surgeries she died. Each time she was reunited with her departed son.

When I came to know Jane she was struggling with the decision of whether or not to have another surgery for another reoccurrence of the cancer. She said that because of the previous deaths and of meeting her child each time, she no longer feared death. She felt that death would be preferable to the pain and suffering that followed each surgery, especially since she now knew that death was not the end of life. She decided not to have further surgery and was still living when we moved from the area two years later.

She had learned, as Dr. Ritchie and many others have discovered through NDEs, that death is only a doorway to an ongoing life with

God and perhaps to a choice to return to another life through reincarnation.

Occasionally an unremembered NDE can produce emotional upheaval. About ten years ago a new client, Robert, came to see me because he was having strange dreams that he couldn't understand[57]. The dreams caused him to feel disoriented and quite uncomfortable because he would be floating above his body. I pointed out that we all have unusual dreams and occasionally they are about flying, but he insisted that something just wasn't right. I trust an individual's inner sense about their emotional state so we began a rather thorough gathering of history around these dreams and recent events in his life. As we completed the first session there seemed to be no external causative factor that would produce such recurring dreams of floating above his body.

At our next session Robert said the dreams seemed to be even more vivid. I asked him to relax and drift back to the most recent memory of such a dream. It took him only a moment to be in the dream, as was evident from rapid eye movements under his closed eyelids. I asked him to describe in detail what he was seeing. He said, "I am just floating around above my body. I am anxious, and I want to wake up." I asked him to move away from the emotions for a moment and remember that he was sitting in my office, and that he could return to the image of floating above his body and see what else he could observe.

Robert seemed to relax and then reported, "I am moving up higher, almost to the overhanging limbs of the tree above." I suggested that he stay with that dream for a little longer and see if anything else happened (in the past he always forced himself to awaken at this point because he was so troubled by the floating sensation). He then said, "Wait a minute. My daughter just rode up on her horse and jumped off. She has run to my side and I can now see I'm lying on the ground. She is crying and saying, 'Daddy, wake up, wake up,' and now my wife has just ridden up and is kneeling next to me. Oh

---

[57] As mentioned in the Introduction, when discussing cases from my counseling practice or parishes, some details are always disguised to protect the privacy of the clients or parishioners.

my God, I think I'm dead, but now I'm being drawn back down into my body. And now I'm looking up into my daughter's face. O Lord, my body hurts," and his body became very tense. I assured him that this was just a memory and that taking a few deep breaths he could put the pain aside. He did this and his body visibly relaxed. I then instructed him to bring those memories back into his fully awake and aware state as I counted from one to five.

When Robert was totally awake and conscious he had a great smile on his face. "Now I understand," he said. "Several weeks ago my daughter, my wife and I were participating in a fox hunt in Albemarle County. I had gone down into a ravine and had hit an overhanging branch of a tree because I was watching the ground immediately in front of the horse. I was thrown from the horse and assumed that I had just been knocked unconscious. However, I believe I was actually dead for a few minutes, until my daughter and my wife came to my side and started calling for me to wake up. I feel like it was their love that was drawing me back into my body. I can see now my dreams were actually of me reliving the memories of being dead and floating above my body. Is that unusual?"

I explained to Robert that often when individuals have near-death experiences they hover over their bodies for a while, and occasionally see things that only could be seen from that particular perspective. He said, "Yes, I was seeing the back of my daughter's head, and I could see where she had jumped from her horse, where she dropped her reins ... her horse was trained to be ground hitched just by doing that. I couldn't have seen that from where I was on the ground." This man called me several days later to report that his dreams had disappeared and that he thought he needed no further sessions but would call if he had any future problems. I never heard from him again.

I think this is a clear example of the therapeutic effects of bringing to the conscious mind memories that have been somehow lost or repressed. Dr. Brian Weiss reports on cases from his psychiatric practice where the recall of past-life memories has had similar healing outcomes.

Some of the most convincing NDE stories come from children. Many books have been written on the topic, most of which include numerous accounts from young children. Listed below are a few of those texts.[58]

Serious questions have been asked about whether or not such experiences are "real" or are in conflict with major religions. In my studies of these topics, I do not find that near-death experiences or reincarnation, or encounters with recently departed loved ones, is counter to my Christian faith or theology. Some theologians may disagree.

It is important to remember that these are real experiences that people have had. I think we should first honor the validity of their experiences. We may question their interpretation of what they encountered, but I do not question the honesty of the individuals making the reports, especially when they are young children not yet indoctrinated with adult ideas or religious prejudices. Clearly, the massive number of accounts of near-death experiences, past-life memories, and visits from those recently departed, all point to the reasonable possibility that what can be seen about death and measured by modern science may not be a complete description of the nature of reality. And theologians may be wise to step back from the perspective of their orthodoxy to acknowledge that our God and our universe is truly infinite. We do not know all there is, and the more we learn the broader our horizons become.

J. B. Phillips, a canon of the Anglican Church who died in 1982, once published a book entitled, *Your God is Too Small*. Phillips did

[58] Ian Stevenson, M.D., *Children Who Remember Previous Lives, A question of Reincarnation* , McFarland & Co., 2000.

P.M.H. Atwater, *The New Children and Near-Death Experiences*, Bear & Co., 2003.

Brad Steiger and Sherry Hansen Steiger, *Children of the Light: The Startling and Inspiring Truth About Children's Near-Death Experiences and How They Illumine the Beyond*, Signet Books, 1995.

Dr. Melvin L. Morse, *Closer to the Light: Learning from Near-Death Experiences of Children*, Villard, 1990.

Cherie Sutherland, *Children of the Light: The Near-Death Experiences of Children*, Souvenir Press, 1996.

a good job helping the reader see how we can hold limited or unreal views of God. Just the title of his book can help us acknowledge a much greater view of God. Many theologians have recognized that anything we say about the nature of our infinite God will be inadequate and incomplete. However, I do think we get glimpses of the nature of God in how others have experienced that Infinite Mystery. And part of that mystery appears to be related the nature of His/Her children. Our existence does not seem to be necessarily limited to only this one life. The experiences of thousands of individuals like you and me point to the high probability that life does not end at the death of our physical bodies.

Dr. Werner Von Braun, well known for his part in the US space program, once said he has "essentially scientific" reasons for believing in eternal life. He explained that science has shown that nothing can totally disappear. In nature we do not encounter extinction but transformation. If this "law" applies to the most minute and insignificant parts of the universe, it would seem to make sense that it applies also to the great masterpiece of God's creation--the human soul. That is also my deep faith.

As we come to the conclusion of this brief pilgrimage together I am reminded of an excellent book by Stephen Levine entitled *A Year to Live, How to Live This Year As If It Were Your Last*. When some hear that phrase, "to live this year as if it were your last," they may respond with fear or anxiety. And yet, as I have been with many parishioners who were facing terminal illnesses, they have often come to the realization that they have received a second chance to live more fully than ever before. Some have even commented that their cancer or other illness was the best thing that ever happened to them. They felt that prior to hearing the diagnosis, they had been barely alive ... simply going through the motions of living.

Just knowing that death is near causes us to approach each moment as a precious gift. We wake up to the beauty around us. We begin to see loved ones, to really see them, as never before. One dear friend, who died from cancer a few years ago at age 89, told me she had lived more fully in her last five years than in most of her years prior to that time. She said that food tasted better (except when going through chemo), the air felt fresher, the sound of birds was more precious. She was more awake, and she didn't put up with the "crap" that others tried to shove in her direction.

George Ritchie, mentioned above, has recently been diagnosed with a terminal illness. In talking with him a few weeks ago, he said, "You know, I love life and am in no hurry to leave, but at the same time I am looking forward to moving again into what we call death. Many of my friends and family have already moved across that boundary … so I think it really is going to be a joyous reunion."

What a wonderful way to think about death – "a joyous reunion!"

Just a month ago another member of my parish was facing eminent death. She had been in and out of a coma for several days and her doctors had told her son that she had only about 12 to 24 hours. Her son, who had taken care of his mother for the last few years of her life, was now at her bedside day and night. He says that just a short time before her death, while still seeming to be in a coma, his mother said very clearly, "Beautiful. Oh so beautiful." Granted, such a comment could have been about anything. But both her son and I agree that she was probably then moving into her new heavenly home, although the final death of her physical body would not occur for another two hours. Although this is not what is usually thought of as a "NDE, I do think it could qualify for what I call an "Approaching Death Experience" or "ADE."

Another ADE I remember happened about 30 years ago while I was doing my clinical training as a Chaplain at the University of Virginia Medical Center. One of my assignments had been to the Coronary Care Unit where we encountered quite a few deaths. While I was in that unit one day a nun I worked with came out of the room of a patient who had just died. She said, "I need to talk for a minute." So we got some coffee and sat in the staff room. She said the man who had just died had been in a coma for several days. The MDs had said the patient only had a few hours remaining, so his large family had been called and all had gathered around his bed. The nun was present, off to one side. Just before this patient died, he sat bolt upright in the bed and said, "Hi Mable! Hi Joan! Hi Bob!" Then he fell back in the bed and died. The nun asked the stunned family, "Which of you are Mable and Joan and Bob?" One of them reported, "Mable and Joan were his sisters and Bob was his brother. They all had died many years ago." Again it seems this patient had started making the transition to the next life prior to his physical death.

Over the years I have been with many people at the time of their deaths. And I would say that in the majority of those cases, a short while before physical death occurred, I have seen a clear smile cross a persons face, or some other clear indication that some kind of wonderful transition had begun. Even when individuals have been in pain, often those last moments seem to contain some kind of special joy or peace. That has not been true with every person at the time of death. In some cases death was a battle, a struggle right to the end. For them death seemed to be more of a blessed release than a transition. It often seemed the struggle so dominated the person's conscious or semi-conscious awareness that nothing else could be seen or appreciated. In quite a few other cases the individuals had been in a coma for several days to several weeks. When I would visit near the end, it often seemed that the person's soul was no longer there. As I talked with family members I frequently learned that they could tell me exactly when their loved one had departed, although the body continued to live. They had seen some outward, visible sign of peace or joy or release. I trust these reports. I don't believe they were just imaginings or wishful thinking. I truly believe, death is not something to fear.

In one Gospel account, at the time of his death Jesus told one of the prisoners being crucified with him, "Truly I tell you, today you will be with me in Paradise." (Luke 23:43) According to this report, it seems clear that Jesus knew that death is not the end of life but simply a doorway into the next adventure.

I believe our studies of past life recall, NDEs, ADEs, and the rich variety of spiritual experiences discussed in this book also helps reduce our fear of death. And the absence of such fear helps us run the race of life that is set before us with as much joy as possible. When we are free from the fear of death then all of life truly becomes a joyous celebration.

Over the years I have collected quotations that reflect a similar awareness. There are also many excellent collections of quotes (see Bibliography). I recommend pasting quotes that have special meaning for you on your bathroom mirror, above your computer screen, on the wall above your desk, on the dashboard of your car, etc. Place them anywhere they can serve as reminders of the importance of living every moment with as much joy as possible. We must remember that we are not dead until we die, and even then we have life.

"Be glad of life because it gives you the chance to love, and to work, and to play and to look up at the stars." *Henry Van Dyke*

"I like living. I have sometimes been wildly, despairingly, acutely miserable, racked with sorrow, but through it all I still know quite certainly that just to be alive is a grand thing." *Agatha Christie*

"The mere sense of living is joy enough." *Emily Dickinson*

"I went to the woods because I wished to live deliberately, to front only the essential facts of life, and see if I could not learn what it had to teach, and not, when I came to die, discover that I had not lived. . . . I wanted to live deep and suck out all the marrow of life...." *Henry David Thoreau*

"This is the day which the Lord has made. Let us rejoice and be glad in it." *Psalm 118:24*

∞

I pray that you will dream some impossible dreams, suck out the marrow of life, and, in the joy of living each moment, that you truly experience *limitless living*.

May God bless you with Peace and hold you in Love. Amen.

Appendix A
TESTING SPIRITUAL GUIDANCE

The following procedures provide a way to test the spiritual guidance, directions, hunches or nudges we receive, whether it be from dreams, guidance from the Holy Spirit, conversations with Guardian Angels and Ascended Masters, automatic writing or typing, or however else we might feel we have received information or guidance from outside of what might be called "normal" or "ordinary" means.

EXERCISE A.1 – Testing Spiritual Guidance
The Three Light Test

I call this activity the "Three Light Test." There is a port off the Mediterranean Sea that has a small channel into the harbor. In the harbor are three lights set on posts, forming a line toward the open channel. When a boat starts to enter the channel, it must line up the three lights so they look like one light. If any one light is not in line, the proper channel is not being followed.

Likewise when we are testing guidance we may apply a kind of "Three Light Test" that can lead us into a peaceful harbor of spiritual truth.

1) **Test One – Prior Revelation**

The **first light** in the line is prior revelation from God. For Christians that of course is our Bible and the historical traditions of our faith. Those of other religions or faiths may look to their Holy Scriptures and find the collected wisdom of their faith. Study the history of your religion and the ongoing revelation from God. Is your guidance in accordance with this previous revelation, as best you can determine? This is not always an easy question to answer. Some biblical scholars have said that you can justify almost any human act if you take the right piece of scripture out of context. A good case in point is how, for many years, segregation was biblically justified. Likewise, certain factions of extreme Muslim terrorists claim their murders are done in the name of Allah, which other Muslims say is actually abhorrent to their faith.

Nevertheless, I have found that God will never tell us, and our Guardian Angels will never lead us, to break the laws of God. For example, God will not tell us to commit adultery, or to steal, or to kill.

However, in this imperfect world and as imperfect people, we must sometimes make decisions that seem contrary to God's laws. There have been times when I have had to help individuals choose an action that was the lesser evil, e.g., whether or not to stop life support of a terminally ill loved one when it only furthers suffering and prolongs the natural dying process. Death is not always the worst that can happen in this life. Also, members of my parishes have served in the military, police, and other law enforcement agencies, where it is sometimes necessary to take the life of another human being -- which seems to be contrary to the previous revelation of God, but they may be defending the people of this nation. I think of these courageous souls as peacekeepers, individuals who follow the example of Christ who offered his life so others could have life.

So we cannot blindly read the holy scriptures of our faith and assume that a literal reading is always adequate. We must look at the context of the writings, the purpose of the writer and the nature of the audience for those writings, and the religious traditions that have grown up through the history of that faith community. All of this comes from serious scholarship, not blind obedience.

I have heard it said that religious doctrine is analogous to a three-legged stool, the three legs being: 1) Holy Scripture; 2) Church tradition or history; and, 3) human intelligence. All legs of that stool must be equal if our doctrine is to be reasonable, balanced, and faithful to our Creator.

I do believe that guidance from God or through our Guardian Angels will always help us keep the great commandments: to love the Lord our God with all our heart, with all our soul, with all our mind, with all our strength, and our neighbor as ourselves.

When we receive assistance or direction, we need to ask ourselves whether or not that guidance will further love for God, love for others, and love for ourselves.

If our guidance is in accordance with this law of love then it will usually fit one of the following ideals: a) it will increase our physical, spiritual or emotional health or that of others; b) it will benefit humankind; c) it will increase joy in our lives or in the lives of others; d) it will increase our awareness of God; or, e) it will increase love, hope, forgiveness and reconciliation in our lives, in our community or in our world. Love will help bring about these things.

I believe you can trust this higher law of love.

2) **Test Two – Check with a spiritual friend or guide**

If you run into a problem here, trying to interpret this law of love in a specific situation, I suggest you go to your priest, pastor, rabbi, or other spiritual guide for assistance, which is the **second light** in the "Three Light Test." Visit with a spiritual friend or guide who is also trying to listen to the guidance of God. Share what has been received and ask for help in "testing" it.

My wife is especially gifted in this area and has frequently helped me decide whether or not what I receive is of God. I sometimes talk with an outside spiritual director who is actively exploring these spiritual dimensions and who has had more experience. In his book on spiritual direction, *Soul Friend*, Kenneth Leech states that the main tasks of a director are: a) to help an individual move toward self-knowledge; b) to assist a person in finding self-acceptance; c) to further the detachment of a person from his/her own ego; and, d) to help one find the will of God. Such a soul friend can be a vital part of our spiritual growth. Such a friend can also help us determine if we are moving away from common sense and rational thought. Granted, some experiences of "non-ordinary reality" may seem very irrational. Still, we must be able to return to "ordinary reality" so we can try to communicate our experiences to others using the symbols of our language, music, art, poetry, liturgy and stories.

I remember when I was being evaluated by a Bishop's committee to determine whether or not I should be admitted as a candidate for Holy Orders, I was asked by a committee member, "Have you ever had any unusual spiritual experiences?" When I replied that I had, I was then asked, "Have you discussed these with your priest and/or spiritual director?" I replied in the affirmative, and that they had not believed I was delusional or disordered. That was sufficient.

We know, from the evidence of recent events such as the tragedies of 9/11 and the religious fanaticism that leads terrorists to commit suicide bombings in the name of their faith, that our minds are quite capable of deceiving us. Never forget that fact.

3) **Test Three- Inner Feeling or Intuition**

So finally, we come to the **third light** of our test that is our inner, gut feeling. How does the guidance make us feel? Is there a sense of light and joy and peace? If so it <u>may</u> be of the Holy Spirit, it <u>may</u> be authentic information or genuine conversations with non-ordinary reality. If there is a feeling of heaviness or darkness, or if there is a compulsive urgency about the guidance or information, e.g., "this MUST be done right now," then it is probably not of God, and/or is not for our highest good. I have felt nausea in the pit of my stomach when something is not right (what I call a "spiritual check"), although logically everything seemed just fine.

If the guidance received is truly of God, or is allowable within the will of Divine Grace, there will be an inner peace about it. There will be a feeling of "knowing" what is right or correct. In my account in Chapter Nine, when I was in conversation with what I understood to be Ascended Masters, I "knew" on an inner, intuitive level that this was genuine and was not forbidden by God.

One of the final words the Christ left with his disciples was, "Peace I give to you, my peace I leave with you." There must be that sense of peace about spiritual guidance. If there is no peace, then something is wrong.

However, please do not confuse peace with an absence of apprehension or concern. I am often aware of heightened concern prior to delivering a sermon, even after almost thirty years of preaching. I believe such an increase in focus and attention is valuable if I am to be most effective as a preacher. I think preaching is a sacramental element in our worship, i.e., it is a moment in which the Living Word of God is encountered. I want to be faithful to the message I feel called to deliver. That gets my attention, which feels somewhat like anxiety, but there is also a deep sense of peace in my soul as I start to preach. Actors and surgeons also speak of that heightened alertness. Anyone striving to do his or her best may feel some of that concern, which is quite different from the absence of peace. We can be concerned and, at the same time, feel great peace.

So, as we are testing spiritual guidance, we can usually be assured that what we have received MAY be from God or from a spiritual source that is working for our highest good if those three lights are lined up and in agreement with: **1) prior revelation from God; 2) a spiritual friend or guide; and, 3) our inner feeling or intuitive awareness**.

I intentionally use the word "MAY" because in all this, especially in trying to find and follow spiritual truth, we need to remain humble and recognize that we are not the final judge of truth, i.e., we may be wrong.

Often I am asked, "Is that a true experience, i.e., did it really happen?" As mentioned in Chapter One, when dealing with spiritual matters, I think that is a question that cannot be objectively answered by scientific method or double-blind studies. However, we can ask, "Does that experience convey truth?" That is the heart of the matter. Do our spiritual explorations and the spiritual guidance we receive bring us closer to truth, open us further to the truth of God's infinite mystery flowing through us and through others around us? These spiritual tests help us measure such truth.

RELAXATION AND CENTERING

Do not practice these exercises while driving a car or operating dangerous equipment! Do not use these exercises if you have been diagnosed as having a Dissociative Disorder, Borderline Personality Disorder, Schizophrenia, or have psychotic episodes, or hallucinations. If you have any other emotional disorder, talk with your mental health professional before using these exercises. Also, please see WARNING at the end of this Appendix for when you complete your time of meditation.

EXERCISE B.1 – A Detailed Full Body Relaxation

1) Prepare your space. Take the phone off the hook, move pets out of the room, close the shades if you like it dark, be sure your clothing is loose and there are no binding points. I also like to have a clean, dry wash cloth to place over my eyes to further block out light – unless I am doing a session at my computer session or sitting in a chair. If you have contact lenses, use a wetting solution before and after the session. I have a kneeling bench, which I find very useful for Buddhist types of meditation, and a prayer cushion, which is quite comfortable for longer, cross-legged meditations. The prayer cushion I purchased from Heritage Book Store in Virginia Beach (there are two sizes, I prefer the larger, Mary Ann likes the smaller).

2) Lie down or sit and to be comfortable. I like to have gentle, meditative music softly playing in the background. My favorites are: "Silver Wings" or "The Fairy Ring" by Mike Rowland; "Earth Spirit" by Carlos Nakai, which is more Native American; and "Music for Zen Meditation" by Scott, Yuize, and Yamamoto. There are many, many other excellent cassettes, CDs, and now music for iPods and MP3 players, so find something that you like.

3) Once you have prepared your space and begun to quiet your mind, begin to focus on your body. Notice your feet; move them around and let them relax. Move up to your calves and then your thighs; tighten each muscle group and let them relax. Move your attention to your buttocks and pelvis; tighten muscles and then let

them relax. Focus on your abdomen; tighten and relax. Focus on your chest and back; tighten and relax. Focus on your shoulders, neck and down one arm and then the other. Shoulders and necks are often places of collected tension. Imagine tension moving out of your neck, across your shoulders, down your arms -- like a heavy molasses that finally drips off the end of your fingers. You may feel a throbbing or tingling sensation in your hands as the relaxation increases. Now move that relaxation up to the back of your neck and up over your scalp, and let the muscles in your scalp relax. Move to your face and tighten, squeeze your lips then open your mouth into a great yawn and allow your face to totally relax. Now feel the warmth of relaxation that has spread over your entire body; breathe in that relaxation, soak up the warmth.

4) In this state of relaxation, take a moment to imagine that a pure white light is shining down on you (I think of it as the Light of Christ). Allow this Light to flow around your entire body. Sometimes I imagine stepping back from my body so that I can observe the Light totally surrounding me. Be in this cocoon of this pure, white, protective Light. You are now centered and protected, ready to begin your session of meditation, healing, channeling, prayer, etc.

EXERCISE B.2 – A Quick Full Body Relaxation

1) Prepare your space as above.

2) Focus on your right arm. Imagine that the warm light of the sun is shining down on this arm. Feel the warmth penetrating through your skin, into the muscles and down to the bone. Take a deep breath, and as you breath in through your nose tighten the muscles in this right arm; hold your breath for the count of four, open your mouth and breath out as you relax these muscles.

3) Focus on your left arm and repeat the above procedure.

4) Focus on your right leg and repeat.

5) Focus on your left leg and repeat.

6) Focus on your abdomen and repeat.

7) Focus on your chest and repeat.

8) Now imagine that White Light is shining down through your head, down into your heart and then spreading out through all your body, so that you are gently filled with pure, white Light. Let this white, cleansing Light move into every corner of your body, until you feel filled with this Light. Finally, be so filled with Light that it spills out around your body (your cup overflows), and your body becomes surrounded by this protective Light.

9) You are now calm, centered, surrounded by protection and ready to begin.

EXERCISE B.3: A Chakra Meditation

One of the most powerful centering exercises I have discovered is the Chakra Meditation outlined in Chapter 6. This technique includes some elements of the relaxation and centering techniques above. For a full discussion of the location and colors of the chakras, see Chapter Six. I duplicate the Chakra Meditation here for your quick reference.

Get comfortable, either sitting or lying. Use a relaxation or centering exercise found above (B.1 or B.2).

1) Now, focus your attention on the **1st or Root Chakra** and become aware of its red color. I imagine the red color of a fire truck. Allow your consciousness to move from that Root Chakra down through the surface below you, down into the earth, down through the dirt, down through the rocks and deeper bedrock, down to the red-hot center of the earth. Now bring up some of that clear, pure red, energy of the earth along the same path to your Root Chakra, energizing that 1st chakra. Take some of that swirling, rotating energy out to an area about one foot below your feet and let it begin to surround your body, as though surrounded by a red cocoon or giant egg with a thin shell of red energy. Be sure the red energy totally surrounds your body.

2) Now bring your attention back to the Root Chakra and the red ball of energy. Allow some of that energy to move upward in a spiraling movement up to the **Sacral, 2nd, or Sexual Chakra**, where the red changes into a beautiful orange. I think of the color of

a fresh Florida or California orange. This time allow some of the energy to emerge from your body just below your umbilicus and let it move out in front of you to the red cocoon of energy, but now let the orange energy form a second layer on top of the red energy, again totally surrounding your body.

3) Now return to the 2nd chakra, and allow some of that orange energy to spiral upward to the **3rd or Solar Plexus Chakra**, with the energy taking on the color of yellow. I imagine the color of a fresh lemon. Increase the energy of this chakra and permit some of the yellow energy to move out in front of your body to cover the orange layer of the cocoon with a layer of yellow energy.

4) Return to the 3rd chakra and bring some of the yellow energy spiraling upward to the **4th or Heart Chakra**, with the color becoming green. I think of rich green leaves on a tree. Green is a healing color, so now surround your heart with healing green and let the green 3rd chakra become fully energized. Now take some of that green energy out through the front of your chest to the cocoon of energy, covering over the yellow layer of energy with this green energy, totally surrounding your body with the green.

5) Return to the Heart Chakra and allow some of the green energy to spiral upward to the **5th or Throat Chakra**, with the color becoming blue. Think of deep sky blue on a clear day. Increase the blue energy of the Throat Chakra, and take some of that energy out to the energy cocoon, totally covering over the surface with a layer of blue energy.

6) Return to the Throat Chakra and allow some of the blue energy to move deep into the center of the brain to the area of the pituitary gland and the **6th or Third Eye Chakra** which is the color of indigo. Mix pure blue and red to arrive at a beautiful, rich indigo color. Increase the energy of the Third Eye Chakra and then take some of the indigo energy out through the forehead at the place of the third eye and move to the energy cocoon, covering it over with another layer of energy, this time colored indigo.

7) Now return your consciousness to the Third Eye Chakra and the ball of indigo energy there. Allow some of that energy to spiral up to the **7th or Crown Chakra** at the top of your head, with the color

becoming purple or violet. I think of the color of a Bishop's shirt or a purple pansy. Here I sense my connection to the Infinite Mystery, and I allow the purple energy to move up, over my head, to the surface of the energy cocoon, now covering the surface with purple energy. As this energy spreads over the surface it begins a process of blending all the colors so the cocoon now becomes a vibrating surface of pure white energy.

8) This opens up my Crown Chakra to a **Transpersonal Chakra** or energy center about a foot above my head. I think of this as the Light of Christ, which now begins to flow over the surface of the energy cocoon and pour into my body, filling my entire body and all of its energy systems with this pure white, cleansing Light of Christ. This pure white energy now streams through my body and down into the earth, with my body forming a connecting point between heaven and earth and the energy flowing back and forth between these two polarities, cleansing, healing, renewing, energizing my chakras, my body, my soul, my entire being. I am now completely filled with and surrounded by the Light of Christ. Sometimes the flow of energy is so intense that there is a trembling as though electricity were moving through my body.

As I complete this meditation, I feel that "my cup is overflowing" with the Light, Energy, Love and Healing of Christ. I stay in this cocoon of flowing, loving energy until I feel it is time for the meditation to come to an end. Sometimes this takes on a short while, just a few minutes, and sometimes I remain in this wonderful, healing space for 30 minutes or more.

9) Finally, I check each of the chakras to be sure each color is clear, rich, and vibrant. For me that means the chakras are not blocked but open, and the energies of my body and soul are now flowing freely.

10) I next thank the presence of Christ and my Higher Self for this time of healing. I can then move into another spiritual exploration or meditation, or I can gradually move back into ordinary reality, usually by slowing counting from one to five. When I get to five I take a deep, cleansing breath, briefly recalling the colors of energy flowing through my body, and open my eyes, back in my day-to-day world.

After you have done this meditation a few times you can abbreviate it by not building the cocoon of energy. Just go through the process of re-energizing the chakras with energy from the earth and then moving quickly up through each chakra, ending with the energy of the Light of Christ flowing from above and back down through your body and each of the chakras.

Occasionally I alter my centering process by taking just a moment to focus my consciousness on each of the chakras and their colors. By the time I have gotten to the Crown Chakra I am centered … in my space, in my body, and in my soul.

IMPORTANT WARNING

Following a heart attack in 1989 and while still in the hospital, I frequently stayed in this kind of healing space for hours at a time, inviting the peace, energy and light of God to promote my physical and spiritual healing. I remember a nurse once came in to take my blood pressure. She assumed I was sleeping and went ahead to quietly surround my arm with the cuff and get the vital data she needed for her chart. Suddenly she dashed from the room and in a few moments the chief resident was shaking me and saying, "Father Kinser, Father Kinser, wake up! Your blood pressure has dropped quite low." I explained that I was deep in meditation and that often, while in such a deep state, a person's blood pressure drops.

That is why I issue this warning with these meditations: *Do not stand up quickly after coming back into ordinary space and time. You can conclude by slowly counting 1 to 5. When you get to 5, move your arms and legs. Take a few deep breaths, and stretch a little before standing or continuing with your day's activities.*

Note: Both Dr. Herbert Benson and Dr. Jon Kabat-Zinn have found that after several months of daily relaxation and meditation exercises, some people who are taking blood pressure medications may be able to reduce the dosage of medication. However, *do not change any medications without first talking with your physician, nurse practitioner, or other health care provider!*

Appendix C
A CONTEMPLATIVE EXERCISE

EXERCISE C.1 - Praying The Scriptures

This exercise follows the pattern of "Lectio Devina" (Latin: "divine reading").

We read (lectio), under the eye of God (meditatio), until the heart is touched (oratio), and leaps into flame (contemplatio).

1) **Enter into God's presence – open to Grace**

> Relax and center yourself before God
>
> Perform a reverent act, e.g., sign self with +
>
> Be conscious of your human condition (thoughts, concerns, feelings, needs)
>
> Ask God for the Grace needed to receive God's Word
>
> Open yourself to this Grace and imagine God providing it for you

2) **Read the Scripture – which you have selected for this contemplative exercise; "lectio"**

> Read the lesson (perhaps from two or three translations, e.g., New Revised Standard Version, Jerusalem, New International Version; I usually do not recommend the King James Version because of the presence of archaic words which can be misleading and in view of the fact that Biblical archeology has discovered manuscripts more ancient than those used to produce the KJV.)
>
> Be quiet, be attentive, reflect (perhaps check a commentary, e.g., Jerome[59])

---

[59] My favorite version is: *The New Jerome Biblical Commentary* by Raymond E. Brown, et al, Editors, (Prentice Hall; Rei Sub edition, September 1989).

Read the lesson a second time, more slowly, as God's own word for YOU

3) Engage the Scripture

Be present to God's word for you; "meditatio" (Ignatius called this "contemplation")

Imagine the event, the action, the persons, the words or thoughts

Bring your image into the present

Enter into the image and involve your self

Experience it as happening now

Converse with God about your experience; "oratio" (Ignatius: "meditation")

Go before God as Holy Trinity, as a community, as a small group

Engage in a conversation with God as a friend attempting to gain clarity on the implications for your life; "so what?"

Ask for Grace; open your heart to be touched by God

"contemplatio"

Open yourself and imagine God providing this Grace for you; give in to God; allow God to do it for you; leap into the flame of God's Grace

Thank God for your time together

Perform a reverent act, which reflects your deep gratitude to God; when St. Dominic read Holy Scripture (especially the Gospels) alone in this solitary fashion he used to venerate it, then bow to it and kiss it.

4) Reflect (journaling)

Record the passage prayed or used in this contemplative exercise

Where did you dwell?

What was your experience?

Where was God working?

What insights did you receive? What implications emerged; how did you respond? Did you receive the Grace requested? (Why or why not?)

For much more extensive and rigorous contemplative exercises you may want to work with *The Spiritual Exercises of St. Ignatius of Loyola*, trans. Father Elder Mullan, S.J. (New York: P.J. Kenedy & Sons, 1914).

An Adobe Reader version is available at:

www.jesuit.org/images/docs/915dWg.pdf.

ANNOTATED BIBLIOGRAPHY

Healing and Health, Mind-Body Healing (see also T'ai Chi section)

Banks, John Gayner. *Healing Everywhere, A Book of Healing Mission Talks*. St. Luke's Press, 1961.

Benson, M.D., Herbert. *The Mind/Body Effect: How Behavioral Medicine Can Show You the Way to Better Health*. New York: Simon & Schuster, 1979.

Benson, M.D., Herbert. *Timeless Healing, The Power and Biology of Belief*. New York: Scribner, 1996.

Chopra, M.D., Deepak. *Healing the Heart, A Spiritual Approach to Reversing Coronary Artery Disease*. New York: Harmony Books, 1998.

Chopra, M.D., Deepak. *Perfect Health, The Complete Mind/Body Guide*. New York: Harmony Books, 1991.

Chopra, M.D., Deepak. *Quantum Healing, Exploring the Frontiers of Mind/Body Medicine*. New York: Bantam Books, 1989.

Cousins, Norman. *Anatomy of an Illness*. New York: Norton, 1979.

Cousins, Norman. *The Healing Heart, Antidotes to Panic and Helplessness*. New York: W. W. Norton & Company, 1983.

Goldbrunner, Josef. *Holiness Is Wholeness*. New York: Pantheon, 1955.

Goldbrunner, Josef. *Holiness Is Wholeness and Other Essays*. University of Notre Dame Press, 1964.

Kabat-Zinn, Jon. *Full Catastrophe Living, Using the Wisdom of Your Body and Mind to Face Stress, Pain, and Illness*. New York: Delta Book, 1990.

Kavahagh, M.D., Terence. *The Healthy Heart Program, The successful, medically-tested program that will improve your cardiovascular fitness*. Key Porter Books, 1985.

Klein, Allen. *The Healing Power of Humor, Techniques for Getting through Loss, Setbacks, Upsets, Disappointments, Difficulties, Trials, Tribulations, and All That Not-So-Funny Stuff*. New York: Penguin Putnam, 1989.

Lapsley, James N. *Salvation and Health, The Interlocking Processes of Life*. Philadelphia: The Westminster Press, 1972. Based on Lapsley's study of the meaning of the words in the New Testament for "salvation," "to heal," "to cure," and "to save," the argument can be made that "salvation" in a Biblical sense can be understood not just as "being saved" in terms of eternal life but also "finding healing and wholeness" in terms of life here and now. Josef Goldbrunner made a virtual equation of salvation and health in his book *Holiness Is Wholeness*.

Levine, Stephen. *A Year to Live, How to Live This Year As If It Were Your Last*. New York: Bell Tower, 1997.

McLanahan, M.D., Sandra A., and McLanahan, M.D., David J. *Surgery and its Alternatives, How to Make the Right Choices for Your Health.* New York: Twin Stream Books, 2002.

Morse, M.D., Melvin, with Perry, Paul. *Where God Lives, The Science of the Paranormal and How Our Brains are Linked to the Universe.* New York: Cliff Street Books, 2000.

Orloff, M.D., Judith. *Guide to Intuitive Healing, 5 Steps to Physical, Emotional, and Sexual Wellness.* New York: Three Rivers Press, 2000.

Ornish, M.D., Dean. *Stress, Diet and Your Heart.* New York: Holt, Rinehart and Winston, 1982.

Rossi, Ernest Lawrence. *The Psychobiology of Mind-Body Healing.* New York: W. W. Norton & Company, Inc., 1986.

Siegel, M.D., Bernie S. *Love, Medicine & Miracles, Lessons Learned About Self-healing from a Surgeon's experience with Exceptional Patients.* New York: Harper and Row, Publishers, 1986.

Siegel, M.D., Bernie S. *Peace, Love & Healing, Bodymind Communication & the Path to Self-Healing: an Exploration.* New York: Harper and Row, Publishers, 1989.

Simonton, O. C. *Getting Well Again.* Los Angeles: J. P. Tarcher, 1978.

Smith, A. *Powers of the Mind.* New York: Random House, 1975.

Stotland, E. *The Psychology of Hope.* San Francisco: Jossey-Bass, 1969.

Tate, David A. *Health Hope Healing.* New York: M. Evans and Company, 1989.

Weil, M.D., Andrew. *Eight Weeks to Optimum Health, A Proven Program for Taking Full Advantage of Your Body's Natural Healing Power.* New York: Alfred A. Knopf, 1997.

Weil, M.D., Andrew. *Natural Health, Natural Medicine, A Comprehensive Manual for Wellness and Self-care.* New York: Houghton Mifflin Company, 1998.

Guardian Angels and Spirit Guides

Amaa-ra, Solara Antara. *Invoking Your Celestial Guardians.* Charlottesville: Star-Borne Unlimited, 1986.

Maclean, Dorothy. *To Hear the Angels Sing.* Issaquah, Washington: Morningtown Press, 1980.

Taylor, Terry Lynn. *Messengers of Light, The Angels' Guide to Spiritual Growth.* Tiburon, California: H. J. Kramer Inc., 1989.

Meditation, Prayer, Chakras, and Mindfulness

Arya, Pandit Usharbudh. *Mantra & Meditation*. Honesdale, PA: Himalayan International Institute of Yoga Science and Philosophy, 1981.

Benson, Robert. *Living Prayer*. New York: Jeremy P. Tarchaer/Putnam, 1998.

Bloom, Archbishop Anthony. *Living Prayer*. Springfield, Ill: Templegate, Publishers, 1966.

Coburn, John B. *A Life to Live – A Way to Pray*. New York: The Seabury Press, 1973.

Fontana, David. *The Elements of Meditation*. Massachusetts, Rockport: Element, Inc., 1991.

Goleman, Daniel. *The Meditative Mind, The Varieties of Meditative Experience*. Los Angeles: Jeremy P. Tarcher, Inc., 1998 (Distributed by St. Martin's Press, New York).

Hanh, Thich Nhat. *Being Peace*. Berkeley: Parallax Press, 1987.

Hanh, Thich Nhat. *The Miracle of Mindfulness, A Manual on Meditation*. Boston, Beacon Press, 1987 (revised).

Johnston, William. *Silent Music, The Science of Meditation*. New York: Harper & Row, Publishers, 1975.

Kabat-Zinn, Jon. *Wherever You Go There You Are, Mindfulness Meditation in Everyday Life*. New York: Hyperion, 1994.

Kelsey, Morton T. *The Other Side of Silence, A Guide to Christian Meditation*. New York: Paulist Press, 1976.

Lansdowne, Zachary F. *The Chakras & Esoteric Healing*. York Beach, Maine: Samuel Weiser, Inc., 1986.

Leadbeater, C. W. *The Chakras*. Wheaton, Ill.: The Theosophical Publishing House, 1927.

Maclaine, Shirley. *Going Within, A Guide for Inner Transformation*. New York: Bantam Books, 1989.

Merton, Thomas, *The Wisdom of the Desert*. New York: A New Directions Paperbook, 1960.

Nouwen, Henri J. M. *Making All Things New, An Invitation to the Spiritual Life*. San Francisco: Harper & Row, Publishers, 1981.

Nouwen, Henri J. M. *The Way of the Heart*. New York: Ballantine Books, 1981.

Nouwen, Henri J. M. *With Open Hands, Bring Prayer into Your Life*. New York: Ballantine Books, Ave Maria Press, 1972.

Oates, Wayne E. *Nurturing Silence in a Noisy Heart*. Garden City, NY: Doubleday & Company, Inc., 1979.

Peterson, Richard. *Creative Meditation: Inner Peace Is Practically Yours*. Virginia Beach, A.R.E. Press, 1990.

Rama, Swami, et. alle. *Meditation in Christianity*. Honesdale: The Himalayan International Institute of Yoga Science and Philosophy, 1983.

Savary, Lous M. and Berne, Patricia H. *Prayerways*. San Francisco: Harper & Row, Publishers, 1980.

Tugwell, Simon. *Prayer, Living With God*. Springfield: Templegate Publishers,1975.

Near-Death Experiences, Reincarnation, Past Life Recall

Church, W. H. *Edgar Cayce's Story of the Soul*. Virginia Beach: A.R.E. Press, 1989.

Eadie, Betty J. *Embraced by the Light*. New York: Bantam Books, 1994.

Brennan, J. H. *Discover Your Past Lives, A Practical Course*. New York: Sterling Publishing Co., Inc. 1994.

Gershom, Rabbi Yonassan. *Beyond the Ashes, Cases of Reincarnation from the Holocaust*. Virginia Beach: A.R.E. Press, 1992.

Howe, Jr., Quincy. *Reincarnation for the Christian*. Wheaton, Ill: The Theosophical Publishing House, 1974.

Lorimer, David. *Whole in One, The Near-death Experience and the Ethic of Interconnectedness*. London: The Penguin Group, 1990.

MacGregor, Geddes. *Reincarnation in Christianity, A New Vision of the Role of Rebirth in Christian Thought*. Wheaton, Ill: The Theosophical Publishing House, 1978.

McClain, Florence Wagner. *A Practical Guide to Past Life Regression*. St. Pau: Llewellyn Publications, 1987.

Moody, Jr., M.D., Raymond A. *Coming Back, A Psychiatrist Explores Past-Life Journeys*. New York: Bantam Books, 1991.

Moody, Jr., M.D., Raymond A. *Life After Life: The Investigation of a Phenomenon –Survival of Bodily Death*. San Francisco: Harper & Row, Publishers, 2nd Edition, 2001.

Moody M.D., Raymond, with Perry, Paul. *Reunions, Visionary Encounters with Departed Loved Ones*. New York: Ivy Books, 1993.

Praagh, James Van. *Talking to Heaven, A Medium's Message of Life After Death*. New York: Penguin Putnam Inc., Dutton, 1997.

Ritchie, M.D., George G. with Sherrill, Elizabeth. *Return from Tomorrow*. Revell, 1988.

Ritchie, M.D., George G. *Ordered to Return: My Life After Dying*. Charlottesville: Hampton Roads Publishing Company, 1998.

Ritchie, M.D., George G. *The Place We Call Home, Exploring the Soul's Existence After Death*. Virginia Beach: A.R.E. Press, 2000.

Shroder, Tom. *Old Souls, The Scientific Evidence for Past Lives*. New York: Simon & Schuster, 1999.

Sparrow, Lynn Elwell. *Reincarnation, Claiming Your Past, Creating Your Future*. San Francisco: Harper & Row, Publishers, 1988.

Stevenson, M.D., Ian. *Twenty Cases Suggestive of Reincarnation, 2nd Edition, Revised and Enlarged*. Charlottesville: University Press of Virginia, 1974

Weiss, M.D., Brian L. *Many Lives, Many Masters*. New York: Simon & Schuster Inc., 1988.

Weiss, M.D., Brian L. *Messages from the Masters, Tapping into the Power of Love*. New Work: Warner Books, Inc., 2000.

Weiss, M.D., Brian L. *Only Love is Real, A Story of Soulmates Reunited*. New York: Warner Books, Inc., 1996.

Weiss, M.D., Brian L. *Through Time Into Healing*. New York: Simon & Schuster Inc., A Fireside Book, 1993.

Woolger, Roger J. *Other Lives, Other Selves, A Jungian Psychotherapist Discovers Past Lives*. New York: Bantam Books, 1988.

Native American Spirituality

Andrews, Lynn V. *The Woman of Wyrrd*. San Francisco: Harper Collins Publishers, 1990.

Brown, Jr., Tom. *Awakening Spirits*. Berkley Trade, April 1, 1994.

Brown, Jr., Tom. *Grandfather*. Berkley Trade, Reissue, 2001.

Brown, Jr., Tom. *The Tracker*. New York: Penguin Group, 1978.

Brown, Jr., Tom. *The Vision*. New York: Berkley Publishing Group, 1988.

Brown, Jr., Tom. *The Quest: One Man's Search for Peace, Insight, and Healing in an Endangered World*. New York: Berkley Publishing Group, 1998.

Freesoul, John Redtail. *Breath of the Invisible, The Way of the Pipe*. Wheaton, Ill.: The Theosophical Publishing House, 1986.

Neihardt, John G. *Black Elk Speaks, Being the Life Story of a Holy Man of the Oglala Sioux*. Lincoln, Nebraska: University of Nebraska Press, 1961.

Sun Bear, Wabun, and Weinstock, Barry. *The Path of Power*. New York: Prentice Hall Press, 1987.

Quote Collections

Applewhite, Ashton, Evans, III, William R., Frothingham, Andrew, Eds.. *And I Quote*. New York: St. Martin's Press, 1992.

Bartlett, John, Ed.. *Familiar Quotations*. Boston: Little, Brown and Company, 1955.

Cook, John, Ed.. *The Book of Positive Quotations*. New York: Gramercy Books, 1999.

Edwards, Drew, Ed.. *Affirmation & Inspiration, Words of Strength*. Malaysia: Compass Labs, 2001.

Henry, Lewis C., Ed.. *Best Quotations for all Occasions*, Revised. Greenwich, Conn.: Fawcett Publications, Inc., 1966.

Martindale, Wayne, and Root, Jerry, Eds.. *The Quotable Lewis*. Wheaton, Illinois: Tyndale House Publishers, Inc., 1989.

T'ai Chi

Chuen, Master Lam Kam. *Step-by-Step Tai Chi*. New York: Simon & Schuster Inc., 1994.

Galante, Lawrence. *Tai Chi, The Supreme Ultimate*. York Beach, Maine: Samuel Weiser, 1981.

Huang, Al Chung-liang. *Embrace Tiger, Return to Mountain, the essence of T'ai Chi*. Moab, Utah: Real People Press, 1973.

Jahnke, Roger, O.M.D. *The Healing Promise of Qi, Creating Extraordinary Wellness Through Qigong and Tai Chi*. New York: McGraw-Hill, 2002.

Kauz, Herman. *Tai Chi Handbook, exercise, meditation and self-defense*. Garden City, New York: Doubleday & Company, Inc., 1974.

Lee, Douglas. *Tai Chi Chuan, the philosophy of yin and yang and its application*. Burbank, California: Ohara Publications, Inc., 1976.

Liu, Da. *Taoist Health Exercise Book*. New York: The Putnam Publishing Group, 1974.

Pang, Chia Siew, and Hock, Goh Ewe. *Tai Chi, Ten Minutes to Health*. Reno, Nevada: CRCS Publications, 1985.

Tohei, Koichi. *Book of Ki: Co-ordinating Mind and Body in Daily Life*. Tokyo: Japan Publications, Inc., 1976.

The Soul, Death and Other Special Books

Hillman, James. *The Soul's Code, In Search of Character and Calling*. New

York: Random House, 1996.

Johnson, L.D. *The Morning After Death*. Nashville: Broadman Press, 1978.

Kubler-Ross, Elisabeth. *Death, The Final Stage of Growth*. Englewood cliffs, NJ: Prentice-Hall, Inc., 1975.

Kubler-Ross, Elisabeth. *On Death and Dying, What the dying have to teach doctors, nurses, clergy and their own families*. New York: MacMillian Publishing Co., Inc: 1969.

Montgomery, Ruth. *A Search for the Truth*. New York: Fawcett Crest, 1966.

Rinpoche, Sogyal. *The Tibetan Book of Living and Dying*. San Francisco: Harper Collins Publishers, 1992.

Westerhoff III, John H. *Will Our Children Have Faith?*. New York: Seabury Press, 1976. I strongly recommend any and all of John Westerhoff's books. John was a professor at Duke University and is an Episcopal priest.

Zukav, Gary. *The Seat of the Soul*. New York: Simon and Schuster, 1989.

Zukav, Gary. *Soul Stories*. New York: Simon and Schuster, 2000.

Zukav, Gary, and Francis, Linda. *The Heart of the Soul*. New York: Simon and Schuster, 2002.

Theory, Theology, Hypnotherapy, and Psychotherapy

Alexander, Ronald G. "Can a Christian Ethic Condone Behavior Modification?" *Religion in Life*, Vol. XLV, No. 2 (Summer, 1976), pp. 191-203.

Bacal, Howard A. and Newman, Kenneth M. *Theories of Object Relations: Bridges to Self Psychology*. New York: Columbia University Press, 1990.

Bennett, Boyce M. "Visions and Audition in Biblical Prophecy," *Journal of Religion and Psychical Research*, Vol. 3, October, 1980, pp. 245-268.

Beveridge, Irving C. *Hypnotherapy: Its Christian Aspects*. Columbus: Brentwood Christian Press, 1992.

Bourguignon, Erika. *Religion, Altered States of Consciousness, and Social Change*. Columbus: Ohio State University Press, 1973.

Browning, Don S.; Jobe, Thomas; and, Evison, Ian. *Religious and Ethical Factors in Psychiatric Practice*. Chicago: Nelson-Hall, 1990.

Bryan, Jr., William J. *Religious Aspects of Hypnosis*. Springfield: Charles C. Thomas, 1962.

Bufford, Rodger K. "God and Behavior Mod: Some Thoughts Concerning the Relationships Between Biblical Principles and Behavior Modification," *Journal of Psychology and Theology*, Vol. 5, No. 1 (Winter, 1977), pp. 13-21.

Capps, Donald. *Reframing, A New Method In Pastoral Care*. Minneapolis:

Fortress Press, 1990.

Coue, Emile. *How to Practice Suggestion and Auto-Suggestion* New York: American Library Service, 1923. As quoted by Krasner.

Court, John H. "The Lord of the Trance," *Journal of Psychology and Christianity*, Vol. 10, No. 3 (Fall, 1991), pp. 261-265.

Darley, John M., Glucksberg, Sam, and Kinchla, Ronald A. *Psychology* (4th Edition). Englewood Cliffs, New Jersey: Prentice Hall, 1988.

Erickson, Richard C. "Walden III: Toward an Ethics of Changing Behavior," *Journal of Religion and Health*, Vol. 16, No. 1 (January 1977), pp. 7-14.

Erikson, Erik H. *The Life Cycle Completed, A Review*. New York: W. W. Norton & Company, 1985.

Erwin, Edwin. Behavior Therapy: Scientific, Philosophical, and Moral Foundations. Cambridge: Cambridge University Press, 1978.

Feinstein, Moshe. *Iggros Moshe*. Yoreh Deah Vol. 2, No. 29), cited by, David Fox, *Journal of Psychology and Judaism*, Vol. 16, No. 2, Summer 1992.

Flynn, John. "Behavior Modification: Communication and Psychological Manipulation," *Soundings*, Vol. LX, No. 1 (Spring 1977), pp. 88-107.

Gardner, E. Clinton. *Biblical Faith and Social Ethics*. New York and Evanston: Harper & Row, Publishers, 1960.

Gedo, John E. *Beyond Interpretation, Toward a Revised Theory for Psychoanalysis* (Rev.). Hillsdale, NJ: The Analytic Press, 1993.

Haley, Jay. *Uncommon Therapy: The Psychiatric Techniques of Milton H. Erickson, M.D.* New York: W. W. Norton & Co., 1973.

Haring, Berhnard. *Manipulation: Ethical Boundaries of Medical, Behavioral & Genetic Manipulation*. Slough: St. Paul Publications, 1975.

Holmes, III, Urban T. *The Priest in Community, Exploring the Roots of Ministry*. New York: The Seabury Press, 1978.

Holmes III, Urban T. *To Speak of God, Theology for Beginners*. New York: The Seabury Press, 1974. This is the best introduction to theological topics I have ever encountered! Strongly recommended for all readers.

Johanson, Greg, and Kurtz, Ron. *Grace Unfolding*. New York: Bell Tower, 1991.

Kinser, III, Prentice. "Hypnosis and Pastoral Hypnotherapy," *Interlink, National Board for Certified Clinical Hypnotherapists*, July 20, 2006.

Kinser III, Prentice. *Prophecy, Trance and Transference: Hypnosis as a Pastoral Counseling Modality*. Evanston, Ill: Garrett-Evangelical Theological Seminary Press, 1997. Doctoral thesis.

Kohut, Heinz, ed. by Arnold Goldberg. *How Does Analysis Cure?* Chicago: University of Chicago Press, 1984.

Krasner, A. M. *The Wizard Within*. Santa Ana: American Board of Hypnotherapy Press, 1991.

Lamm, Rabbi Maurice. *The Power of Hope, The One Essential of Life and Love.* New York: Rawson Associates, 1995.

Malony, H. Newton. "A Theology for Hypnosis: A Beginning Inquiry", *Journal of Psychology and Christianity*, Vol. 2, No. 1 (Spring 1983).

Matheson, George. "Hypnotic Aspects of Religious Experiences," *Journal of Psychology and Theology*, Vol 7(1) (Spring 1979), pp. 13-21.

McAdams, Dan P. *Stories We Live By, Personal Myths and the Making of the Self.* New York: William Morrow and Company, Inc., 1993.

Meissner, William W. *Psychoanalysis and Religious Experience.* New Haven: Yale University Press, 1984.

Merton, Thomas. *No Man is an Island.* New York: Harcort, Inc., 1955).

Pfaff, Donald W. (Ed.). *Ethical Questions in Brain and Behavior: Problems and Opportunities.* New York: Springer-Verlag, 1983.

Sanders, Shirley. *Clinical Self-Hypnosis, The Power of Words and Images.* New York: The Guilford Press, 1991.

Sorenson, Anita Lehmann. "Psychoanalytic Perspectives on Religion: The Illusion Has a Future," *Journal of Psychology and Theology*, Vol. 18, No. 3 (Fall, 1990), pp. 209-217.

Tappeiner, Daniel A. "Psychological Paradigm for the Interpretation of the Charismatic Phenomenon of Prophecy," *Journal of Psychology and Theology*, Vol. 5, Winter, 1977.

Wilhelm, Richard, translation from Chinese into German; Baynes, Cary F., translation from German into English. *The I Ching or Book of Changes.* Princeton: The Princeton University Press, 1977.

Wilson, R. "Prophecy and Ecstasy, " *JBL*, 1979.

Winnicott, D. W. *Psychoanalytic Explorations.* Edited by: Clare Winnicott, Ray Shephered, and Madeleine Davis. Cambridge: Harvard University Press, 1989.

Winnicott, D. W. *Through Paediatrics to Psycho-Analysis, Collected Papers.* New York: Brunner/Mazel, 1992.

Wolinsky, Stephen. *Trances People Live.* Falls Village, Connecticut: The Bramble Company, 1991.

INDEX

ABOUT THE AUTHOR

The Rev. Dr. Prentice Kinser III

The author of *Limitless Living, A Guide to Unconventional Spiritual Exploration and Growth*, Prentice Kinser III, D.Min., currently serves full-time as the Rector of two Episcopal parishes in Virginia.

Dr. Kinser has been an ordained minister (Episcopal priest) for almost 30 years. He received a Doctor of Ministry degree in pastoral counseling and psychotherapy from Garrett-Evangelical Theological Seminary, Evanston, Illinois, in cooperation with the Virginia Institute of Pastoral Care, Richmond, Virginia. He earned a M.Div. degree from the School of Theology, University of the South, Sewanee, Tennessee, an M.B.A. from the University of Virginia Darden Graduate School of Business Administration, Charlottesville, Virginia, and a B.A. degree from Randolph-Macon College, Ashland, Virginia. He is certified as a Pastoral Counselor and Fellow by the American Association of Pastoral Counselors, serves on the Board of the National Board for Certified Clinical Hypnotherapists, and is himself a National Board Certified Clinical Hypnotherapist.

After college Dr. Kinser explored a variety of vocations as a chemistry and physics teacher, as administrative assistant to the Dean of the University of Virginia Darden Graduate School of Business Administration, as vice president of Motivational Concepts, Inc., as a real estate broker in Charlottesville, Virginia, and even attended medical school for three semesters.

Dr. Kinser is also the author of the doctoral thesis *Prophecy, Trance and Transference: Hypnosis as a Pastoral Counseling Modality*, and of the soon to be completed novel: *Hawksbill.*

He and his wife now reside on the Northern Neck of Virginia and are parents of three children and four grandchildren.

∞

MORE LIMITLESS LIVING

Dr. Kinser has already begun a sequel to this book that will be entitled: *MORE LIMITLESS LIVING.* Some of the topics he hopes to include are:

1) The Experience of Faith, Hope and Non-ordinary Reality
2) Precognition, Time Warps, Chaos Theory and the Heisenberg Principle
3) ESP: Extra-Sensory Perception
4) The Healing Power of Yoga
5) The Mystery of Reiki
6) Holotropic Breathwork
7) Soul Healing and the Healing of Memories
8) Holy Play and Holy Humor
9) Medicine Cards, Tarot, and the I-Ching
10) Talking with Nature
11) Out of Body Explorations and Shamanic Journeys
12) Kabbalah and Jewish Mysticism
13) Christian Mysticism and Following the Way
14) Harmony, Balance, and Cosmic Consciousness
15) More Past Life Recalls and NDEs: No Death - No Fear

Believing that truth is often stranger than fiction, and that some of the best stories of *limitless living* come from the experiences of people like you who have read this book, Dr. Kinser invites you to share your special spiritual experiences or stories from your life related to one or more of the topics above (or suggest your own topic). Your stories may be chosen to appear in this next book.

Other authors and researchers in the field of non-ordinary reality are also invited to submit stories from their studies (appropriate credit will be given).

Please send story, along with the following *signed* permission, to:

The Rev. Dr. Prentice Kinser III
c/o Ancient Otter Publishing
PO Box 53
Montross, VA 22520-0053

Copy this page then cut along line. Complete one copy and send with each story you submit.

Copyright Permission Release

I hereby certify that the attached story comes from my own personal experience, and I give Prentice Kinser III non-exclusive rights to use the story in any and all editions of his next book, *MORE LIMITLESS LIVING*, in derivative works, in English and in foreign translations, in all formats, including CD ROM & electronic media. I [ ]*do* or [ ]*do not* want attribution by name in the text.

Your Signature: _____

Print Your Name:_____
Date:_____ 20____

Address:_____
City:_____ State:_____ ZIP:_____
Phone:_____ Email:_____

No story can be used unless this permission is also received. Please *do not* send stories about someone other than yourself unless you receive written permission to do so and send that permission along with the story.

∞

Even if you do not have an unusual spiritual story to share, Dr. Kinser would love to hear from you. Send a note to the address above.

Printed in the United States
200130BV00008B/115-198/A